יהושע

THE
ISRAEL
BIBLE

JOSHUA

EDITED BY

Rabbi Tuly Weisz

The Israel Bible: Joshua

First Edition, 2021

The Israel Bible was produced by Israel365 in cooperation with Teach for Israel and is used with permission from Teach for Israel. All rights reserved. The English translation was adapted by Israel365 from the JPS Tanakh. Copyright © 1985 by the Jewish Publication Society. All rights reserved.

Cover image used under license from Shutterstock.com

ISBN 978-1-957109-31-2

A CIP catalogue record for this title is available from the British Library

The Israel Bible: Joshua is a holy book that contains the name of God and should be treated with respect.

Table of Contents

Introduction

The Hebrew Bible is commonly known as the *Tanakh* which stands for *Torah* (the Five Books of Moses), *Neviim* (the Prophets) and *Ketuvim* (the Writings). The *Tanakh* consists of 24 books that are considered by Jews to be the word of God. While these books have been referred to as the "Old Testament," many Jews reject this label since it implies the replacement of the Hebrew Bible with something newer and prefer the more authentic Jewish name.

The *Tanakh* is not only the most important book known to man, it is God's word that is perfect and absolute. It is therefore a daunting undertaking to publish an edition of the *Tanakh*, and the responsibilities are awesome. There is no room for error or carelessness in dealing with the eternal word of God. Further, upon embarking on such a serious initiative, we ask ourselves if our efforts are gratuitous. Considering the many editions of the Bible in print, is there truly a need for yet another one?

While there are numerous Bibles in circulation today, its most central aspect – the Land of Israel – has often been overlooked. References to Israel appear on nearly every page, and the city of Jerusalem is specifically referred to hundreds of times throughout the Bible. The essential link between Israel and *Torah* is emphasized repeatedly in verses such as, "For instruction (*Torah*) shall come forth from *Tzion*, the word of *Hashem* from *Yerushalayim*" (Micah 4:2).

The miraculous return of the People of Israel to the Land of Israel in our own generation provides the perfect moment for a new volume to fill this void in biblical literature. *The Israel Bible* includes many special features elucidating God's focus on Israel throughout *Tanakh* and there are many additional, multimedia features available on our website **www.theisraelbible.com**.

Ordering and Presentation – In presenting *The Israel Bible*, our goal is to spread awareness of the biblical significance of the Land of Israel as well as the Jewish people's eternal connection to the land, based on the text of the *Tanakh*, the Hebrew Bible. We aim to honor "the God, the People and the Land of Israel" from an Orthodox Jewish perspective. To that end, *The Israel Bible* follows the traditional Jewish ordering of the books and the customary Hebrew division of chapters. Therefore, for example, we count 24 books of *Tanakh* with *Sefer Divrei Hayamim* (Chronicles) appearing last. It is our hope that our rich content will speak to all Jews and non-Jews who appreciate Israel as the God given land of the Jewish people.

English Translation – Throughout history, Jews have studied the Bible in Hebrew, as any form of translation would miss much of the nuance of the original holy tongue in which *Torah* has been transmitted since the days of Moses. However, as many Jews settled in America in the 19th Century, the need for an English translation became necessary. To be sure, there were already English translations prepared over the centuries by Christians, but in the words of the original editors of the Jewish Publication Society (JPS), "The Jew cannot afford to have his Bible translation prepared for him by others. He cannot have it as a gift, even as he cannot borrow his soul from others."

JPS set out in the late 1800s to publish an authoritative English translation "in the spirit of Jewish tradition." It was compiled over decades by some of the leading Jewish scholars of the time. They formed committees and subcommittees to compare existing English versions, considering medieval and modern Jewish commentators. The monumental JPS translation, originally published in 1917, has been updated in recent years, and *The Israel Bible* is proud to utilize the 1984 New Jewish Publication Society (NJPS) version with its modern, clear language, as well as its wide-ranging acceptance as an accurate and high-quality translation. We applied the NJPS translation verbatim, except for a select list of nouns which we replaced with their traditional Hebrew names. This is true even when we found the NJPS translation to be different than the popular translation of a word or phrase and when the NJPS switched the order of the text for the sake of clarity (see, for example, Ezekiel 24:22–24).

Hebrew Transliteration – To give our readers an authentic *Tanakh* experience, every verse that has commentary is transliterated from Hebrew into English. The Hebrew alphabet chart includes our standards for transliteration and pronunciation of Hebrew verses, enabling readers of *The Israel Bible* to decipher key biblical passages in the holy language. Readers can hear the entire Bible read in Hebrew on our website **www.theisraelbible.com**.

There are various standards when it comes to transliterating Hebrew words into English letters. While we have relied primarily on the classical Hebrew transliteration, we have occasionally deviated for the sake of simplicity, clarity and to reflect common usage.

In addition to whole verses, we have also transliterated many proper nouns in the English translation so that our readers can learn the names of key biblical figures and locations in their Hebrew form. As a rule, we chose to transliterate names of people that were central in the establishment and functioning of the nation of Israel, as well as significant places in the Holy Land. Therefore, regarding Adam's sons, for example, only *Shet* (Seth) is transliterated since

it was from him that *Noach* (Noah), and ultimately *Avraham* (Abraham), descended. For this reason, there might be verses or sections of *The Israel Bible* that contains multiple names and only some of them are transliterated.

For the same reason, we have transliterated the names of the books of *Tanakh* when referring to them in our introductions and commentary. When referencing a specific chapter or verse, however, we use the English names of the books in our citations for clarity. We also transliterated ideas and concepts that are central to Judaism such as *Shabbat* (Sabbath), the names of the Jewish holidays and the *Beit Hamikdash* (Temple), as well as biblical measurements. Finally, the name of God is transliterated. Out of respect, Orthodox Jews generally refer to the Lord as *Hashem*, which literally means 'the Name.' Referring to God as *Hashem* reminds us that we feel close to Him but also recognize our distance at the same time. To stress this moniker, we transliterated both the Tetragrammaton as well as the name *Elohim* as *Hashem*.

Study Notes – Our unique commentary was compiled by Orthodox Jewish scholars who live in Israel. It is an anthology in the sense that most of the commentary is not original, but draws from traditional teachings of early Jewish Sages and modern rabbinic commentators. We also include quotations from individuals who have played a significant part in the past century of modern Israeli history including Israeli prime ministers, poets and military leaders.

Our commentary can be broken into four categories, three of which are identified by an icon at the beginning of the study note:

 Israel lessons are indicated with an icon bearing the map of Israel and focus on the Land of Israel and the modern State of Israel.

 Jewish lessons are indicated with a *Torah* scroll and teach a concept in Judaism or a classic idea from rabbinic thought.

 Hebrew lessons are represented by an icon bearing the letter *aleph* and focus on the meaning of a Hebrew word or phrase.

All other comments are considered general comments and are not assigned an icon.

Supplemental Material – In addition to our unique translation and original commentary, *The Israel Bible* offers supplementary material to enrich the learning experience of our readers. Before every book of *Tanakh,* we provide

an introduction, as well as information, generally in the form of a map, a chart or a list, which is central to the specific book.

Maps – As the purpose of *The Israel Bible* is to highlight the biblical significance of the Land of Israel, significant time was spent researching and preparing maps to bring the physical contours of the holy land to life with great accuracy. However, since there is a lack of information regarding the precise locations of certain ancient cities, some of the places on our maps are approximate or subject to debate. In these cases, we followed the opinion that we are most comfortable with, but acknowledge that there is room for disagreement. We continue to produce new maps, which are available on our website **www.theisraelbible.com/maps**.

Torah **Readings** – The *Torah* is not just a work that is studied privately, it is also read out loud in synagogue. Every *Shabbat* and holiday a portion of the *Torah* is read, as well as a related section from *Neviim*, the prophets, called the *haftarah*. We included the blessings recited before and after the reading of the *Torah*, a list of the weekly *Torah* portions and their corresponding *haftarot*, and a chart of the *Torah* readings for special days with their corresponding *haftarot*. Readers can always find the current week's *Torah* portion by visiting **www.theisraelbible.com/weekly-torah-portion**. In this volume, we indicate where a new *Torah* portion begins by highlighting the Hebrew verse number with a gray box so readers can follow along with the communal *Torah* readings. Furthermore, we have included prayers for the State of Israel and the soldiers of the Israel Defense Forces (IDF) that are generally recited following the *Torah* reading in synagogue. It is our constant prayer that God watch over the State of Israel and the members of the IDF, who defend Israel every hour of every day.

In 1948, the State of Israel was created providing a modern answer to Isaiah's ancient question, "Is a nation born all at once?" (Isaiah 66:8). *The Israel Bible* was first published in the 70th year of God's miraculous restoration of the People of Israel to the Land of Israel. Jewish wisdom teaches that 70 is a significant number: *Moshe* (Moses) translated the *Torah* into 70 languages for all 70 nations of the world. From our very origins, the Jewish people were meant to be a light unto the 70 nations, spreading God's truth to the masses.

In the seven decades since the modern rebirth of the State of Israel, God's plan has been unfolding with unprecedented speed, dramatic highs and heartbreaking lows. Never has Israel been at the forefront of the world's attention as it is in our generation. Efforts to vilify the Jewish State seem to spread every

day across the globe. At the same time, so does the growing movement of millions of non-Jewish biblical Zionists who stand with the nation of Israel as an expression of their commitment to God's word. As we seek to understand the clash of these two conflicting worldviews, the need for *The Israel Bible* has never been so important.

Standing on the great shoulders of those who came before us and emanating from the land that has always served as the birthplace for the Bible, we conclude with a heartfelt prayer: May the Almighty bless our efforts in offering this *Tanakh* to influence the hearts, minds and actions of its readers. In this way, it is our hope to spread God's name so that the publication of *The Israel Bible* brings us one step closer to the final redemption of Israel and the entire world.

Rabbi Tuly Weisz
Editor, *The Israel Bible*

Foreword

The mandate to study God's word daily is interestingly not found in the Five Books of Moses (Pentateuch), but rather in the first book of our prophetic writings: "Let not this Book of the Teaching cease from your lips, but recite it day and night, so that you may observe faithfully all that is written in it. Only then will you prosper in your undertakings and only then will you be successful" (Joshua 1:8). Charged with bringing the Israelites into the land covenantally promised to Abraham, Isaac and Jacob, God ensures Joshua of His protection if the nation observes His ways as dictated in the Divine constitution known as the *Torah*.

In Jewish tradition, Joshua (1:8) is directly linked with Deuteronomy (11:14), "You shall gather in your new grain and wine, and oil."[1] Our Sages deduced from this scriptural combination the importance of merging *Torah* study with a profession. Completely dedicating oneself to the study of *Torah* without having the financial means to sustain this lifestyle can lead one to eventually straying from observance of God's will. Poverty and crime can have an intimate relationship.

We must also be careful that our work does not affect our daily study of Scripture. The addiction of becoming a workaholic and not making *Torah* study a priority can also lead one into temptations that can violate our personal relationship with Him as well as our fellow human beings. The goal is to achieve a healthy balance between our study of God's word and our daily work.

The Deuteronomic verse quoted above is part of the second section of the Shema[2] that discusses the concept of reward and punishment. Sanctifying God by fulfilling His commandments results in the Land of Israel practically benefitting from rains that occur in the right season and reaping the abundance from the fields. However, if the nation follows pagan gods and practices, the consequences are devastating – famine and death. The Land of Israel is intrinsically linked with the keeping of the *Torah*. Covenant Land comes with covenant responsibility.

---

1. Talmud Bavli Berachot 35b
2. Consisting of three sections within the Five Books of Moses (Deut. 6:4–8; 11:13–22 and Numbers 15:37–42), the *Shema* is proclamation of accepting God's Kingdom in our lives, loyalty to His commandments and remembering His redemptive act of liberating us from Egypt. Jews recite the *Shema* twice a day as stated in Deut. 6:7.

Born into slavery, Joshua is now leading His people into the Promised Land. More than 500 years separates him from his ancestral forefather Abraham. The historical narratives that took place between Abraham leaving everything behind to follow God in Genesis 12 and the death of Moses in the last chapter of Deuteronomy are filled with intrigue, suspense, joy, sorrow and hope. What began as a family is now a nation actualizing its mission to be a kingdom of priests to the world. However, for the Israelites to succeed in the Land of Israel, they must see the *Torah* as the only compass to direct their lives.

The biblical episodes after our first entry into the land are well known. Our ancestors' triumphs and sins are all on public record. We learned the harsh reality of Leviticus (18:28) "So let not the land spew you out for defiling it as it spewed out the nation that came before you." Twice, we lost the privilege to be stewards of the Land of Israel and to fulfill our nation state mandate to be a light to the world. However, when the annals of history were ready to archive the Jewish people after the Holocaust, God kept His covenantal promise and gathered us from the four corners of the globe to come home. The year 1948 was a game changer. Biblical prophecies were and are being realized. We are now living in the birth pangs of the messianic era.

In our morning prayers, we recite a series of blessings over the *Torah* that include petitioning God to have a sweet tooth for His word, to study it without any ulterior motive and to have Him to teach it to us. They are some congregations that invoke the following liturgical prayer after the completion of these blessings: *May the Torah be my faith and El Shaddai my help. Blessed be the name of His glorious kingdom forever and all time.*

According to Jewish tradition, the neglect of not blessing the *Torah* before engaging in its study was one of the reasons for the destruction of the Temple.[3] This is deduced from the redundancy of words in Jeremiah (9:12) that talks about Israel not following God: "... Because they forsook the teaching I had set before them. They did not obey Me and they did not follow it [did not make a blessing before studying it]." Our inability to properly cherish God's greatest gift to the world, the *Torah*, led to our eventual exile from our land.

On Israel's Independence Day, Jews around the world recite Psalms 113–118 to express our gratitude to God for His Divine hand in helping establish the State of Israel. We have learned from our past and realize the privilege to see firsthand the land, people and *Torah* operating all together in our generation.

---

3. Babylonian Talmud Nedarim 81a

When Rabbi Tuly Weisz approached me about his intent to publish *The Israel Bible* that would highlight commentary about the special relationship between the land and people, I saw this project as another way to publicly demonstrate our appreciation to God for having the State of Israel. In addition, it is another educational tool to ensure biblical literacy. If we are to truly enjoy the Land of Israel, it is incumbent upon us to continually study the *Torah*. Isaiah once prophesied that the Jewish people would return to Zion with songs, "crowned with everlasting joy" (35:10). *The Israel Bible* provides us the lyrical content to express our joy in living in the land that God calls holy.

Rabbi Shlomo Riskin
Chief Rabbi of Efrat
Founder of the Center for Jewish-Christian
Understanding & Cooperation (cjcuc)

Introduction to Sefer Yehoshua
The Book of Joshua

Introduction and commentary by Rabbi Shmuel Jablon

Sefer Yehoshua (Joshua) is the first book of the Prophets. Though the People of Israel had many prophets, almost none of their writings are recorded. The rabbis of the Talmud (*Megillah* 14a) teach that only prophetic messages that would be relevant for later generations were written down and included in the *Tanakh*, the Hebrew Bible.

In his commentary to *Sefer Yehoshua*, Rabbi Shlomo Aviner notes that this does not mean that every prophecy in *Tanakh* is necessary in every period. Only the five books of the *Torah,* given by God Himself, have this eternal quality. The other prophecies written in the Bible, while relevant at some point in the future, are not relevant at all times.

Which future generation would need the messages of the book of *Yehoshua*? Rabbi Aviner answers that it is certainly our generation, which has witnessed the creation, building and flowering of the State of Israel, the ingathering of the exiles and the miraculous military victories. We are the ones who must derive inspiration and instruction from *Sefer Yehoshua*.

Sefer Yehoshua contains a number of central themes:

1. We are reminded that *Yehoshua* was *Moshe*'s loyal student, and that his leadership is a direct continuation of that of *Moshe*. The People of Israel are repeatedly instructed to remain loyal to the *Torah* of *Moshe*, and we are constantly reminded that *Yehoshua*'s actions and the nation's victories are due to the promises of the past.

2. We are taught that the entire Land of Israel belongs to the Children of Israel. We learn of the borders of the land, and of many key cities.

3. We learn that unlike the life the Israelites led in the desert, in the Land of Israel *Hashem* will not do all the work Himself. Whereas in the desert, *Hashem* fought their battles and sent them manna from heaven, the Children of Israel will have to engage in battles to take possession of the

Promised Land and work the land in order to have food to eat. Human actions, in addition to divine miracles, are necessary to survive and to thrive in *Eretz Yisrael*.

4. We are taught that the proper place for the Children of Israel is *Eretz Yisrael* under the reign of the Kingdom of Israel. Each tribe has its own inheritance, with the land divided according to divine lots, and they must all see themselves as sections of one great nation.

Each of these themes resonates with any contemporary person who feels a connection to the State of Israel. After more than two thousand years of bitter exile, the Jewish People have returned home and can serve *Hashem* as a free people in its own land. This dream of generations of Jewish history has now become a reality. *Sefer Yehoshua* surely speaks to our generation.

Map of 12 Tribal Allotments

This is a map of of the twelve tribal allotments in the Land of Israel, based of *Sefer Yehoshua* (chapters 14–19).

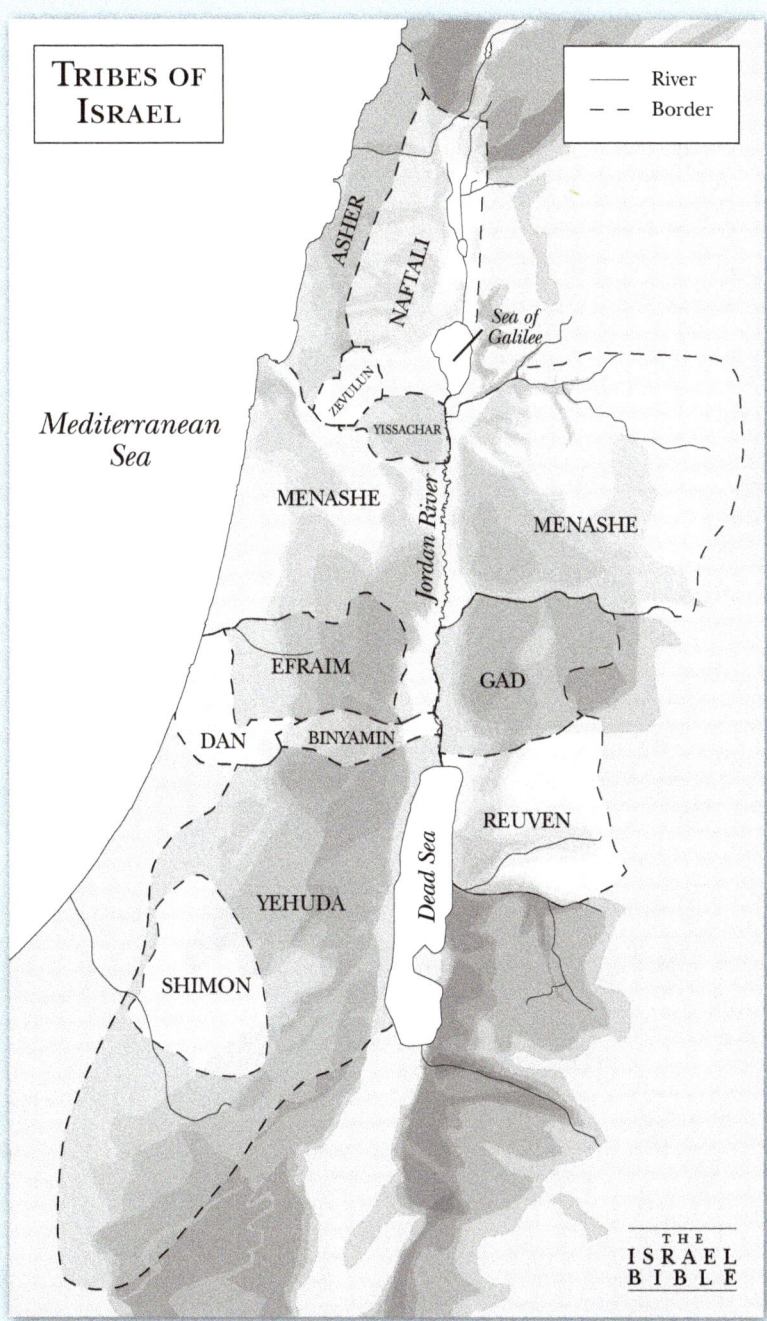

Joshua

1 **¹** After the death of *Moshe* the servant of *Hashem*, *Hashem* said to *Yehoshua* son of Nun, *Moshe's* attendant:

א וַיְהִי אַחֲרֵי מוֹת מֹשֶׁה עֶבֶד יְהֹוָה
וַיֹּאמֶר יְהֹוָה אֶל־יְהוֹשֻׁעַ בִּן־נוּן מְשָׁרֵת
מֹשֶׁה לֵאמֹר:

vai-HEE a-kha-RAY MOT mo-SHEH E-ved a-do-NAI va-YO-mer a-do-NAI el y'-ho-SHU-a bin NUN m'-sha-RAYT mo-SHEH lay-MOR

² "My servant *Moshe* is dead. Prepare to cross the *Yarden*, together with all this people, into the land that I am giving to the Israelites.

ב מֹשֶׁה עַבְדִּי מֵת וְעַתָּה קוּם עֲבֹר
אֶת־הַיַּרְדֵּן הַזֶּה אַתָּה וְכָל־הָעָם הַזֶּה
אֶל־הָאָרֶץ אֲשֶׁר אָנֹכִי נֹתֵן לָהֶם לִבְנֵי
יִשְׂרָאֵל:

mo-SHEH av-DEE MAYT v'-a-TAH KUM a-VOR et ha-yar-DAYN ha-ZEH a-TAH v'-khol ha-AM ha-ZEH el ha-A-retz a-SHER a-no-KHEE no-TAYN la-HEM liv-NAY yis-ra-AYL

³ Every spot on which your foot treads I give to you, as I promised *Moshe*.

ג כָּל־מָקוֹם אֲשֶׁר תִּדְרֹךְ כַּף־רַגְלְכֶם בּוֹ
לָכֶם נְתַתִּיו כַּאֲשֶׁר דִּבַּרְתִּי אֶל־מֹשֶׁה:

⁴ Your territory shall extend from the wilderness and the Lebanon to the Great River, the River Euphrates [on the east] – the whole Hittite country – and up to the Mediterranean Sea on the west.

ד מֵהַמִּדְבָּר וְהַלְּבָנוֹן הַזֶּה וְעַד־הַנָּהָר
הַגָּדוֹל נְהַר־פְּרָת כֹּל אֶרֶץ הַחִתִּים
וְעַד־הַיָּם הַגָּדוֹל מְבוֹא הַשָּׁמֶשׁ יִהְיֶה
גְּבוּלְכֶם:

⁵ No one shall be able to resist you as long as you live. As I was with *Moshe*, so I will be with you; I will not fail you or forsake you.

ה לֹא־יִתְיַצֵּב אִישׁ לְפָנֶיךָ כֹּל יְמֵי חַיֶּיךָ
כַּאֲשֶׁר הָיִיתִי עִם־מֹשֶׁה אֶהְיֶה עִמָּךְ לֹא
אַרְפְּךָ וְלֹא אֶעֶזְבֶךָּ:

⁶ "Be strong and resolute, for you shall apportion to this people the land that I swore to their fathers to assign to them.

ו חֲזַק וֶאֱמָץ כִּי אַתָּה תַּנְחִיל אֶת־
הָעָם הַזֶּה אֶת־הָאָרֶץ אֲשֶׁר־נִשְׁבַּעְתִּי
לַאֲבוֹתָם לָתֵת לָהֶם:

⁷ But you must be very strong and resolute to observe faithfully all the Teaching that My servant *Moshe* enjoined upon you. Do not deviate from it to the right or to the left, that you may be successful wherever you go.

ז רַק חֲזַק וֶאֱמַץ מְאֹד לִשְׁמֹר לַעֲשׂוֹת
כְּכָל־הַתּוֹרָה אֲשֶׁר צִוְּךָ מֹשֶׁה עַבְדִּי
אַל־תָּסוּר מִמֶּנּוּ יָמִין וּשְׂמֹאול לְמַעַן
תַּשְׂכִּיל בְּכֹל אֲשֶׁר תֵּלֵךְ:

1:1 *Hashem* **said to** *Yehoshua* **son of Nun** The Talmud (*Nedarim* 22b) teaches that *Sefer Yehoshua* has a unique quality which sets it apart from all of the other books of the Prophets. Books like *Sefer Yeshayahu, Sefer Yirmiyahu, Sefer Melachim* and *Sefer Shoftim* were necessary only to rebuke the people as a response to their behavior. Had they not sinned, they would have needed only the five books of the *Torah* and *Sefer Yehoshua*, for it describes the borders and boundaries of Israel. May our study of *Sefer Yehoshua* increase our love for, and appreciation of, the Land of Israel.

1:2 **Prepare to cross the** *Yarden* *Hashem* instructs *Yehoshua*, the new leader of the Nation of Israel, to rise up and lead them across the *Yarden*, and to inhabit the land that *Hashem* is giving them. Taking possession of *Eretz Yisrael* will require human actions, which will be supported by God's miracles. At the very beginning of *Yehoshua's* leadership, the nation is reminded that the entire *Eretz Yisrael* belongs to the Jewish people, and that they must do their part to take possession of this special gift from *Hashem*.

Jordan River

8 Let not this Book of the Teaching cease from your lips, but recite it day and night, so that you may observe faithfully all that is written in it. Only then will you prosper in your undertakings and only then will you be successful.

ח לֹא־יָמוּשׁ סֵפֶר הַתּוֹרָה הַזֶּה מִפִּיךָ וְהָגִיתָ בּוֹ יוֹמָם וָלַיְלָה לְמַעַן תִּשְׁמֹר לַעֲשׂוֹת כְּכָל־הַכָּתוּב בּוֹ כִּי־אָז תַּצְלִיחַ אֶת־דְּרָכֶךָ וְאָז תַּשְׂכִּיל:

9 "I charge you: Be strong and resolute; do not be terrified or dismayed, for *Hashem* your God is with you wherever you go."

ט הֲלוֹא צִוִּיתִיךָ חֲזַק וֶאֱמָץ אַל־תַּעֲרֹץ וְאַל־תֵּחָת כִּי עִמְּךָ יְהוָה אֱלֹהֶיךָ בְּכֹל אֲשֶׁר תֵּלֵךְ:

10 *Yehoshua* thereupon gave orders to the officials of the people:

י וַיְצַו יְהוֹשֻׁעַ אֶת־שֹׁטְרֵי הָעָם לֵאמֹר:

11 "Go through the camp and charge the people thus: Get provisions ready, for in three days' time you are to cross the *Yarden*, in order to enter and possess the land that *Hashem* your God is giving you as a possession."

יא עִבְרוּ בְּקֶרֶב הַמַּחֲנֶה וְצַוּוּ אֶת־הָעָם לֵאמֹר הָכִינוּ לָכֶם צֵידָה כִּי בְּעוֹד שְׁלֹשֶׁת יָמִים אַתֶּם עֹבְרִים אֶת־הַיַּרְדֵּן הַזֶּה לָבוֹא לָרֶשֶׁת אֶת־הָאָרֶץ אֲשֶׁר יְהוָה אֱלֹהֵיכֶם נֹתֵן לָכֶם לְרִשְׁתָּהּ:

12 Then *Yehoshua* said to the Reubenites, the Gadites, and the half-tribe of *Menashe*,

יב וְלָרְאוּבֵנִי וְלַגָּדִי וְלַחֲצִי שֵׁבֶט הַמְנַשֶּׁה אָמַר יְהוֹשֻׁעַ לֵאמֹר:

13 "Remember what *Moshe* the servant of *Hashem* enjoined upon you, when he said: '*Hashem* your God is granting you a haven; He has assigned this territory to you.'

יג זָכוֹר אֶת־הַדָּבָר אֲשֶׁר צִוָּה אֶתְכֶם מֹשֶׁה עֶבֶד־יְהוָה לֵאמֹר יְהוָה אֱלֹהֵיכֶם מֵנִיחַ לָכֶם וְנָתַן לָכֶם אֶת־הָאָרֶץ הַזֹּאת:

14 Let your wives, children, and livestock remain in the land that *Moshe* assigned to you on this side of the *Yarden*; but every one of your fighting men shall go across armed in the van of your kinsmen. And you shall assist them

יד נְשֵׁיכֶם טַפְּכֶם וּמִקְנֵיכֶם יֵשְׁבוּ בָּאָרֶץ אֲשֶׁר נָתַן לָכֶם מֹשֶׁה בְּעֵבֶר הַיַּרְדֵּן וְאַתֶּם תַּעַבְרוּ חֲמֻשִׁים לִפְנֵי אֲחֵיכֶם כֹּל גִּבּוֹרֵי הַחַיִל וַעֲזַרְתֶּם אוֹתָם:

15 until *Hashem* has given your kinsmen a haven, such as you have, and they too have gained possession of the land that *Hashem* your God has assigned to them. Then you may return to the land on the east side of the *Yarden*, which *Moshe* the servant of *Hashem* assigned to you as your possession, and you may possess it."

טו עַד אֲשֶׁר־יָנִיחַ יְהוָה לַאֲחֵיכֶם כָּכֶם וְיָרְשׁוּ גַם־הֵמָּה אֶת־הָאָרֶץ אֲשֶׁר־יְהוָה אֱלֹהֵיכֶם נֹתֵן לָהֶם וְשַׁבְתֶּם לְאֶרֶץ יְרֻשַּׁתְכֶם וִירִשְׁתֶּם אוֹתָהּ אֲשֶׁר נָתַן לָכֶם מֹשֶׁה עֶבֶד יְהוָה בְּעֵבֶר הַיַּרְדֵּן מִזְרַח הַשָּׁמֶשׁ:

16 They answered *Yehoshua*, "We will do everything you have commanded us and we will go wherever you send us.

טז וַיַּעֲנוּ אֶת־יְהוֹשֻׁעַ לֵאמֹר כֹּל אֲשֶׁר־צִוִּיתָנוּ נַעֲשֶׂה וְאֶל־כָּל־אֲשֶׁר תִּשְׁלָחֵנוּ נֵלֵךְ:

17 We will obey you just as we obeyed *Moshe*; let but *Hashem* your God be with you as He was with *Moshe*!

יז כְּכֹל אֲשֶׁר־שָׁמַעְנוּ אֶל־מֹשֶׁה כֵּן נִשְׁמַע אֵלֶיךָ רַק יִהְיֶה יְהוָה אֱלֹהֶיךָ עִמָּךְ כַּאֲשֶׁר הָיָה עִם־מֹשֶׁה:

18 Any man who flouts your commands and does not obey every order you give him shall be put to death. Only be strong and resolute!"

יח כָּל־אִישׁ אֲשֶׁר־יַמְרֶה אֶת־פִּיךָ וְלֹא־יִשְׁמַע אֶת־דְּבָרֶיךָ לְכֹל אֲשֶׁר־תְּצַוֶּנּוּ יוּמָת רַק חֲזַק וֶאֱמָץ:

kol EESH a-sher yam-REH et PEE-kha v'-lo yish-MA et d'-va-RE-kha l'-KHOL a-sher t'-tza-VE-nu yu-MAT RAK kha-ZAK ve-e-MATZ

Joshua

2 ¹ *Yehoshua* son of *Nun* secretly sent two spies from Shittim, saying, "Go, reconnoiter the region of *Yericho*." So they set out, and they came to the house of a harlot named Rahab and lodged there.

ב א וַיִּשְׁלַח יְהוֹשֻׁעַ־בִּן־נוּן מִן־הַשִּׁטִּים שְׁנַיִם־אֲנָשִׁים מְרַגְּלִים חֶרֶשׁ לֵאמֹר לְכוּ רְאוּ אֶת־הָאָרֶץ וְאֶת־יְרִיחוֹ וַיֵּלְכוּ וַיָּבֹאוּ בֵּית־אִשָּׁה זוֹנָה וּשְׁמָהּ רָחָב וַיִּשְׁכְּבוּ־שָׁמָּה:

² The king of *Yericho* was told, "Some men have come here tonight, Israelites, to spy out the country."

ב וַיֵּאָמַר לְמֶלֶךְ יְרִיחוֹ לֵאמֹר הִנֵּה אֲנָשִׁים בָּאוּ הֵנָּה הַלַּיְלָה מִבְּנֵי יִשְׂרָאֵל לַחְפֹּר אֶת־הָאָרֶץ:

³ The king of *Yericho* thereupon sent orders to Rahab: "Produce the men who came to you and entered your house, for they have come to spy out the whole country."

ג וַיִּשְׁלַח מֶלֶךְ יְרִיחוֹ אֶל־רָחָב לֵאמֹר הוֹצִיאִי הָאֲנָשִׁים הַבָּאִים אֵלַיִךְ אֲשֶׁר־בָּאוּ לְבֵיתֵךְ כִּי לַחְפֹּר אֶת־כָּל־הָאָרֶץ בָּאוּ:

⁴ The woman, however, had taken the two men and hidden them. "It is true," she said, "the men did come to me, but I didn't know where they were from.

ד וַתִּקַּח הָאִשָּׁה אֶת־שְׁנֵי הָאֲנָשִׁים וַתִּצְפְּנוֹ וַתֹּאמֶר כֵּן בָּאוּ אֵלַי הָאֲנָשִׁים וְלֹא יָדַעְתִּי מֵאַיִן הֵמָּה:

⁵ And at dark, when the gate was about to be closed, the men left; and I don't know where the men went. Quick, go after them, for you can overtake them."

ה וַיְהִי הַשַּׁעַר לִסְגּוֹר בַּחֹשֶׁךְ וְהָאֲנָשִׁים יָצָאוּ לֹא יָדַעְתִּי אָנָה הָלְכוּ הָאֲנָשִׁים רִדְפוּ מַהֵר אַחֲרֵיהֶם כִּי תַשִּׂיגוּם:

⁶ Now she had taken them up to the roof and hidden them under some stalks of flax which she had lying on the roof.

ו וְהִיא הֶעֱלָתַם הַגָּגָה וַתִּטְמְנֵם בְּפִשְׁתֵּי הָעֵץ הָעֲרֻכוֹת לָהּ עַל־הַגָּג:

⁷ So the men pursued them in the direction of the *Yarden* down to the fords; and no sooner had the pursuers gone out than the gate was shut behind them.

ז וְהָאֲנָשִׁים רָדְפוּ אַחֲרֵיהֶם דֶּרֶךְ הַיַּרְדֵּן עַל הַמַּעְבְּרוֹת וְהַשַּׁעַר סָגָרוּ אַחֲרֵי כַּאֲשֶׁר יָצְאוּ הָרֹדְפִים אַחֲרֵיהֶם:

⁸ The spies had not yet gone to sleep when she came up to them on the roof.

ח וְהֵמָּה טֶרֶם יִשְׁכָּבוּן וְהִיא עָלְתָה עֲלֵיהֶם עַל־הַגָּג:

⁹ She said to the men, "I know that *Hashem* has given the country to you, because dread of you has fallen upon us, and all the inhabitants of the land are quaking before you.

ט וַתֹּאמֶר אֶל־הָאֲנָשִׁים יָדַעְתִּי כִּי־נָתַן יְהוָה לָכֶם אֶת־הָאָרֶץ וְכִי־נָפְלָה אֵימַתְכֶם עָלֵינוּ וְכִי נָמֹגוּ כָּל־יֹשְׁבֵי הָאָרֶץ מִפְּנֵיכֶם:

*va-TO-mer el ha-a-na-SHEEM ya-DA-tee kee na-TAN a-do-NAI
la-KHEM et ha-A-retz v'-khee na-f'-LAH ay-mat-KHEM a-LAY-nu
v'-KHEE na-MO-gu kol yo-sh'-VAY ha-A-retz mi-p'-nay-KHEM*

Golan Heights – biblical Bashan

2:9 I know that *Hashem* has given the country to you When Rahab speaks to the spies, she reports that the Canaanites are afraid of the Children of Israel. They are well aware of the miracles *Hashem* has done for the Israelites – both forty years earlier during the time of the exodus, and more recently in the battles against the Amorite kings Sihon and Og (Numbers 21). They know that God has given the land to the Children of Israel and therefore, they are afraid. Not only does Rahab report this to the spies, but she even casts her lot with the Israelites. Rahab is a prime example of a righteous gentile. Understanding that these men are representatives of *Hashem*'s chosen people who will receive the chosen land, she singlehandedly undertakes to protect the

10 For we have heard how *Hashem* dried up the waters of the Sea of Reeds for you when you left Egypt, and what you did to Sihon and Og, the two Amorite kings across the *Yarden*, whom you doomed.

11 When we heard about it, we lost heart, and no man had any more spirit left because of you; for *Hashem* your God is the only *Hashem* in heaven above and on earth below.

12 Now, since I have shown loyalty to you, swear to me by *Hashem* that you in turn will show loyalty to my family. Provide me with a reliable sign

13 that you will spare the lives of my father and mother, my brothers and sisters, and all who belong to them, and save us from death."

14 The men answered her, "Our persons are pledged for yours, even to death! If you do not disclose this mission of ours, we will show you true loyalty when *Hashem* gives us the land."

י כִּי שָׁמַעְנוּ אֵת אֲשֶׁר־הוֹבִישׁ יְהֹוָה אֶת־מֵי יַם־סוּף מִפְּנֵיכֶם בְּצֵאתְכֶם מִמִּצְרָיִם וַאֲשֶׁר עֲשִׂיתֶם לִשְׁנֵי מַלְכֵי הָאֱמֹרִי אֲשֶׁר בְּעֵבֶר הַיַּרְדֵּן לְסִיחֹן וּלְעוֹג אֲשֶׁר הֶחֱרַמְתֶּם אוֹתָם:

יא וַנִּשְׁמַע וַיִּמַּס לְבָבֵנוּ וְלֹא־קָמָה עוֹד רוּחַ בְּאִישׁ מִפְּנֵיכֶם כִּי יְהֹוָה אֱלֹהֵיכֶם הוּא אֱלֹהִים בַּשָּׁמַיִם מִמַּעַל וְעַל־הָאָרֶץ מִתָּחַת:

יב וְעַתָּה הִשָּׁבְעוּ־נָא לִי בַּיהֹוָה כִּי־עָשִׂיתִי עִמָּכֶם חָסֶד וַעֲשִׂיתֶם גַּם־אַתֶּם עִם־בֵּית אָבִי חֶסֶד וּנְתַתֶּם לִי אוֹת אֱמֶת:

יג וְהַחֲיִתֶם אֶת־אָבִי וְאֶת־אִמִּי וְאֶת־אַחַי וְאֶת־אַחְיוֹתַי [אַחְיוֹתַי] וְאֵת כָּל־אֲשֶׁר לָהֶם וְהִצַּלְתֶּם אֶת־נַפְשֹׁתֵינוּ מִמָּוֶת:

יד וַיֹּאמְרוּ לָהּ הָאֲנָשִׁים נַפְשֵׁנוּ תַחְתֵּיכֶם לָמוּת אִם לֹא תַגִּידוּ אֶת־דְּבָרֵנוּ זֶה וְהָיָה בְּתֵת־יְהֹוָה לָנוּ אֶת־הָאָרֶץ וְעָשִׂינוּ עִמָּךְ חֶסֶד וֶאֱמֶת:

va-YO-m'-ru LAH ha-a-na-SHEEM naf-SHAY-nu takh-tay-KHEM la-MUT IM LO ta-GEE-du et d'-va-RAY-nu ZEH v'-ha-YAH b'-tayt a-do-NAI LA-nu et ha-A-retz v'-a-SEE-nu i-MAKH KHE-sed ve-e-MET

15 She let them down by a rope through the window – for her dwelling was at the outer side of the city wall and she lived in the actual wall.

16 She said to them, "Make for the hills, so that the pursuers may not come upon you. Stay there in hiding three days, until the pursuers return; then go your way."

17 But the men warned her, "We will be released from this oath which you have made us take

טו וַתּוֹרִדֵם בַּחֶבֶל בְּעַד הַחַלּוֹן כִּי בֵיתָהּ בְּקִיר הַחוֹמָה וּבַחוֹמָה הִיא יוֹשָׁבֶת:

טז וַתֹּאמֶר לָהֶם הָהָרָה לֵּכוּ פֶּן־יִפְגְּעוּ בָכֶם הָרֹדְפִים וְנַחְבֵּתֶם שָׁמָּה שְׁלֹשֶׁת יָמִים עַד שׁוֹב הָרֹדְפִים וְאַחַר תֵּלְכוּ לְדַרְכְּכֶם:

יז וַיֹּאמְרוּ אֵלֶיהָ הָאֲנָשִׁים נְקִיִּם אֲנַחְנוּ מִשְּׁבֻעָתֵךְ הַזֶּה אֲשֶׁר הִשְׁבַּעְתָּנוּ:

Banias waterfall landscape

spies. The Children of Israel are not the only ones who understand that God is giving them the Promised Land; the righteous among the nations also recognize that this is the will of *Hashem*. God gave the Children of Israel the Land of Israel then, and He gives it to them now as well.

א **2:14 We will show you true loyalty** The spies promise that they will repay Rahab with 'true loyalty,' *chesed v'emet* (חסד ואמת). Rabbi Benjamin Blech, in his book *The Secrets of Hebrew Words*, teaches that *emet* (אמת), the Hebrew word for 'truth,' contains a deep lesson. The word is comprised of three letters and "requires for its essence the first letter *alef* (א), the "One" standing for the Almighty. Remove the initial letter *alef* and all that remains is *met* (מת), meaning death. Without *Hashem* there can be no truth. In its place only death and destruction remain." אמת

18 [unless,] when we invade the country, you tie this length of crimson cord to the window through which you let us down. Bring your father, your mother, your brothers, and all your family together in your house;

19 and if anyone ventures outside the doors of your house, his blood will be on his head, and we shall be clear. But if a hand is laid on anyone who remains in the house with you, his blood shall be on our heads.

20 And if you disclose this mission of ours, we shall likewise be released from the oath which you made us take."

21 She replied, "Let it be as you say." She sent them on their way, and they left; and she tied the crimson cord to the window.

22 They went straight to the hills and stayed there three days, until the pursuers turned back. And so the pursuers, searching all along the road, did not find them.

23 Then the two men came down again from the hills and crossed over. They came to *Yehoshua* son of *Nun* and reported to him all that had happened to them.

24 They said to *Yehoshua*, "*Hashem* has delivered the whole land into our power; in fact, all the inhabitants of the land are quaking before us."

3 1 Early next morning, *Yehoshua* and all the Israelites set out from Shittim and marched to the *Yarden*. They did not cross immediately, but spent the night there.

2 Three days later, the officials went through the camp

3 and charged the people as follows: "When you see the *Aron Brit Hashem* your God being borne by the levitical *Kohanim*, you shall move forward. Follow it

4 but keep a distance of some two thousand *amot* from it, never coming any closer to it – so that you may know by what route to march, since it is a road you have not traveled before."

יח הִנֵּה אֲנַחְנוּ בָאִים בָּאָרֶץ אֶת־תִּקְוַת חוּט הַשָּׁנִי הַזֶּה תִּקְשְׁרִי בַּחַלּוֹן אֲשֶׁר הוֹרַדְתֵּנוּ בוֹ וְאֶת־אָבִיךְ וְאֶת־אִמֵּךְ וְאֶת־אַחַיִךְ וְאֵת כָּל־בֵּית אָבִיךְ תַּאַסְפִי אֵלַיִךְ הַבָּיְתָה:

יט וְהָיָה כֹּל אֲשֶׁר־יֵצֵא מִדַּלְתֵי בֵיתֵךְ הַחוּצָה דָּמוֹ בְרֹאשׁוֹ וַאֲנַחְנוּ נְקִיִּם וְכֹל אֲשֶׁר יִהְיֶה אִתָּךְ בַּבַּיִת דָּמוֹ בְרֹאשֵׁנוּ אִם־יָד תִּהְיֶה־בּוֹ:

כ וְאִם־תַּגִּידִי אֶת־דְּבָרֵנוּ זֶה וְהָיִינוּ נְקִיִּם מִשְּׁבֻעָתֵךְ אֲשֶׁר הִשְׁבַּעְתָּנוּ:

כא וַתֹּאמֶר כְּדִבְרֵיכֶם כֶּן־הוּא וַתְּשַׁלְּחֵם וַיֵּלֵכוּ וַתִּקְשֹׁר אֶת־תִּקְוַת הַשָּׁנִי בַּחַלּוֹן:

כב וַיֵּלְכוּ וַיָּבֹאוּ הָהָרָה וַיֵּשְׁבוּ שָׁם שְׁלֹשֶׁת יָמִים עַד־שָׁבוּ הָרֹדְפִים וַיְבַקְשׁוּ הָרֹדְפִים בְּכָל־הַדֶּרֶךְ וְלֹא מָצָאוּ:

כג וַיָּשֻׁבוּ שְׁנֵי הָאֲנָשִׁים וַיֵּרְדוּ מֵהָהָר וַיַּעַבְרוּ וַיָּבֹאוּ אֶל־יְהוֹשֻׁעַ בִּן־נוּן וַיְסַפְּרוּ־לוֹ אֵת כָּל־הַמֹּצְאוֹת אוֹתָם:

כד וַיֹּאמְרוּ אֶל־יְהוֹשֻׁעַ כִּי־נָתַן יְהוָה בְּיָדֵנוּ אֶת־כָּל־הָאָרֶץ וְגַם־נָמֹגוּ כָּל־יֹשְׁבֵי הָאָרֶץ מִפָּנֵינוּ:

ג א וַיַּשְׁכֵּם יְהוֹשֻׁעַ בַּבֹּקֶר וַיִּסְעוּ מֵהַשִּׁטִּים וַיָּבֹאוּ עַד־הַיַּרְדֵּן הוּא וְכָל־בְּנֵי יִשְׂרָאֵל וַיָּלִנוּ שָׁם טֶרֶם יַעֲבֹרוּ:

ב וַיְהִי מִקְצֵה שְׁלֹשֶׁת יָמִים וַיַּעַבְרוּ הַשֹּׁטְרִים בְּקֶרֶב הַמַּחֲנֶה:

ג וַיְצַוּוּ אֶת־הָעָם לֵאמֹר כִּרְאוֹתְכֶם אֵת אֲרוֹן בְּרִית־יְהוָה אֱלֹהֵיכֶם וְהַכֹּהֲנִים הַלְוִיִּם נֹשְׂאִים אֹתוֹ וְאַתֶּם תִּסְעוּ מִמְּקוֹמְכֶם וַהֲלַכְתֶּם אַחֲרָיו:

ד אַךְ רָחוֹק יִהְיֶה בֵּינֵיכֶם ובינו [וּבֵינָיו] כְּאַלְפַּיִם אַמָּה בַּמִּדָּה אַל־תִּקְרְבוּ אֵלָיו לְמַעַן אֲשֶׁר־תֵּדְעוּ אֶת־הַדֶּרֶךְ אֲשֶׁר תֵּלְכוּ־בָהּ כִּי לֹא עֲבַרְתֶּם בַּדֶּרֶךְ מִתְּמוֹל שִׁלְשׁוֹם:

5 And *Yehoshua* said to the people, "Purify yourselves, for tomorrow *Hashem* will perform wonders in your midst."

ה וַיֹּאמֶר יְהוֹשֻׁעַ אֶל־הָעָם הִתְקַדָּשׁוּ כִּי מָחָר יַעֲשֶׂה יְהוָה בְּקִרְבְּכֶם נִפְלָאוֹת:

va-YO-mer y'-ho-SHU-a el ha-AM hit-ka-DA-shu KEE ma-KHAR
ya-a-SEH a-do-NAI b'-kir-b'-KHEM nif-la-OT

6 Then *Yehoshua* ordered the *Kohanim*, "Take up the *Aron HaBrit* and advance to the head of the people." And they took up the *Aron HaBrit* and marched at the head of the people.

ו וַיֹּאמֶר יְהוֹשֻׁעַ אֶל־הַכֹּהֲנִים לֵאמֹר שְׂאוּ אֶת־אֲרוֹן הַבְּרִית וְעִבְרוּ לִפְנֵי הָעָם וַיִּשְׂאוּ אֶת־אֲרוֹן הַבְּרִית וַיֵּלְכוּ לִפְנֵי הָעָם:

7 *Hashem* said to *Yehoshua*, "This day, for the first time, I will exalt you in the sight of all *Yisrael*, so that they shall know that I will be with you as I was with *Moshe*.

ז וַיֹּאמֶר יְהוָה אֶל־יְהוֹשֻׁעַ הַיּוֹם הַזֶּה אָחֵל גַּדֶּלְךָ בְּעֵינֵי כָּל־יִשְׂרָאֵל אֲשֶׁר יֵדְעוּן כִּי כַּאֲשֶׁר הָיִיתִי עִם־מֹשֶׁה אֶהְיֶה עִמָּךְ:

8 For your part, command the *Kohanim* who carry the *Aron HaBrit* as follows: When you reach the edge of the waters of the *Yarden*, make a halt in the *Yarden*."

ח וְאַתָּה תְּצַוֶּה אֶת־הַכֹּהֲנִים נֹשְׂאֵי אֲרוֹן־הַבְּרִית לֵאמֹר כְּבֹאֲכֶם עַד־קְצֵה מֵי הַיַּרְדֵּן בַּיַּרְדֵּן תַּעֲמֹדוּ:

9 And *Yehoshua* said to the Israelites, "Come closer and listen to the words of *Hashem* your God.

ט וַיֹּאמֶר יְהוֹשֻׁעַ אֶל־בְּנֵי יִשְׂרָאֵל גֹּשׁוּ הֵנָּה וְשִׁמְעוּ אֶת־דִּבְרֵי יְהוָה אֱלֹהֵיכֶם:

10 By this," *Yehoshua* continued, "you shall know that a living *Hashem* is among you, and that He will dispossess for you the Canaanites, Hittites, Hivites, Perizzites, Girgashites, Amorites, and Jebusites:

י וַיֹּאמֶר יְהוֹשֻׁעַ בְּזֹאת תֵּדְעוּן כִּי אֵל חַי בְּקִרְבְּכֶם וְהוֹרֵשׁ יוֹרִישׁ מִפְּנֵיכֶם אֶת־הַכְּנַעֲנִי וְאֶת־הַחִתִּי וְאֶת־הַחִוִּי וְאֶת־הַפְּרִזִּי וְאֶת־הַגִּרְגָּשִׁי וְהָאֱמֹרִי וְהַיְבוּסִי:

11 the *Aron HaBrit* of the Sovereign of all the earth is advancing before you into the *Yarden*.

יא הִנֵּה אֲרוֹן הַבְּרִית אֲדוֹן כָּל־הָאָרֶץ עֹבֵר לִפְנֵיכֶם בַּיַּרְדֵּן:

12 Now select twelve men from the tribes of *Yisrael*, one man from each tribe.

יב וְעַתָּה קְחוּ לָכֶם שְׁנֵי עָשָׂר אִישׁ מִשִּׁבְטֵי יִשְׂרָאֵל אִישׁ־אֶחָד אִישׁ־אֶחָד לַשָּׁבֶט:

13 When the feet of the *Kohanim* bearing the *Aron* of *Hashem*, the Sovereign of all the earth, come to rest in the waters of the *Yarden*, the waters of the *Yarden* – the water coming from upstream – will be cut off and will stand in a single heap."

יג וְהָיָה כְּנוֹחַ כַּפּוֹת רַגְלֵי הַכֹּהֲנִים נֹשְׂאֵי אֲרוֹן יְהוָה אֲדוֹן כָּל־הָאָרֶץ בְּמֵי הַיַּרְדֵּן מֵי הַיַּרְדֵּן יִכָּרֵתוּן הַמַּיִם הַיֹּרְדִים מִלְמָעְלָה וְיַעַמְדוּ נֵד אֶחָד:

3:5 Tomorrow *Hashem* will perform wonders Yehoshua instructs the people to sanctify themselves, as *Hashem* will perform miracles for them. Typically, miracles require a partnership between God and man. Though ultimately *Hashem* performs the miracle, He expects us to do our part to merit His acting on our behalf. Hence, the Children of Israel need to prepare themselves spiritually and physically, in order to merit the miracles of the parting of the *Yarden* and the victories in the conquest of the Promised Land. In our own era as well, the partnership between man and *Hashem* has resulted in the rebirth and flourishing of the State of Israel. As a result of God's blessings, together with man's hard work, the desert literally blooms, the economy grows, the army defends and the nation continues to absorb countless immigrants from the four corners of the earth. As in the days of *Yehoshua*, the fulfillment of these miracles has demanded both spiritual and physical effort by human beings.

A blossoming kibbutz field

Joshua

14 When the people set out from their encampment to cross the *Yarden*, the *Kohanim* bearing the *Aron HaBrit* were at the head of the people.

יד וַיְהִי בִּנְסֹעַ הָעָם מֵאָהֳלֵיהֶם לַעֲבֹר אֶת־הַיַּרְדֵּן וְהַכֹּהֲנִים נֹשְׂאֵי הָאָרוֹן הַבְּרִית לִפְנֵי הָעָם:

15 Now the *Yarden* keeps flowing over its entire bed throughout the harvest season. But as soon as the bearers of the *Aron* reached the *Yarden*, and the feet of the *Kohanim* bearing the *Aron* dipped into the water at its edge,

טו וּכְבוֹא נֹשְׂאֵי הָאָרוֹן עַד־הַיַּרְדֵּן וְרַגְלֵי הַכֹּהֲנִים נֹשְׂאֵי הָאָרוֹן נִטְבְּלוּ בִּקְצֵה הַמָּיִם וְהַיַּרְדֵּן מָלֵא עַל־כָּל־גְּדוֹתָיו כֹּל יְמֵי קָצִיר:

16 the waters coming down from upstream piled up in a single heap a great way off, at *Adam*, the town next to Zarethan; and those flowing away downstream to the Sea of the Arabah (the Dead Sea) ran out completely. So the people crossed near *Yericho*.

טז וַיַּעַמְדוּ הַמַּיִם הַיֹּרְדִים מִלְמַעְלָה קָמוּ נֵד־אֶחָד הַרְחֵק מְאֹד באדם [מֵאָדָם] הָעִיר אֲשֶׁר מִצַּד צָרְתָן וְהַיֹּרְדִים עַל יָם הָעֲרָבָה יָם־הַמֶּלַח תַּמּוּ נִכְרָתוּ וְהָעָם עָבְרוּ נֶגֶד יְרִיחוֹ:

17 The *Kohanim* who bore the *Aron Brit Hashem* stood on dry land exactly in the middle of the *Yarden*, while all *Yisrael* crossed over on dry land, until the entire nation had finished crossing the *Yarden*.

יז וַיַּעַמְדוּ הַכֹּהֲנִים נֹשְׂאֵי הָאָרוֹן בְּרִית־יְהוָה בֶּחָרָבָה בְּתוֹךְ הַיַּרְדֵּן הָכֵן וְכָל־יִשְׂרָאֵל עֹבְרִים בֶּחָרָבָה עַד אֲשֶׁר־תַּמּוּ כָּל־הַגּוֹי לַעֲבֹר אֶת־הַיַּרְדֵּן:

4 1 When the entire nation had finished crossing the *Yarden*, *Hashem* said to *Yehoshua*,

ד א וַיְהִי כַּאֲשֶׁר־תַּמּוּ כָל־הַגּוֹי לַעֲבוֹר אֶת־הַיַּרְדֵּן וַיֹּאמֶר יְהוָה אֶל־יְהוֹשֻׁעַ לֵאמֹר:

2 "Select twelve men from among the people, one from each tribe,

ב קְחוּ לָכֶם מִן־הָעָם שְׁנֵים עָשָׂר אֲנָשִׁים אִישׁ־אֶחָד אִישׁ־אֶחָד מִשָּׁבֶט:

3 and instruct them as follows: Pick up twelve stones from the spot exactly in the middle of the *Yarden*, where the *Kohanim*' feet are standing; take them along with you and deposit them in the place where you will spend the night."

ג וְצַוּוּ אוֹתָם לֵאמֹר שְׂאוּ־לָכֶם מִזֶּה מִתּוֹךְ הַיַּרְדֵּן מִמַּצַּב רַגְלֵי הַכֹּהֲנִים הָכִין שְׁתֵּים־עֶשְׂרֵה אֲבָנִים וְהַעֲבַרְתֶּם אוֹתָם עִמָּכֶם וְהִנַּחְתֶּם אוֹתָם בַּמָּלוֹן אֲשֶׁר־תָּלִינוּ בוֹ הַלָּיְלָה:

4 *Yehoshua* summoned the twelve men whom he had designated among the Israelites, one from each tribe;

ד וַיִּקְרָא יְהוֹשֻׁעַ אֶל־שְׁנֵים הֶעָשָׂר אִישׁ אֲשֶׁר הֵכִין מִבְּנֵי יִשְׂרָאֵל אִישׁ־אֶחָד אִישׁ־אֶחָד מִשָּׁבֶט:

5 and *Yehoshua* said to them, "Walk up to the *Aron* of *Hashem* your God, in the middle of the *Yarden*, and each of you lift a stone onto his shoulder – corresponding to the number of the tribes of *Yisrael*.

ה וַיֹּאמֶר לָהֶם יְהוֹשֻׁעַ עִבְרוּ לִפְנֵי אֲרוֹן יְהוָה אֱלֹהֵיכֶם אֶל־תּוֹךְ הַיַּרְדֵּן וְהָרִימוּ לָכֶם אִישׁ אֶבֶן אַחַת עַל־שִׁכְמוֹ לְמִסְפַּר שִׁבְטֵי בְנֵי־יִשְׂרָאֵל:

6 This shall serve as a symbol among you: in time to come, when your children ask, 'What is the meaning of these stones for you?'

ו לְמַעַן תִּהְיֶה זֹאת אוֹת בְּקִרְבְּכֶם כִּי־יִשְׁאָלוּן בְּנֵיכֶם מָחָר לֵאמֹר מָה הָאֲבָנִים הָאֵלֶּה לָכֶם:

7 you shall tell them, 'The waters of the *Yarden* were cut off because of the *Aron Brit Hashem*; when it passed through the *Yarden*, the waters of the *Yarden* were cut off.' And so these stones shall serve the people of *Yisrael* as a memorial for all time."

ז וַאֲמַרְתֶּם לָהֶם אֲשֶׁר נִכְרְתוּ מֵימֵי הַיַּרְדֵּן מִפְּנֵי אֲרוֹן בְּרִית־יְהוָה בְּעָבְרוֹ בַּיַּרְדֵּן נִכְרְתוּ מֵי הַיַּרְדֵּן וְהָיוּ הָאֲבָנִים הָאֵלֶּה לְזִכָּרוֹן לִבְנֵי יִשְׂרָאֵל עַד־עוֹלָם:

8 The Israelites did as *Yehoshua* ordered. They picked up twelve stones, corresponding to the number of the tribes of *Yisrael*, from the middle of the *Yarden* – as *Hashem* had charged *Yehoshua* – and they took them along with them to their night encampment and deposited them there.

9 *Yehoshua* also set up twelve stones in the middle of the *Yarden*, at the spot where the feet of the *Kohanim* bearing the *Aron HaBrit* had stood; and they have remained there to this day.

10 The *Kohanim* who bore the *Aron* remained standing in the middle of the *Yarden* until all the instructions that *Hashem* had ordered *Yehoshua* to convey to the people had been carried out. And so the people speedily crossed over, just as *Moshe* had assured *Yehoshua* in his charge to him.

11 And when all the people finished crossing, the *Aron* of *Hashem* and the *Kohanim* advanced to the head of the people.

12 The Reubenites, the Gadites, and the half-tribe of *Menashe* went across armed in the van of the Israelites, as *Moshe* had charged them.

13 About forty thousand shock troops went across, at the instance of *Hashem*, to the steppes of *Yericho* for battle.

14 On that day *Hashem* exalted *Yehoshua* in the sight of all *Yisrael*, so that they revered him all his days as they had revered *Moshe*.

15 *Hashem* said to *Yehoshua*,

16 "Command the *Kohanim* who bear the *Aron HaBrit* to come up out of the *Yarden*."

17 So *Yehoshua* commanded the *Kohanim*, "Come up out of the *Yarden*."

18 As soon as the *Kohanim* who bore the *Aron Brit Hashem* came up out of the *Yarden*, and the feet of the *Kohanim* stepped onto the dry ground, the waters of the *Yarden* resumed their course, flowing over its entire bed as before.

19 The people came up from the *Yarden* on the tenth day of the first month, and encamped at *Gilgal* on the eastern border of *Yericho*.

ח וַיַּעֲשׂוּ־כֵן בְּנֵי־יִשְׂרָאֵל כַּאֲשֶׁר צִוָּה יְהוֹשֻׁעַ וַיִּשְׂאוּ שְׁתֵּי־עֶשְׂרֵה אֲבָנִים מִתּוֹךְ הַיַּרְדֵּן כַּאֲשֶׁר דִּבֶּר יְהֹוָה אֶל־יְהוֹשֻׁעַ לְמִסְפַּר שִׁבְטֵי בְנֵי־יִשְׂרָאֵל וַיַּעֲבִרוּם עִמָּם אֶל־הַמָּלוֹן וַיַּנִּחוּם שָׁם:

ט וּשְׁתֵּים עֶשְׂרֵה אֲבָנִים הֵקִים יְהוֹשֻׁעַ בְּתוֹךְ הַיַּרְדֵּן תַּחַת מַצַּב רַגְלֵי הַכֹּהֲנִים נֹשְׂאֵי אֲרוֹן הַבְּרִית וַיִּהְיוּ שָׁם עַד הַיּוֹם הַזֶּה:

י וְהַכֹּהֲנִים נֹשְׂאֵי הָאָרוֹן עֹמְדִים בְּתוֹךְ הַיַּרְדֵּן עַד תֹּם כָּל־הַדָּבָר אֲשֶׁר־צִוָּה יְהֹוָה אֶת־יְהוֹשֻׁעַ לְדַבֵּר אֶל־הָעָם כְּכֹל אֲשֶׁר־צִוָּה מֹשֶׁה אֶת־יְהוֹשֻׁעַ וַיְמַהֲרוּ הָעָם וַיַּעֲבֹרוּ:

יא וַיְהִי כַּאֲשֶׁר־תַּם כָּל־הָעָם לַעֲבוֹר וַיַּעֲבֹר אֲרוֹן־יְהֹוָה וְהַכֹּהֲנִים לִפְנֵי הָעָם:

יב וַיַּעַבְרוּ בְּנֵי־רְאוּבֵן וּבְנֵי־גָד וַחֲצִי שֵׁבֶט הַמְנַשֶּׁה חֲמֻשִׁים לִפְנֵי בְּנֵי יִשְׂרָאֵל כַּאֲשֶׁר דִּבֶּר אֲלֵיהֶם מֹשֶׁה:

יג כְּאַרְבָּעִים אֶלֶף חֲלוּצֵי הַצָּבָא עָבְרוּ לִפְנֵי יְהֹוָה לַמִּלְחָמָה אֶל עַרְבוֹת יְרִיחוֹ:

יד בַּיּוֹם הַהוּא גִּדַּל יְהֹוָה אֶת־יְהוֹשֻׁעַ בְּעֵינֵי כָּל־יִשְׂרָאֵל וַיִּרְאוּ אֹתוֹ כַּאֲשֶׁר יָרְאוּ אֶת־מֹשֶׁה כָּל־יְמֵי חַיָּיו:

טו וַיֹּאמֶר יְהֹוָה אֶל־יְהוֹשֻׁעַ לֵאמֹר:

טז צַוֵּה אֶת־הַכֹּהֲנִים נֹשְׂאֵי אֲרוֹן הָעֵדוּת וְיַעֲלוּ מִן־הַיַּרְדֵּן:

יז וַיְצַו יְהוֹשֻׁעַ אֶת־הַכֹּהֲנִים לֵאמֹר עֲלוּ מִן־הַיַּרְדֵּן:

יח וַיְהִי בַּעֲלוֹת [כַּעֲלוֹת] הַכֹּהֲנִים נֹשְׂאֵי אֲרוֹן בְּרִית־יְהֹוָה מִתּוֹךְ הַיַּרְדֵּן נִתְּקוּ כַּפּוֹת רַגְלֵי הַכֹּהֲנִים אֶל הֶחָרָבָה וַיָּשֻׁבוּ מֵי־הַיַּרְדֵּן לִמְקוֹמָם וַיֵּלְכוּ כִתְמוֹל־שִׁלְשׁוֹם עַל־כָּל־גְּדוֹתָיו:

יט וְהָעָם עָלוּ מִן־הַיַּרְדֵּן בֶּעָשׂוֹר לַחֹדֶשׁ הָרִאשׁוֹן וַיַּחֲנוּ בַּגִּלְגָּל בִּקְצֵה מִזְרַח יְרִיחוֹ:

20 And *Yehoshua* set up in *Gilgal* the twelve stones they had taken from the *Yarden*.

כ וְאֵת שְׁתֵּים עֶשְׂרֵה הָאֲבָנִים הָאֵלֶּה אֲשֶׁר לָקְחוּ מִן־הַיַּרְדֵּן הֵקִים יְהוֹשֻׁעַ בַּגִּלְגָּל:

v'-AYT sh'-TAYM es-RAY ha-a-va-NEEM ha-AY-leh a-SHER la-k'-KHU min ha-yar-DAYN hay-KEEM y'-ho-SHU-a ba-gil-GAL

21 He charged the Israelites as follows: "In time to come, when your children ask their fathers, 'What is the meaning of those stones?'

כא וַיֹּאמֶר אֶל־בְּנֵי יִשְׂרָאֵל לֵאמֹר אֲשֶׁר יִשְׁאָלוּן בְּנֵיכֶם מָחָר אֶת־אֲבוֹתָם לֵאמֹר מָה הָאֲבָנִים הָאֵלֶּה:

22 tell your children: 'Here the Israelites crossed the *Yarden* on dry land.'

כב וְהוֹדַעְתֶּם אֶת־בְּנֵיכֶם לֵאמֹר בַּיַּבָּשָׁה עָבַר יִשְׂרָאֵל אֶת־הַיַּרְדֵּן הַזֶּה:

23 For *Hashem* your God dried up the waters of the *Yarden* before you until you crossed, just as *Hashem* your God did to the Sea of Reeds, which He dried up before us until we crossed.

כג אֲשֶׁר־הוֹבִישׁ יְהוָה אֱלֹהֵיכֶם אֶת־מֵי הַיַּרְדֵּן מִפְּנֵיכֶם עַד־עָבְרְכֶם כַּאֲשֶׁר עָשָׂה יְהוָה אֱלֹהֵיכֶם לְיַם־סוּף אֲשֶׁר־הוֹבִישׁ מִפָּנֵינוּ עַד־עָבְרֵנוּ:

24 Thus all the peoples of the earth shall know how mighty is the hand of *Hashem*, and you shall fear *Hashem* your God always."

כד לְמַעַן דַּעַת כָּל־עַמֵּי הָאָרֶץ אֶת־יַד יְהוָה כִּי חֲזָקָה הִיא לְמַעַן יְרָאתֶם אֶת־יְהוָה אֱלֹהֵיכֶם כָּל־הַיָּמִים:

5 1 When all the kings of the Amorites on the western side of the *Yarden*, and all the kings of the Canaanites near the Sea, heard how *Hashem* had dried up the waters of the *Yarden* for the sake of the Israelites until they crossed over, they lost heart, and no spirit was left in them because of the Israelites.

ה א וַיְהִי כִשְׁמֹעַ כָּל־מַלְכֵי הָאֱמֹרִי אֲשֶׁר בְּעֵבֶר הַיַּרְדֵּן יָמָּה וְכָל־מַלְכֵי הַכְּנַעֲנִי אֲשֶׁר עַל־הַיָּם אֵת אֲשֶׁר־הוֹבִישׁ יְהוָה אֶת־מֵי הַיַּרְדֵּן מִפְּנֵי בְנֵי־יִשְׂרָאֵל עַד־עׇבְרָנוּ [עָבְרָם] וַיִּמַּס לְבָבָם וְלֹא־הָיָה בָם עוֹד רוּחַ מִפְּנֵי בְּנֵי־יִשְׂרָאֵל:

2 At that time *Hashem* said to *Yehoshua*, "Make flint knives and proceed with a second circumcision of the Israelites."

ב בָּעֵת הַהִיא אָמַר יְהוָה אֶל־יְהוֹשֻׁעַ עֲשֵׂה לְךָ חַרְבוֹת צֻרִים וְשׁוּב מֹל אֶת־בְּנֵי־יִשְׂרָאֵל שֵׁנִית:

3 So *Yehoshua* had flint knives made, and the Israelites were circumcised at Gibeath-haaraloth.

ג וַיַּעַשׂ־לוֹ יְהוֹשֻׁעַ חַרְבוֹת צֻרִים וַיָּמָל אֶת־בְּנֵי יִשְׂרָאֵל אֶל־גִּבְעַת הָעֲרָלוֹת:

4 This is the reason why *Yehoshua* had the circumcision performed: All the people who had come out of Egypt, all the males of military age, had died during the desert wanderings after leaving Egypt.

ד וְזֶה הַדָּבָר אֲשֶׁר־מָל יְהוֹשֻׁעַ כָּל־הָעָם הַיֹּצֵא מִמִּצְרַיִם הַזְּכָרִים כֹּל אַנְשֵׁי הַמִּלְחָמָה מֵתוּ בַמִּדְבָּר בַּדֶּרֶךְ בְּצֵאתָם מִמִּצְרָיִם:

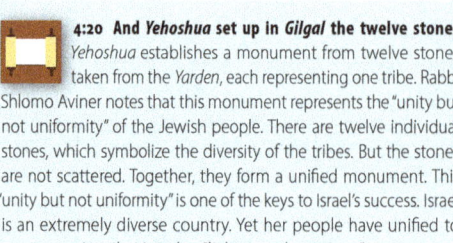

4:20 And *Yehoshua* set up in *Gilgal* the twelve stones *Yehoshua* establishes a monument from twelve stones taken from the *Yarden*, each representing one tribe. Rabbi Shlomo Aviner notes that this monument represents the "unity but not uniformity" of the Jewish people. There are twelve individual stones, which symbolize the diversity of the tribes. But the stones are not scattered. Together, they form a unified monument. This "unity but not uniformity" is one of the keys to Israel's success. Israel is an extremely diverse country. Yet her people have unified to create a society that is truly a "light unto the nations."

Proposed location of biblical *Gilgal*

5 Now, whereas all the people who came out
of Egypt had been circumcised, none of the
people born after the exodus, during the desert
wanderings, had been circumcised.

ה כִּי־מֻלִים הָיוּ כָּל־הָעָם הַיֹּצְאִים וְכָל־
הָעָם הַיִּלֹּדִים בַּמִּדְבָּר בַּדֶּרֶךְ בְּצֵאתָם
מִמִּצְרַיִם לֹא־מָלוּ:

6 For the Israelites had traveled in the wilderness
forty years, until the entire nation – the men of
military age who had left Egypt – had perished;
because they had not obeyed *Hashem*, and *Hashem*
had sworn never to let them see the land that
Hashem had sworn to their fathers to assign to us, a
land flowing with milk and honey.

ו כִּי אַרְבָּעִים שָׁנָה הָלְכוּ בְנֵי־יִשְׂרָאֵל
בַּמִּדְבָּר עַד־תֹּם כָּל־הַגּוֹי אַנְשֵׁי
הַמִּלְחָמָה הַיֹּצְאִים מִמִּצְרַיִם אֲשֶׁר לֹא־
שָׁמְעוּ בְּקוֹל יְהוָֹה אֲשֶׁר נִשְׁבַּע יְהוָֹה
לָהֶם לְבִלְתִּי הַרְאוֹתָם אֶת־הָאָרֶץ אֲשֶׁר
נִשְׁבַּע יְהוָֹה לַאֲבוֹתָם לָתֶת לָנוּ אֶרֶץ
זָבַת חָלָב וּדְבָשׁ:

7 But He had raised up their sons in their stead; and
it was these that *Yehoshua* circumcised, for they
were uncircumcised, not having been circumcised
on the way.

ז וְאֶת־בְּנֵיהֶם הֵקִים תַּחְתָּם אֹתָם מָל
יְהוֹשֻׁעַ כִּי־עֲרֵלִים הָיוּ כִּי לֹא־מָלוּ
אוֹתָם בַּדָּרֶךְ:

8 After the circumcising of the whole nation was
completed, they remained where they were, in the
camp, until they recovered.

ח וַיְהִי כַּאֲשֶׁר־תַּמּוּ כָל־הַגּוֹי לְהִמּוֹל
וַיֵּשְׁבוּ תַחְתָּם בַּמַּחֲנֶה עַד חֲיוֹתָם:

9 And *Hashem* said to *Yehoshua*, "Today I have rolled
away from you the disgrace of Egypt." So that place
was called *Gilgal*, as it still is.

ט וַיֹּאמֶר יְהוָֹה אֶל־יְהוֹשֻׁעַ הַיּוֹם גַּלּוֹתִי
אֶת־חֶרְפַּת מִצְרַיִם מֵעֲלֵיכֶם וַיִּקְרָא
שֵׁם הַמָּקוֹם הַהוּא גִּלְגָּל עַד הַיּוֹם הַזֶּה:

10 Encamped at *Gilgal*, in the steppes of *Yericho*,
the Israelites offered the *Pesach* sacrifice on the
fourteenth day of the month, toward evening.

י וַיַּחֲנוּ בְנֵי־יִשְׂרָאֵל בַּגִּלְגָּל וַיַּעֲשׂוּ אֶת־
הַפֶּסַח בְּאַרְבָּעָה עָשָׂר יוֹם לַחֹדֶשׁ
בָּעֶרֶב בְּעַרְבוֹת יְרִיחוֹ:

11 On the day after the *Pesach* offering, on that
very day, they ate of the produce of the country,
unleavened bread and parched grain.

יא וַיֹּאכְלוּ מֵעֲבוּר הָאָרֶץ מִמָּחֳרַת הַפֶּסַח
מַצּוֹת וְקָלוּי בְּעֶצֶם הַיּוֹם הַזֶּה:

12 On that same day, when they ate of the produce of
the land, the manna ceased. The Israelites got no
more manna; that year they ate of the yield of the
land of Canaan.

יב וַיִּשְׁבֹּת הַמָּן מִמָּחֳרָת בְּאָכְלָם מֵעֲבוּר
הָאָרֶץ וְלֹא־הָיָה עוֹד לִבְנֵי יִשְׂרָאֵל מָן
וַיֹּאכְלוּ מִתְּבוּאַת אֶרֶץ כְּנַעַן בַּשָּׁנָה
הַהִיא:

13 Once, when *Yehoshua* was near *Yericho*, he looked
up and saw a man standing before him, drawn
sword in hand. *Yehoshua* went up to him and asked
him, "Are you one of us or of our enemies?"

יג וַיְהִי בִּהְיוֹת יְהוֹשֻׁעַ בִּירִיחוֹ וַיִּשָּׂא עֵינָיו
וַיַּרְא וְהִנֵּה־אִישׁ עֹמֵד לְנֶגְדּוֹ וְחַרְבּוֹ
שְׁלוּפָה בְּיָדוֹ וַיֵּלֶךְ יְהוֹשֻׁעַ אֵלָיו וַיֹּאמֶר
לוֹ הֲלָנוּ אַתָּה אִם־לְצָרֵינוּ:

14 He replied, "No, I am captain of *Hashem*'s host.
Now I have come!" *Yehoshua* threw himself face
down to the ground and, prostrating himself,
said to him, "What does my lord command his
servant?"

יד וַיֹּאמֶר לֹא כִּי אֲנִי שַׂר־צְבָא־יְהוָֹה עַתָּה
בָאתִי וַיִּפֹּל יְהוֹשֻׁעַ אֶל־פָּנָיו אַרְצָה
וַיִּשְׁתָּחוּ וַיֹּאמֶר לוֹ מָה אֲדֹנִי מְדַבֵּר
אֶל־עַבְדּוֹ:

15 The captain of *Hashem*'s host answered *Yehoshua*, "Remove your sandals from your feet, for the place where you stand is holy." And *Yehoshua* did so.

טו וַיֹּאמֶר שַׂר־צְבָא יְהוָה אֶל־יְהוֹשֻׁעַ שַׁל־נַעַלְךָ מֵעַל רַגְלֶךָ כִּי הַמָּקוֹם אֲשֶׁר אַתָּה עֹמֵד עָלָיו קֹדֶשׁ הוּא וַיַּעַשׂ יְהוֹשֻׁעַ כֵּן:

va-YO-mer sar tz'-VA a-do-NAI el y'-ho-SHU-a shal na-al-KHA may-AL rag-LE-kha KEE ha-ma-KOM a-SHER a-TAH o-MAYD a-LAV KO-desh HU va-YA-as y'-ho-SHU-a KAYN

6 ¹ Now *Yericho* was shut up tight because of the Israelites; no one could leave or enter.

ו א וִירִיחוֹ סֹגֶרֶת וּמְסֻגֶּרֶת מִפְּנֵי בְּנֵי יִשְׂרָאֵל אֵין יוֹצֵא וְאֵין בָּא:

vee-ree-KHO so-GE-ret um-su-GE-ret mi-p'-NAY b'-NAY yis-ra-AYL AYN yo-TZAY v'-AYN ba

² *Hashem* said to *Yehoshua*, "See, I will deliver *Yericho* and her king [and her] warriors into your hands.

ב וַיֹּאמֶר יְהוָה אֶל־יְהוֹשֻׁעַ רְאֵה נָתַתִּי בְיָדְךָ אֶת־יְרִיחוֹ וְאֶת־מַלְכָּהּ גִּבּוֹרֵי הֶחָיִל:

³ Let all your troops march around the city and complete one circuit of the city. Do this six days,

ג וְסַבֹּתֶם אֶת־הָעִיר כֹּל אַנְשֵׁי הַמִּלְחָמָה הַקֵּיף אֶת־הָעִיר פַּעַם אֶחָת כֹּה תַעֲשֶׂה שֵׁשֶׁת יָמִים:

⁴ with seven *Kohanim* carrying seven *shofarot* preceding the *Aron*. On the seventh day, march around the city seven times, with the *Kohanim* blowing the *shofarot*.

ד וְשִׁבְעָה כֹהֲנִים יִשְׂאוּ שִׁבְעָה שׁוֹפְרוֹת הַיּוֹבְלִים לִפְנֵי הָאָרוֹן וּבַיּוֹם הַשְּׁבִיעִי תָּסֹבּוּ אֶת־הָעִיר שֶׁבַע פְּעָמִים וְהַכֹּהֲנִים יִתְקְעוּ בַּשּׁוֹפָרוֹת:

⁵ And when a long blast is sounded on the *shofar* – as soon as you hear that sound of the *shofar* – all the people shall give a mighty shout. Thereupon the city wall will collapse, and the people shall advance, every man straight ahead."

ה וְהָיָה בִּמְשֹׁךְ בְּקֶרֶן הַיּוֹבֵל בשמעכם [כְּשָׁמְעֲכֶם] אֶת־קוֹל הַשּׁוֹפָר יָרִיעוּ כָל־הָעָם תְּרוּעָה גְדוֹלָה וְנָפְלָה חוֹמַת הָעִיר תַּחְתֶּיהָ וְעָלוּ הָעָם אִישׁ נֶגְדּוֹ:

⁶ *Yehoshua* son of *Nun* summoned the *Kohanim* and said to them, "Take up the *Aron HaBrit*, and let seven *Kohanim* carrying seven *shofarot* precede the *Aron* of *Hashem*."

ו וַיִּקְרָא יְהוֹשֻׁעַ בִּן־נוּן אֶל־הַכֹּהֲנִים וַיֹּאמֶר אֲלֵהֶם שְׂאוּ אֶת־אֲרוֹן הַבְּרִית וְשִׁבְעָה כֹהֲנִים יִשְׂאוּ שִׁבְעָה שׁוֹפְרוֹת יוֹבְלִים לִפְנֵי אֲרוֹן יְהוָה:

Desert hills with Jericho in the distance

5:15 Remove your sandals from your feet, for the place where you stand is holy *Yehoshua* is told to remove his shoes because the place where he is standing is reminiscent of the similar command given to *Moshe* while standing at the burning bush on the mountain of God, Mount Sinai (Exodus 3:5). But there is a critical difference. Unlike Sinai, which attained only temporary holiness, the place upon which *Yehoshua* is standing is eternally sacred. He is standing upon the ground of *Eretz Yisrael*.

6:1 Now *Yericho* was shut up tight because of the Israelites Archeological finds of the past 150 years have granted significant understandings

and insights into the world of the Bible, while also leaving us with many unanswered questions. In a 1983 interview, Israel's first Chief of Staff and renowned archaeologist, Yigael Yadin, addressed the limits of biblical archaeology. Describing this passage in *Sefer Yehoshua* about the miraculous nature of the tumbling walls of *Yericho*, Yadin opined: "That's beyond the realm of archaeology, and I think it's beyond the realm of history as well. It's a matter of faith…The fact is that there was a city there, in my opinion, and it was conquered. There can be no doubt." According to many ancient Jewish philosophers, science and nature are not meant to validate our faith, nor is archeology. However, they can serve as powerful tools in bolstering our faith to believe in the truth of God's word in a more complete and complex fashion.

Yigael Yadin (1917–1984)

7 And he instructed the people, "Go forward, march around the city, with the vanguard marching in front of the *Aron* of *Hashem*."

ז וַיֹּאמְרוּ [וַיֹּאמֶר] אֶל־הָעָם עִבְרוּ וְסֹבּוּ אֶת־הָעִיר וְהֶחָלוּץ יַעֲבֹר לִפְנֵי אֲרוֹן יְהֹוָה:

8 When *Yehoshua* had instructed the people, the seven *Kohanim* carrying seven *shofarot* advanced before *Hashem*, blowing their *shofarot*; and the *Aron Brit Hashem* followed them.

ח וַיְהִי כֶּאֱמֹר יְהוֹשֻׁעַ אֶל־הָעָם וְשִׁבְעָה הַכֹּהֲנִים נֹשְׂאִים שִׁבְעָה שׁוֹפְרוֹת הַיּוֹבְלִים לִפְנֵי יְהֹוָה עָבְרוּ וְתָקְעוּ בַּשּׁוֹפָרוֹת וַאֲרוֹן בְּרִית יְהֹוָה הֹלֵךְ אַחֲרֵיהֶם:

9 The vanguard marched in front of the *Kohanim* who were blowing the *shofarot*, and the rear guard marched behind the *Aron*, with the *shofarot* sounding all the time.

ט וְהֶחָלוּץ הֹלֵךְ לִפְנֵי הַכֹּהֲנִים תקעו [תֹּקְעֵי] הַשּׁוֹפָרוֹת וְהַמְאַסֵּף הֹלֵךְ אַחֲרֵי הָאָרוֹן הָלוֹךְ וְתָקוֹעַ בַּשּׁוֹפָרוֹת:

10 But *Yehoshua*'s orders to the rest of the people were, "Do not shout, do not let your voices be heard, and do not let a sound issue from your lips until the moment that I command you, 'Shout!' Then you shall shout."

י וְאֶת־הָעָם צִוָּה יְהוֹשֻׁעַ לֵאמֹר לֹא תָרִיעוּ וְלֹא־תַשְׁמִיעוּ אֶת־קוֹלְכֶם וְלֹא־יֵצֵא מִפִּיכֶם דָּבָר עַד יוֹם אָמְרִי אֲלֵיכֶם הָרִיעוּ וַהֲרִיעֹתֶם:

11 So he had the *Aron* of *Hashem* go around the city and complete one circuit; then they returned to camp and spent the night in camp.

יא וַיַּסֵּב אֲרוֹן־יְהֹוָה אֶת־הָעִיר הַקֵּף פַּעַם אֶחָת וַיָּבֹאוּ הַמַּחֲנֶה וַיָּלִינוּ בַּמַּחֲנֶה:

12 *Yehoshua* rose early the next day; and the *Kohanim* took up the *Aron* of *Hashem*,

יב וַיַּשְׁכֵּם יְהוֹשֻׁעַ בַּבֹּקֶר וַיִּשְׂאוּ הַכֹּהֲנִים אֶת־אֲרוֹן יְהֹוָה:

13 while the seven *Kohanim* bearing the seven *shofarot* marched in front of the *Aron* of *Hashem*, blowing the *shofarot* as they marched. The vanguard marched in front of them, and the rear guard marched behind the *Aron* of *Hashem*, with the *shofarot* sounding all the time.

יג וְשִׁבְעָה הַכֹּהֲנִים נֹשְׂאִים שִׁבְעָה שׁוֹפְרוֹת הַיֹּבְלִים לִפְנֵי אֲרוֹן יְהֹוָה הֹלְכִים הָלוֹךְ וְתָקְעוּ בַּשּׁוֹפָרוֹת וְהֶחָלוּץ הֹלֵךְ לִפְנֵיהֶם וְהַמְאַסֵּף הֹלֵךְ אַחֲרֵי אֲרוֹן יְהֹוָה הולך [הָלוֹךְ] וְתָקוֹעַ בַּשּׁוֹפָרוֹת:

14 And so they marched around the city once on the second day and returned to the camp. They did this six days.

יד וַיָּסֹבּוּ אֶת־הָעִיר בַּיּוֹם הַשֵּׁנִי פַּעַם אַחַת וַיָּשֻׁבוּ הַמַּחֲנֶה כֹּה עָשׂוּ שֵׁשֶׁת יָמִים:

15 On the seventh day, they rose at daybreak and marched around the city, in the same manner, seven times; that was the only day that they marched around the city seven times.

טו וַיְהִי בַּיּוֹם הַשְּׁבִיעִי וַיַּשְׁכִּמוּ כַּעֲלוֹת הַשַּׁחַר וַיָּסֹבּוּ אֶת־הָעִיר כַּמִּשְׁפָּט הַזֶּה שֶׁבַע פְּעָמִים רַק בַּיּוֹם הַהוּא סָבְבוּ אֶת־הָעִיר שֶׁבַע פְּעָמִים:

*vai-HEE ba-YOM ha-sh'-vee-EE va-yash-KI-mu ka-a-LOT ha-SHA-khar
va-ya-SO-bu et ha-EER ka-mish-PAT ha-ZEH SHE-va p'-a-MEEM
RAK ba-YOM ha-HU sa-v'-VU et ha-EER SHE-va p'-a-MEEM*

6:15 On the seventh day On the seventh day, the Children of Israel walk around *Yericho* seven times. They blow the *shofarot* (שופרות), 'rams horns,' the walls miraculously fall, and they are able to take the city. The classical commentator *Rashi* notes that the seventh day of this process was *Shabbat*. This teaches us that war on behalf of defending the people and Land of Israel is permitted and required even on the peaceful and

Joshua

16   On the seventh round, as the *Kohanim* blew the *shofarot*, *Yehoshua* commanded the people, "Shout! For *Hashem* has given you the city.

טז   וַיְהִי בַּפַּעַם הַשְּׁבִיעִית תָּקְעוּ הַכֹּהֲנִים בַּשּׁוֹפָרוֹת וַיֹּאמֶר יְהוֹשֻׁעַ אֶל־הָעָם הָרִיעוּ כִּי־נָתַן יְהוָה לָכֶם אֶת־הָעִיר:

17   The city and everything in it are to be proscribed for *Hashem*; only Rahab the harlot is to be spared, and all who are with her in the house, because she hid the messengers we sent.

יז   וְהָיְתָה הָעִיר חֵרֶם הִיא וְכָל־אֲשֶׁר־בָּהּ לַיהוָה רַק רָחָב הַזּוֹנָה תִּחְיֶה הִיא וְכָל־אֲשֶׁר אִתָּהּ בַּבַּיִת כִּי הֶחְבְּאַתָה אֶת־הַמַּלְאָכִים אֲשֶׁר שָׁלָחְנוּ:

18   But you must beware of that which is proscribed, or else you will be proscribed: if you take anything from that which is proscribed, you will cause the camp of *Yisrael* to be proscribed; you will bring calamity upon it.

יח   וְרַק־אַתֶּם שִׁמְרוּ מִן־הַחֵרֶם פֶּן־תַּחֲרִימוּ וּלְקַחְתֶּם מִן־הַחֵרֶם וְשַׂמְתֶּם אֶת־מַחֲנֵה יִשְׂרָאֵל לְחֵרֶם וַעֲכַרְתֶּם אוֹתוֹ:

19   All the silver and gold and objects of copper and iron are consecrated to *Hashem*; they must go into the treasury of *Hashem*."

יט   וְכֹל כֶּסֶף וְזָהָב וּכְלֵי נְחֹשֶׁת וּבַרְזֶל קֹדֶשׁ הוּא לַיהוָה אוֹצַר יְהוָה יָבוֹא:

20   So the people shouted when the *shofarot* were sounded. When the people heard the sound of the *shofarot*, the people raised a mighty shout and the wall collapsed. The people rushed into the city, every man straight in front of him, and they captured the city.

כ   וַיָּרַע הָעָם וַיִּתְקְעוּ בַּשֹּׁפָרוֹת וַיְהִי כִשְׁמֹעַ הָעָם אֶת־קוֹל הַשּׁוֹפָר וַיָּרִיעוּ הָעָם תְּרוּעָה גְדוֹלָה וַתִּפֹּל הַחוֹמָה תַּחְתֶּיהָ וַיַּעַל הָעָם הָעִירָה אִישׁ נֶגְדּוֹ וַיִּלְכְּדוּ אֶת־הָעִיר:

21   They exterminated everything in the city with the sword: man and woman, young and old, ox and sheep and ass.

כא   וַיַּחֲרִימוּ אֶת־כָּל־אֲשֶׁר בָּעִיר מֵאִישׁ וְעַד־אִשָּׁה מִנַּעַר וְעַד־זָקֵן וְעַד שׁוֹר וָשֶׂה וַחֲמוֹר לְפִי־חָרֶב:

22   But *Yehoshua* bade the two men who had spied out the land, "Go into the harlot's house and bring out the woman and all that belong to her, as you swore to her."

כב   וְלִשְׁנַיִם הָאֲנָשִׁים הַמְרַגְּלִים אֶת־הָאָרֶץ אָמַר יְהוֹשֻׁעַ בֹּאוּ בֵּית־הָאִשָּׁה הַזּוֹנָה וְהוֹצִיאוּ מִשָּׁם אֶת־הָאִשָּׁה וְאֶת־כָּל־אֲשֶׁר־לָהּ כַּאֲשֶׁר נִשְׁבַּעְתֶּם לָהּ:

23   So the young spies went in and brought out Rahab, her father and her mother, her brothers and all that belonged to her – they brought out her whole family and left them outside the camp of *Yisrael*.

כג   וַיָּבֹאוּ הַנְּעָרִים הַמְרַגְּלִים וַיֹּצִיאוּ אֶת־רָחָב וְאֶת־אָבִיהָ וְאֶת־אִמָּהּ וְאֶת־אַחֶיהָ וְאֶת־כָּל־אֲשֶׁר־לָהּ וְאֵת כָּל־מִשְׁפְּחוֹתֶיהָ הוֹצִיאוּ וַיַּנִּיחוּם מִחוּץ לְמַחֲנֵה יִשְׂרָאֵל:

24   They burned down the city and everything in it. But the silver and gold and the objects of copper and iron were deposited in the treasury of the House of *Hashem*.

כד   וְהָעִיר שָׂרְפוּ בָאֵשׁ וְכָל־אֲשֶׁר־בָּהּ רַק הַכֶּסֶף וְהַזָּהָב וּכְלֵי הַנְּחֹשֶׁת וְהַבַּרְזֶל נָתְנוּ אוֹצַר בֵּית־יְהוָה:

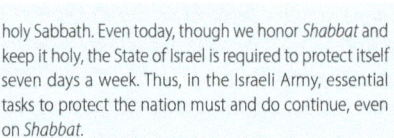

holy Sabbath. Even today, though we honor *Shabbat* and keep it holy, the State of Israel is required to protect itself seven days a week. Thus, in the Israeli Army, essential tasks to protect the nation must and do continue, even on *Shabbat*.

Blowing the rams horn (*shofar*)

25 Only Rahab the harlot and her father's family were spared by *Yehoshua*, along with all that belonged to her, and she dwelt among the Israelites – as is still the case. For she had hidden the messengers that *Yehoshua* sent to spy out *Yericho*.

כה וְאֶת־רָחָב הַזּוֹנָה וְאֶת־בֵּית אָבִיהָ וְאֶת־כָּל־אֲשֶׁר־לָהּ הֶחֱיָה יְהוֹשֻׁעַ וַתֵּשֶׁב בְּקֶרֶב יִשְׂרָאֵל עַד הַיּוֹם הַזֶּה כִּי הֶחְבִּיאָה אֶת־הַמַּלְאָכִים אֲשֶׁר־שָׁלַח יְהוֹשֻׁעַ לְרַגֵּל אֶת־יְרִיחוֹ:

26 At that time *Yehoshua* pronounced this oath: "Cursed of *Hashem* be the man who shall undertake to fortify this city of *Yericho*: he shall lay its foundations at the cost of his first-born, and set up its gates at the cost of his youngest."

כו וַיַּשְׁבַּע יְהוֹשֻׁעַ בָּעֵת הַהִיא לֵאמֹר אָרוּר הָאִישׁ לִפְנֵי יְהוָה אֲשֶׁר יָקוּם וּבָנָה אֶת־הָעִיר הַזֹּאת אֶת־יְרִיחוֹ בִּבְכֹרוֹ יְיַסְּדֶנָּה וּבִצְעִירוֹ יַצִּיב דְּלָתֶיהָ:

27 *Hashem* was with *Yehoshua*, and his fame spread throughout the land.

כז וַיְהִי יְהוָה אֶת־יְהוֹשֻׁעַ וַיְהִי שָׁמְעוֹ בְּכָל־הָאָרֶץ:

7 1 The Israelites, however, violated the proscription: *Achan* son of Carmi son of Zabdi son of *Zerach*, of the tribe of *Yehuda*, took of that which was proscribed, and *Hashem* was incensed with the Israelites.

ז א וַיִּמְעֲלוּ בְנֵי־יִשְׂרָאֵל מַעַל בַּחֵרֶם וַיִּקַּח עָכָן בֶּן־כַּרְמִי בֶן־זַבְדִּי בֶן־זֶרַח לְמַטֵּה יְהוּדָה מִן־הַחֵרֶם וַיִּחַר־אַף יְהוָה בִּבְנֵי יִשְׂרָאֵל:

2 *Yehoshua* sent men from *Yericho* to Ai, which lies close to *Beit Aven* – east of *Beit El* – with orders to go up and spy out the country. So the men went up and spied out Ai.

ב וַיִּשְׁלַח יְהוֹשֻׁעַ אֲנָשִׁים מִירִיחוֹ הָעַי אֲשֶׁר עִם־בֵּית אָוֶן מִקֶּדֶם לְבֵית־אֵל וַיֹּאמֶר אֲלֵיהֶם לֵאמֹר עֲלוּ וְרַגְּלוּ אֶת־הָאָרֶץ וַיַּעֲלוּ הָאֲנָשִׁים וַיְרַגְּלוּ אֶת־הָעָי:

3 They returned to *Yehoshua* and reported to him, "Not all the troops need go up. Let two or three thousand men go and attack Ai; do not trouble all the troops to up there, for [the people] there are few."

ג וַיָּשֻׁבוּ אֶל־יְהוֹשֻׁעַ וַיֹּאמְרוּ אֵלָיו אַל־יַעַל כָּל־הָעָם כְּאַלְפַּיִם אִישׁ אוֹ כִּשְׁלֹשֶׁת אֲלָפִים אִישׁ יַעֲלוּ וְיַכּוּ אֶת־הָעָי אַל־תְּיַגַּע־שָׁמָּה אֶת־כָּל־הָעָם כִּי מְעַט הֵמָּה:

4 So about three thousand of the troops marched up there; but they were routed by the men of Ai.

ד וַיַּעֲלוּ מִן־הָעָם שָׁמָּה כִּשְׁלֹשֶׁת אֲלָפִים אִישׁ וַיָּנֻסוּ לִפְנֵי אַנְשֵׁי הָעָי:

5 The men of Ai killed about thirty-six of them, pursuing them outside the gate as far as Shebarim, and cutting them down along the descent. And the heart of the troops sank in utter dismay.

ה וַיַּכּוּ מֵהֶם אַנְשֵׁי הָעַי כִּשְׁלֹשִׁים וְשִׁשָּׁה אִישׁ וַיִּרְדְּפוּם לִפְנֵי הַשַּׁעַר עַד־הַשְּׁבָרִים וַיַּכּוּם בַּמּוֹרָד וַיִּמַּס לְבַב־הָעָם וַיְהִי לְמָיִם:

6 *Yehoshua* thereupon rent his clothes. He and the elders of *Yisrael* lay until evening with their faces to the ground in front of the *Aron* of *Hashem*; and they strewed earth on their heads.

ו וַיִּקְרַע יְהוֹשֻׁעַ שִׂמְלֹתָיו וַיִּפֹּל עַל־פָּנָיו אַרְצָה לִפְנֵי אֲרוֹן יְהוָה עַד־הָעֶרֶב הוּא וְזִקְנֵי יִשְׂרָאֵל וַיַּעֲלוּ עָפָר עַל־רֹאשָׁם:

7 "Ah, *Hashem*!" cried *Yehoshua*. "Why did You lead this people across the *Yarden* only to deliver us into the hands of the Amorites, to be destroyed by them? If only we had been content to remain on the other side of the *Yarden*!

ז וַיֹּאמֶר יְהוֹשֻׁעַ אֲהָהּ אֲדֹנָי יְהוִה לָמָה הֵעֲבַרְתָּ הַעֲבִיר אֶת־הָעָם הַזֶּה אֶת־הַיַּרְדֵּן לָתֵת אֹתָנוּ בְּיַד הָאֱמֹרִי לְהַאֲבִידֵנוּ וְלוּ הוֹאַלְנוּ וַנֵּשֶׁב בְּעֵבֶר הַיַּרְדֵּן:

8 O *Hashem*, what can I say after *Yisrael* has turned tail before its enemies?

ח בִּי אֲדֹנָי מָה אֹמַר אַחֲרֵי אֲשֶׁר הָפַךְ יִשְׂרָאֵל עֹרֶף לִפְנֵי אֹיְבָיו:

Joshua

9 When the Canaanites and all the inhabitants of the land hear of this, they will turn upon us and wipe out our very name from the earth. And what will You do about Your great name?"

ט וְיִשְׁמְעוּ הַכְּנַעֲנִי וְכֹל יֹשְׁבֵי הָאָרֶץ וְנָסַבּוּ עָלֵינוּ וְהִכְרִיתוּ אֶת־שְׁמֵנוּ מִן־הָאָרֶץ וּמַה־תַּעֲשֵׂה לְשִׁמְךָ הַגָּדוֹל:

10 But *Hashem* answered *Yehoshua*: "Arise! Why do you lie prostrate?

י וַיֹּאמֶר יְהֹוָה אֶל־יְהוֹשֻׁעַ קֻם לָךְ לָמָּה זֶּה אַתָּה נֹפֵל עַל־פָּנֶיךָ:

11 *Yisrael* has sinned! They have broken the covenant by which I bound them. They have taken of the proscribed and put it in their vessels; they have stolen; they have broken faith!

יא חָטָא יִשְׂרָאֵל וְגַם עָבְרוּ אֶת־בְּרִיתִי אֲשֶׁר צִוִּיתִי אוֹתָם וְגַם לָקְחוּ מִן־הַחֵרֶם וְגַם גָּנְבוּ וְגַם כִּחֲשׁוּ וְגַם שָׂמוּ בִכְלֵיהֶם:

kha-TA yis-ra-AYL v'-GAM a-v'-RU et b'-ree-TEE a-SHER tzi-VEE-tee o-TAM v'-GAM la-k'KHU min ha-KHAY-rem v'-GAM ga-n'-VU v'-GAM ki-kha-SHU v'-GAM SA-mu vikh-lay-HEM

12 Therefore, the Israelites will not be able to hold their ground against their enemies; they will have to turn tail before their enemies, for they have become proscribed. I will not be with you any more unless you root out from among you what is proscribed.

יב וְלֹא יֻכְלוּ בְּנֵי יִשְׂרָאֵל לָקוּם לִפְנֵי אֹיְבֵיהֶם עֹרֶף יִפְנוּ לִפְנֵי אֹיְבֵיהֶם כִּי הָיוּ לְחֵרֶם לֹא אוֹסִיף לִהְיוֹת עִמָּכֶם אִם־לֹא תַשְׁמִידוּ הַחֵרֶם מִקִּרְבְּכֶם:

13 Go and purify the people. Order them: Purify yourselves for tomorrow. For thus says *Hashem*, the God of *Yisrael*: Something proscribed is in your midst, O *Yisrael*, and you will not be able to stand up to your enemies until you have purged the proscribed from among you.

יג קֻם קַדֵּשׁ אֶת־הָעָם וְאָמַרְתָּ הִתְקַדְּשׁוּ לְמָחָר כִּי כֹה אָמַר יְהֹוָה אֱלֹהֵי יִשְׂרָאֵל חֵרֶם בְּקִרְבְּךָ יִשְׂרָאֵל לֹא תוּכַל לָקוּם לִפְנֵי אֹיְבֶיךָ עַד־הֲסִירְכֶם הַחֵרֶם מִקִּרְבְּכֶם:

14 Tomorrow morning you shall present yourselves by tribes. Whichever tribe *Hashem* indicates shall come forward by clans; the clan that *Hashem* indicates shall come forward by ancestral houses, and the ancestral house that *Hashem* indicates shall come forward man by man.

יד וְנִקְרַבְתֶּם בַּבֹּקֶר לְשִׁבְטֵיכֶם וְהָיָה הַשֵּׁבֶט אֲשֶׁר־יִלְכְּדֶנּוּ יְהֹוָה יִקְרַב לַמִּשְׁפָּחוֹת וְהַמִּשְׁפָּחָה אֲשֶׁר־יִלְכְּדֶנָּה יְהֹוָה תִּקְרַב לַבָּתִּים וְהַבַּיִת אֲשֶׁר יִלְכְּדֶנּוּ יְהֹוָה יִקְרַב לַגְּבָרִים:

15 Then he who is indicated for proscription, and all that is his, shall be put to the fire, because he broke the Covenant of *Hashem* and because he committed an outrage in *Yisrael*."

טו וְהָיָה הַנִּלְכָּד בַּחֵרֶם יִשָּׂרֵף בָּאֵשׁ אֹתוֹ וְאֶת־כָּל־אֲשֶׁר־לוֹ כִּי עָבַר אֶת־בְּרִית יְהֹוָה וְכִי־עָשָׂה נְבָלָה בְּיִשְׂרָאֵל:

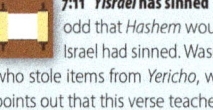

7:11 *Yisrael* has sinned On the surface, it seems odd that *Hashem* would say that the People of Israel had sinned. Wasn't it only *Achan*, the one who stole items from *Yericho*, who sinned? The *Malbim* points out that this verse teaches the critical principle of collective responsibility. The Children of Israel are not simply a collection of individuals. Rather, they are a spiritually united nation where the actions of one impact the fate of all. Therefore, when they entered *Eretz Yisrael* they became responsible for one another. This collective responsibility extends beyond simply avoiding negative things. All are also responsible for the positive welfare of their brothers and sisters, wherever they may be. Successfully meeting this collective responsibility is part of what makes the State of Israel great.

Rabbi Tuly Weisz delivering Purim baskets to Holocaust survivors

16 Early next morning, *Yehoshua* had *Yisrael* come forward by tribes; and the tribe of *Yehuda* was indicated.

17 He then had the clans of *Yehuda* come forward, and the clan of *Zerach* was indicated. Then he had the clan of *Zerach* come forward by ancestral houses, and Zabdi was indicated.

18 Finally he had his ancestral house come forward man by man, and *Achan* son of Carmi, son of Zabdi, son of *Zerach*, of the tribe of *Yehuda*, was indicated.

19 Then *Yehoshua* said to *Achan*, "My son, pay honor to *Hashem*, the God of *Yisrael*, and make confession to Him. Tell me what you have done; do not hold anything back from me."

20 *Achan* answered *Yehoshua*, "It is true, I have sinned against *Hashem*, the God of *Yisrael*. This is what I did:

21 I saw among the spoil a fine Shinar mantle, two hundred *shekalim* of silver, and a wedge of gold weighing fifty *shekalim*, and I coveted them and took them. They are buried in the ground in my tent, with the silver under it."

22 *Yehoshua* sent messengers, who hurried to the tent; and there it was, buried in his tent, with the silver underneath.

23 They took them from the tent and brought them to *Yehoshua* and all the Israelites, and displayed them before *Hashem*.

24 Then *Yehoshua*, and all *Yisrael* with him, took *Achan* son of *Zerach* – and the silver, the mantle, and the wedge of gold – his sons and daughters, and his ox, his ass, and his flock, and his tent, and all his belongings, and brought them up to the Valley of Achor.

25 And *Yehoshua* said, "What calamity you have brought upon us! *Hashem* will bring calamity upon you this day." And all *Yisrael* pelted him with stones. They put them to the fire and stoned them.

26 They raised a huge mound of stones over him, which is still there. Then the anger of *Hashem* subsided. That is why that place was named the Valley of Achor – as is still the case.

טז וַיַּשְׁכֵּם יְהוֹשֻׁעַ בַּבֹּקֶר וַיַּקְרֵב אֶת־יִשְׂרָאֵל לִשְׁבָטָיו וַיִּלָּכֵד שֵׁבֶט יְהוּדָה:

יז וַיַּקְרֵב אֶת־מִשְׁפַּחַת יְהוּדָה וַיִּלְכֹּד אֵת מִשְׁפַּחַת הַזַּרְחִי וַיַּקְרֵב אֶת־מִשְׁפַּחַת הַזַּרְחִי לַגְּבָרִים וַיִּלָּכֵד זַבְדִּי:

יח וַיַּקְרֵב אֶת־בֵּיתוֹ לַגְּבָרִים וַיִּלָּכֵד עָכָן בֶּן־כַּרְמִי בֶן־זַבְדִּי בֶּן־זֶרַח לְמַטֵּה יְהוּדָה:

יט וַיֹּאמֶר יְהוֹשֻׁעַ אֶל־עָכָן בְּנִי שִׂים־נָא כָבוֹד לַיהֹוָה אֱלֹהֵי יִשְׂרָאֵל וְתֶן־לוֹ תוֹדָה וְהַגֶּד־נָא לִי מֶה עָשִׂיתָ אַל־תְּכַחֵד מִמֶּנִּי:

כ וַיַּעַן עָכָן אֶת־יְהוֹשֻׁעַ וַיֹּאמַר אָמְנָה אָנֹכִי חָטָאתִי לַיהֹוָה אֱלֹהֵי יִשְׂרָאֵל וְכָזֹאת וְכָזֹאת עָשִׂיתִי:

כא ואראה [וָאֵרֶא] בַשָּׁלָל אַדֶּרֶת שִׁנְעָר אַחַת טוֹבָה וּמָאתַיִם שְׁקָלִים כֶּסֶף וּלְשׁוֹן זָהָב אֶחָד חֲמִשִּׁים שְׁקָלִים מִשְׁקָלוֹ וָאֶחְמְדֵם וָאֶקָּחֵם וְהִנָּם טְמוּנִים בָּאָרֶץ בְּתוֹךְ הָאָהֳלִי וְהַכֶּסֶף תַּחְתֶּיהָ:

כב וַיִּשְׁלַח יְהוֹשֻׁעַ מַלְאָכִים וַיָּרֻצוּ הָאֹהֱלָה וְהִנֵּה טְמוּנָה בְּאָהֳלוֹ וְהַכֶּסֶף תַּחְתֶּיהָ:

כג וַיִּקָּחוּם מִתּוֹךְ הָאֹהֶל וַיְבִאוּם אֶל־יְהוֹשֻׁעַ וְאֶל כָּל־בְּנֵי יִשְׂרָאֵל וַיַּצִּקֻם לִפְנֵי יְהֹוָה:

כד וַיִּקַּח יְהוֹשֻׁעַ אֶת־עָכָן בֶּן־זֶרַח וְאֶת־הַכֶּסֶף וְאֶת־הָאַדֶּרֶת וְאֶת־לְשׁוֹן הַזָּהָב וְאֶת־בָּנָיו וְאֶת־בְּנֹתָיו וְאֶת־שׁוֹרוֹ וְאֶת־חֲמֹרוֹ וְאֶת־צֹאנוֹ וְאֶת־אָהֳלוֹ וְאֶת־כָּל־אֲשֶׁר־לוֹ וְכָל־יִשְׂרָאֵל עִמּוֹ וַיַּעֲלוּ אֹתָם עֵמֶק עָכוֹר:

כה וַיֹּאמֶר יְהוֹשֻׁעַ מֶה עֲכַרְתָּנוּ יַעְכָּרְךָ יְהֹוָה בַּיּוֹם הַזֶּה וַיִּרְגְּמוּ אֹתוֹ כָל־יִשְׂרָאֵל אֶבֶן וַיִּשְׂרְפוּ אֹתָם בָּאֵשׁ וַיִּסְקְלוּ אֹתָם בָּאֲבָנִים:

כו וַיָּקִימוּ עָלָיו גַּל־אֲבָנִים גָּדוֹל עַד הַיּוֹם הַזֶּה וַיָּשָׁב יְהֹוָה מֵחֲרוֹן אַפּוֹ עַל־כֵּן קָרָא שֵׁם הַמָּקוֹם הַהוּא עֵמֶק עָכוֹר עַד הַיּוֹם הַזֶּה:

8 ¹ *Hashem* said to *Yehoshua*, "Do not be frightened or dismayed. Take all the fighting troops with you, go and march against Ai. See, I will deliver the king of Ai, his people, his city, and his land into your hands.

ח א וַיֹּאמֶר יְהוָה אֶל־יְהוֹשֻׁעַ אַל־תִּירָא וְאַל־תֵּחָת קַח עִמְּךָ אֵת כָּל־עַם הַמִּלְחָמָה וְקוּם עֲלֵה הָעָי רְאֵה נָתַתִּי בְיָדְךָ אֶת־מֶלֶךְ הָעַי וְאֶת־עַמּוֹ וְאֶת־עִירוֹ וְאֶת־אַרְצוֹ:

² You shall treat Ai and her king as you treated *Yericho* and her king; however, you may take the spoil and the cattle as booty for yourselves. Now set an ambush against the city behind it."

ב וְעָשִׂיתָ לָעַי וּלְמַלְכָּהּ כַּאֲשֶׁר עָשִׂיתָ לִירִיחוֹ וּלְמַלְכָּהּ רַק־שְׁלָלָהּ וּבְהֶמְתָּהּ תָּבֹזּוּ לָכֶם שִׂים־לְךָ אֹרֵב לָעִיר מֵאַחֲרֶיהָ:

³ So *Yehoshua* and all the fighting troops prepared for the march on Ai. *Yehoshua* chose thirty thousand men, valiant warriors, and sent them ahead by night.

ג וַיָּקָם יְהוֹשֻׁעַ וְכָל־עַם הַמִּלְחָמָה לַעֲלוֹת הָעָי וַיִּבְחַר יְהוֹשֻׁעַ שְׁלֹשִׁים אֶלֶף אִישׁ גִּבּוֹרֵי הַחַיִל וַיִּשְׁלָחֵם לָיְלָה:

⁴ He instructed them as follows: "Mind, you are to lie in ambush behind the city; don't stay too far from the city, and all of you be on the alert.

ד וַיְצַו אֹתָם לֵאמֹר רְאוּ אַתֶּם אֹרְבִים לָעִיר מֵאַחֲרֵי הָעִיר אַל־תַּרְחִיקוּ מִן־הָעִיר מְאֹד וִהְיִיתֶם כֻּלְּכֶם נְכֹנִים:

⁵ I and all the troops with me will approach the city; and when they come out against us, as they did the first time, we will flee from them.

ה וַאֲנִי וְכָל־הָעָם אֲשֶׁר אִתִּי נִקְרַב אֶל־הָעִיר וְהָיָה כִּי־יֵצְאוּ לִקְרָאתֵנוּ כַּאֲשֶׁר בָּרִאשֹׁנָה וְנַסְנוּ לִפְנֵיהֶם:

⁶ They will come rushing after us until we have drawn them away from the city. They will think, 'They are fleeing from us the same as last time'; but while we are fleeing before them,

ו וְיָצְאוּ אַחֲרֵינוּ עַד הַתִּיקֵנוּ אוֹתָם מִן־הָעִיר כִּי יֹאמְרוּ נָסִים לְפָנֵינוּ כַּאֲשֶׁר בָּרִאשֹׁנָה וְנַסְנוּ לִפְנֵיהֶם:

⁷ you will dash out from your ambush and seize the city, and *Hashem* your God will deliver it into your hands.

ז וְאַתֶּם תָּקֻמוּ מֵהָאוֹרֵב וְהוֹרַשְׁתֶּם אֶת־הָעִיר וּנְתָנָהּ יְהוָה אֱלֹהֵיכֶם בְּיֶדְכֶם:

⁸ And when you take the city, set it on fire. Do as *Hashem* has commanded. Mind, I have given you your orders."

ח וְהָיָה כְּתָפְשְׂכֶם אֶת־הָעִיר תַּצִּיתוּ אֶת־הָעִיר בָּאֵשׁ כִּדְבַר יְהוָה תַּעֲשׂוּ רְאוּ צִוִּיתִי אֶתְכֶם:

⁹ *Yehoshua* then sent them off, and they proceeded to the ambush; they took up a position between Ai and *Beit El* – west of Ai – while *Yehoshua* spent the night with the rest of the troops.

ט וַיִּשְׁלָחֵם יְהוֹשֻׁעַ וַיֵּלְכוּ אֶל־הַמַּאְרָב וַיֵּשְׁבוּ בֵּין בֵּית־אֵל וּבֵין הָעַי מִיָּם לָעָי וַיָּלֶן יְהוֹשֻׁעַ בַּלַּיְלָה הַהוּא בְּתוֹךְ הָעָם:

¹⁰ Early in the morning, *Yehoshua* mustered the troops; then he and the elders of *Yisrael* marched upon Ai at the head of the troops.

י וַיַּשְׁכֵּם יְהוֹשֻׁעַ בַּבֹּקֶר וַיִּפְקֹד אֶת־הָעָם וַיַּעַל הוּא וְזִקְנֵי יִשְׂרָאֵל לִפְנֵי הָעָם הָעָי:

¹¹ All the fighting force that was with him advanced near the city and encamped to the north of Ai, with a hollow between them and Ai.

יא וְכָל־הָעָם הַמִּלְחָמָה אֲשֶׁר אִתּוֹ עָלוּ וַיִּגְּשׁוּ וַיָּבֹאוּ נֶגֶד הָעִיר וַיַּחֲנוּ מִצְּפוֹן לָעַי וְהַגַּי בֵּינוֹ [בֵּינָיו] וּבֵין־הָעָי:

¹² He selected about five thousand men and stationed them as an ambush between *Beit El* and Ai, west of the city.

יב וַיִּקַּח כַּחֲמֵשֶׁת אֲלָפִים אִישׁ וַיָּשֶׂם אוֹתָם אֹרֵב בֵּין בֵּית־אֵל וּבֵין הָעַי מִיָּם לָעִיר:

13 Thus the main body of the army was disposed on the north of the city, but the far end of it was on the west. (This was after *Yehoshua* had spent the night in the valley.)

יג וַיָּשִׂ֣ימוּ הָעָ֗ם אֶת־כׇּל־הַֽמַּחֲנֶה֙ אֲשֶׁ֣ר מִצְּפ֣וֹן לָעִ֔יר וְאֶת־עֲקֵב֖וֹ מִיָּ֣ם לָעִ֑יר וַיֵּ֧לֶךְ יְהוֹשֻׁ֛עַ בַּלַּ֥יְלָה הַה֖וּא בְּת֥וֹךְ הָעֵֽמֶק׃

14 When the king of Ai saw them, he and all his people, the inhabitants of the city, rushed out in the early morning to the meeting place, facing the Arabah, to engage the Israelites in battle; for he was unaware that a force was lying in ambush behind the city.

יד וַיְהִ֞י כִּרְא֣וֹת מֶֽלֶךְ־הָעַ֗י וַֽיְמַהֲר֡וּ וַיַּשְׁכִּ֡ימוּ וַיֵּצְא֣וּ אַנְשֵׁי־הָעִ֣יר לִקְרַֽאת־יִ֠שְׂרָאֵ֠ל לַֽמִּלְחָמָ֞ה ה֧וּא וְכׇל־עַמּ֛וֹ לַמּוֹעֵ֖ד לִפְנֵ֣י הָֽעֲרָבָ֑ה וְהוּא֙ לֹ֣א יָדַ֔ע כִּי־אֹרֵ֥ב ל֖וֹ מֵאַחֲרֵ֥י הָעִֽיר׃

15 *Yehoshua* and all *Yisrael* fled in the direction of the wilderness, as though routed by them.

טו וַיִּנָּֽגְע֛וּ יְהוֹשֻׁ֥עַ וְכׇל־יִשְׂרָאֵ֖ל לִפְנֵיהֶ֑ם וַיָּנֻ֖סוּ דֶּ֥רֶךְ הַמִּדְבָּֽר׃

16 All the troops in the city gathered to pursue them; pursuing *Yehoshua*, they were drawn out of the city.

טז וַיִּזָּעֲק֗וּ כׇּל־הָעָם֙ אֲשֶׁ֣ר בָּעִ֔יר [בָּעַ֑י] לִרְדֹּ֖ף אַחֲרֵיהֶ֑ם וַֽיִּרְדְּפוּ֙ אַחֲרֵ֣י יְהוֹשֻׁ֔עַ וַיִּנָּתְק֖וּ מִן־הָעִֽיר׃

17 Not a man was left in Ai or in *Beit El* who did not go out after *Yisrael*; they left the city open while they pursued *Yisrael*.

יז וְלֹֽא־נִשְׁאַ֣ר אִ֗ישׁ בָּעַי֙ וּבֵ֣ית אֵ֔ל אֲשֶׁ֥ר לֹֽא־יָצְא֖וּ אַחֲרֵ֣י יִשְׂרָאֵ֑ל וַיַּעַזְב֤וּ אֶת־הָעִיר֙ פְּתוּחָ֔ה וַֽיִּרְדְּפ֖וּ אַחֲרֵ֥י יִשְׂרָאֵֽל׃

18 *Hashem* then said to *Yehoshua*, "Hold out the javelin in your hand toward Ai, for I will deliver it into your hands." So *Yehoshua* held out the javelin in his hand toward the city.

יח וַיֹּ֨אמֶר יְהֹוָ֜ה אֶל־יְהוֹשֻׁ֗עַ נְ֠טֵ֠ה בַּכִּיד֤וֹן אֲשֶׁר־בְּיָֽדְךָ֙ אֶל־הָעַ֔י כִּ֥י בְיָֽדְךָ֖ אֶתְּנֶ֑נָּה וַיֵּ֧ט יְהוֹשֻׁ֛עַ בַּכִּיד֥וֹן אֲשֶׁר־בְּיָד֖וֹ אֶל־הָעִֽיר׃

19 As soon as he held out his hand, the ambush came rushing out of their station. They entered the city and captured it; and they swiftly set fire to the city.

יט וְהָאוֹרֵ֡ב קָם֩ מְהֵרָ֨ה מִמְּקוֹמ֜וֹ וַיָּר֗וּצוּ כִּנְטוֹת֙ יָד֔וֹ וַיָּבֹ֥אוּ הָעִ֖יר וַֽיִּלְכְּד֑וּהָ וַֽיְמַהֲר֔וּ וַיַּצִּ֥יתוּ אֶת־הָעִ֖יר בָּאֵֽשׁ׃

20 The men of Ai looked back and saw the smoke of the city rising to the sky; they had no room for flight in any direction. The people who had been fleeing to the wilderness now became the pursuers.

כ וַיִּפְנ֣וּ אַנְשֵׁי֩ הָעַ֨י אַחֲרֵיהֶ֜ם וַיִּרְא֗וּ וְהִנֵּ֨ה עָלָ֜ה עֲשַׁ֤ן הָעִיר֙ הַשָּׁמַ֔יְמָה וְלֹא־הָיָ֨ה בָהֶ֥ם יָדַ֛יִם לָנ֖וּס הֵ֣נָּה וָהֵ֑נָּה וְהָעָם֙ הַנָּ֣ס הַמִּדְבָּ֔ר נֶהְפַּ֖ךְ אֶל־הָרוֹדֵֽף׃

21 For when *Yehoshua* and all *Yisrael* saw that the ambush had captured the city, and that smoke was rising from the city, they turned around and attacked the men of Ai.

כא וִיהוֹשֻׁ֨עַ וְכׇל־יִשְׂרָאֵ֜ל רָא֗וּ כִּֽי־לָכַ֤ד הָאֹרֵב֙ אֶת־הָעִ֔יר וְכִ֥י עָלָ֖ה עֲשַׁ֣ן הָעִ֑יר וַיָּשֻׁ֕בוּ וַיַּכּ֖וּ אֶת־אַנְשֵׁ֥י הָעָֽי׃

22 Now the other [Israelites] were coming out of the city against them, so that they were between two bodies of Israelites, one on each side of them. They were slaughtered, so that no one escaped or got away.

כב וְאֵ֨לֶּה יָצְא֤וּ מִן־הָעִיר֙ לִקְרָאתָ֔ם וַיִּהְי֤וּ לְיִשְׂרָאֵל֙ בַּתָּ֔וֶךְ אֵ֥לֶּה מִזֶּ֖ה וְאֵ֣לֶּה מִזֶּ֑ה וַיַּכּ֣וּ אוֹתָ֔ם עַד־בִּלְתִּ֥י הִשְׁאִֽיר־ל֖וֹ שָׂרִ֥יד וּפָלִֽיט׃

23 The king of Ai was taken alive and brought to *Yehoshua*.

כג וְאֶת־מֶ֥לֶךְ הָעַ֖י תָּ֣פְשׂוּ חָ֑י וַיַּקְרִ֥בוּ אֹת֖וֹ אֶל־יְהוֹשֻֽׁעַ׃

Joshua

24 When *Yisrael* had killed all the inhabitants of Ai who had pursued them into the open wilderness, and all of them, to the last man, had fallen by the sword, all the Israelites turned back to Ai and put it to the sword.

כד וַיְהִי כְּכַלּוֹת יִשְׂרָאֵל לַהֲרֹג אֶת־כָּל־יֹשְׁבֵי הָעַי בַּשָּׂדֶה בַּמִּדְבָּר אֲשֶׁר רְדָפוּם בּוֹ וַיִּפְּלוּ כֻלָּם לְפִי־חֶרֶב עַד־תֻּמָּם וַיָּשֻׁבוּ כָל־יִשְׂרָאֵל הָעַי וַיַּכּוּ אֹתָהּ לְפִי־חָרֶב:

25 The total of those who fell that day, men and women, the entire population of Ai, came to twelve thousand.

כה וַיְהִי כָל־הַנֹּפְלִים בַּיּוֹם הַהוּא מֵאִישׁ וְעַד־אִשָּׁה שְׁנֵים עָשָׂר אָלֶף כֹּל אַנְשֵׁי הָעָי:

26 *Yehoshua* did not draw back the hand with which he held out his javelin until all the inhabitants of Ai had been exterminated.

כו וִיהוֹשֻׁעַ לֹא־הֵשִׁיב יָדוֹ אֲשֶׁר נָטָה בַּכִּידוֹן עַד אֲשֶׁר הֶחֱרִים אֵת כָּל־יֹשְׁבֵי הָעָי:

27 However, the Israelites took the cattle and the spoil of the city as their booty, in accordance with the instructions that *Hashem* had given to *Yehoshua*.

כז רַק הַבְּהֵמָה וּשְׁלַל הָעִיר הַהִיא בָּזְזוּ לָהֶם יִשְׂרָאֵל כִּדְבַר יְהֹוָה אֲשֶׁר צִוָּה אֶת־יְהוֹשֻׁעַ:

28 Then *Yehoshua* burned down Ai, and turned it into a mound of ruins for all time, a desolation to this day.

כח וַיִּשְׂרֹף יְהוֹשֻׁעַ אֶת־הָעָי וַיְשִׂימֶהָ תֵּל־עוֹלָם שְׁמָמָה עַד הַיּוֹם הַזֶּה:

29 And the king of Ai was impaled on a stake until the evening. At sunset, *Yehoshua* had the corpse taken down from the stake and it was left lying at the entrance to the city gate. They raised a great heap of stones over it, which is there to this day.

כט וְאֶת־מֶלֶךְ הָעַי תָּלָה עַל־הָעֵץ עַד־עֵת הָעֶרֶב וּכְבוֹא הַשֶּׁמֶשׁ צִוָּה יְהוֹשֻׁעַ וַיֹּרִידוּ אֶת־נִבְלָתוֹ מִן־הָעֵץ וַיַּשְׁלִיכוּ אוֹתָהּ אֶל־פֶּתַח שַׁעַר הָעִיר וַיָּקִימוּ עָלָיו גַּל־אֲבָנִים גָּדוֹל עַד הַיּוֹם הַזֶּה:

30 At that time *Yehoshua* built a *Mizbayach* to *Hashem*, the God of *Yisrael*, on *Har Eival*,

ל אָז יִבְנֶה יְהוֹשֻׁעַ מִזְבֵּחַ לַיהֹוָה אֱלֹהֵי יִשְׂרָאֵל בְּהַר עֵיבָל:

31 as *Moshe*, the servant of *Hashem*, had commanded the Israelites – as is written in the Book of the Teaching of *Moshe* – a *Mizbayach* of unhewn stone upon which no iron had been wielded. They offered on it burnt offerings to *Hashem*, and brought sacrifices of well-being.

לא כַּאֲשֶׁר צִוָּה מֹשֶׁה עֶבֶד־יְהֹוָה אֶת־בְּנֵי יִשְׂרָאֵל כַּכָּתוּב בְּסֵפֶר תּוֹרַת מֹשֶׁה מִזְבַּח אֲבָנִים שְׁלֵמוֹת אֲשֶׁר לֹא־הֵנִיף עֲלֵיהֶן בַּרְזֶל וַיַּעֲלוּ עָלָיו עֹלוֹת לַיהֹוָה וַיִּזְבְּחוּ שְׁלָמִים:

32 And there, on the stones, he inscribed a copy of the Teaching that *Moshe* had written for the Israelites.

לב וַיִּכְתָּב־שָׁם עַל־הָאֲבָנִים אֵת מִשְׁנֵה תּוֹרַת מֹשֶׁה אֲשֶׁר כָּתַב לִפְנֵי בְּנֵי יִשְׂרָאֵל:

33 All *Yisrael* – stranger and citizen alike – with their elders, officials, and magistrates, stood on either side of the *Aron*, facing the levitical *Kohanim* who carried the *Aron Brit Hashem*. Half of them faced Mount Gerizim and half of them faced *Har Eival*, as *Moshe* the servant of *Hashem* had commanded them of old, in order to bless the people of *Yisrael*.

לג וְכָל־יִשְׂרָאֵל וּזְקֵנָיו וְשֹׁטְרִים וְשֹׁפְטָיו עֹמְדִים מִזֶּה וּמִזֶּה לָאָרוֹן נֶגֶד הַכֹּהֲנִים הַלְוִיִּם נֹשְׂאֵי אֲרוֹן בְּרִית־יְהֹוָה כַּגֵּר כָּאֶזְרָח חֶצְיוֹ אֶל־מוּל הַר־גְּרִזִים וְהַחֶצְיוֹ אֶל־מוּל הַר־עֵיבָל כַּאֲשֶׁר צִוָּה מֹשֶׁה עֶבֶד־יְהֹוָה לְבָרֵךְ אֶת־הָעָם יִשְׂרָאֵל בָּרִאשֹׁנָה:

34 After that, he read all the words of the Teaching, the blessing and the curse, just as it is written in the Book of the Teaching.

לד וְאַחֲרֵי־כֵן קָרָא אֶת־כָּל־דִּבְרֵי הַתּוֹרָה הַבְּרָכָה וְהַקְּלָלָה כְּכָל־הַכָּתוּב בְּסֵפֶר הַתּוֹרָה:

v'-a-kha-ray KHAYN ka-RA et kol div-RAY ha-to-RAH ha-b'-ra-KHAH
v'-ha-k'-la-LAH k'-khol ha-ka-TUV b'-SAY-fer ha-to-RAH

35 There was not a word of all that *Moshe* had commanded that *Yehoshua* failed to read in the presence of the entire assembly of *Yisrael*, including the women and children and the strangers who accompanied them.

לה לֹא־הָיָה דָבָר מִכֹּל אֲשֶׁר־צִוָּה מֹשֶׁה אֲשֶׁר לֹא־קָרָא יְהוֹשֻׁעַ נֶגֶד כָּל־קְהַל יִשְׂרָאֵל וְהַנָּשִׁים וְהַטַּף וְהַגֵּר הַהֹלֵךְ בְּקִרְבָּם:

9 ¹ When all the kings west of the *Yarden* – in the hill country, in the Shephelah, and along the entire coast of the Mediterranean Sea up to the vicinity of Lebanon, the [land of the] Hittites, Amorites, Canaanites, Perizzites, Hivites, and Jebusites – learned of this,

ט א וַיְהִי כִשְׁמֹעַ כָּל־הַמְּלָכִים אֲשֶׁר בְּעֵבֶר הַיַּרְדֵּן בָּהָר וּבַשְּׁפֵלָה וּבְכֹל חוֹף הַיָּם הַגָּדוֹל אֶל־מוּל הַלְּבָנוֹן הַחִתִּי וְהָאֱמֹרִי הַכְּנַעֲנִי הַפְּרִזִּי הַחִוִּי וְהַיְבוּסִי:

² they gathered with one accord to fight against *Yehoshua* and *Yisrael*.

ב וַיִּתְקַבְּצוּ יַחְדָּו לְהִלָּחֵם עִם־יְהוֹשֻׁעַ וְעִם־יִשְׂרָאֵל פֶּה אֶחָד:

³ But when the inhabitants of *Givon* learned how *Yehoshua* had treated *Yericho* and Ai,

ג וְיֹשְׁבֵי גִבְעוֹן שָׁמְעוּ אֵת אֲשֶׁר עָשָׂה יְהוֹשֻׁעַ לִירִיחוֹ וְלָעָי:

⁴ they for their part resorted to cunning. They set out in disguise: they took worn-out sacks for their asses, and worn-out waterskins that were cracked and patched;

ד וַיַּעֲשׂוּ גַם־הֵמָּה בְּעָרְמָה וַיֵּלְכוּ וַיִּצְטַיָּרוּ וַיִּקְחוּ שַׂקִּים בָּלִים לַחֲמוֹרֵיהֶם וְנֹאדוֹת יַיִן בָּלִים וּמְבֻקָּעִים וּמְצֹרָרִים:

⁵ they had worn-out, patched sandals on their feet, and threadbare clothes on their bodies; and all the bread they took as provision was dry and crumbly.

ה וּנְעָלוֹת בָּלוֹת וּמְטֻלָּאוֹת בְּרַגְלֵיהֶם וּשְׂלָמוֹת בָּלוֹת עֲלֵיהֶם וְכֹל לֶחֶם צֵידָם יָבֵשׁ הָיָה נִקֻּדִים:

⁶ And so they went to *Yehoshua* in the camp at *Gilgal* and said to him and to the men of *Yisrael*, "We come from a distant land; we propose that you make a pact with us."

ו וַיֵּלְכוּ אֶל־יְהוֹשֻׁעַ אֶל־הַמַּחֲנֶה הַגִּלְגָּל וַיֹּאמְרוּ אֵלָיו וְאֶל־אִישׁ יִשְׂרָאֵל מֵאֶרֶץ רְחוֹקָה בָּאנוּ וְעַתָּה כִּרְתוּ־לָנוּ בְרִית:

8:34 He read all the words of the Teaching The goal of settling the Land of Israel is not simply for the Children of Israel to be a nation like all other nations. For that, any land would have been sufficient; the Holy Land would not be necessary. Rather, the purpose of being in *Eretz Yis-rael* is to be a holy nation living freely in its land. Therefore, it stands to reason that *Yehoshua* would teach the entire *Torah* again to every man, woman and child at this early point of the nation's entrance into *Eretz Yisrael*. Rabbi Meir Bar Ilan, an early Religious Zionist, taught that the goal must be "the Land of Israel for the People of Israel according to the *Torah* of Israel." Similarly, commenting on the special relationship between the land and the Bible, former President and Prime Minister Shimon Peres said of his mentor David Ben Gurion, "he restored the Bible to its people, and he restored the people to the Bible."

Man reading from the *Torah* at the Western Wall

7 The men of *Yisrael* replied to the Hivites, "But perhaps you live among us; how then can we make a pact with you?"

ז וַיֹּאמְרוּ [וַיֹּאמֶר] אִישׁ־יִשְׂרָאֵל אֶל־הַחִוִּי אוּלַי בְּקִרְבִּי אַתָּה יוֹשֵׁב וְאֵיךְ אכרות־[אֶכְרָת־] לְךָ בְרִית:

8 They said to *Yehoshua*, "We will be your subjects." But *Yehoshua* asked them, "Who are you and where do you come from?"

ח וַיֹּאמְרוּ אֶל־יְהוֹשֻׁעַ עֲבָדֶיךָ אֲנָחְנוּ וַיֹּאמֶר אֲלֵהֶם יְהוֹשֻׁעַ מִי אַתֶּם וּמֵאַיִן תָּבֹאוּ:

9 They replied, "Your servants have come from a very distant country, because of the fame of *Hashem* your God. For we heard the report of Him: of all that He did in Egypt,

ט וַיֹּאמְרוּ אֵלָיו מֵאֶרֶץ רְחוֹקָה מְאֹד בָּאוּ עֲבָדֶיךָ לְשֵׁם יְהוָה אֱלֹהֶיךָ כִּי־שָׁמַעְנוּ שָׁמְעוֹ וְאֵת כָּל־אֲשֶׁר עָשָׂה בְּמִצְרָיִם:

10 and of all that He did to the two Amorite kings on the other side of the *Yarden*, King Sihon of Heshbon and King Og of Bashan who lived in Ashtaroth.

י וְאֵת כָּל־אֲשֶׁר עָשָׂה לִשְׁנֵי מַלְכֵי הָאֱמֹרִי אֲשֶׁר בְּעֵבֶר הַיַּרְדֵּן לְסִיחוֹן מֶלֶךְ חֶשְׁבּוֹן וּלְעוֹג מֶלֶךְ־הַבָּשָׁן אֲשֶׁר בְּעַשְׁתָּרוֹת:

11 So our elders and all the inhabitants of our country instructed us as follows, 'Take along provisions for a trip, and go to them and say: We will be your subjects; come make a pact with us.'

יא וַיֹּאמְרוּ אֵלֵינוּ זְקֵינֵינוּ וְכָל־יֹשְׁבֵי אַרְצֵנוּ לֵאמֹר קְחוּ בְיֶדְכֶם צֵידָה לַדֶּרֶךְ וּלְכוּ לִקְרָאתָם וַאֲמַרְתֶּם אֲלֵיהֶם עַבְדֵיכֶם אֲנַחְנוּ וְעַתָּה כִּרְתוּ־לָנוּ בְרִית:

12 This bread of ours, which we took from our houses as provision, was still hot when we set out to come to you; and see how dry and crumbly it has become.

יב זֶה לַחְמֵנוּ חָם הִצְטַיַּדְנוּ אֹתוֹ מִבָּתֵּינוּ בְּיוֹם צֵאתֵנוּ לָלֶכֶת אֲלֵיכֶם וְעַתָּה הִנֵּה יָבֵשׁ וְהָיָה נִקֻּדִים:

13 These wineskins were new when we filled them, and see how they have cracked. These clothes and sandals of ours are worn out from the very long journey."

יג וְאֵלֶּה נֹאדוֹת הַיַּיִן אֲשֶׁר מִלֵּאנוּ חֲדָשִׁים וְהִנֵּה הִתְבַּקָּעוּ וְאֵלֶּה שַׂלְמוֹתֵינוּ וּנְעָלֵינוּ בָּלוּ מֵרֹב הַדֶּרֶךְ מְאֹד:

14 The men took [their word] because of their provisions, and did not inquire of *Hashem*.

יד וַיִּקְחוּ הָאֲנָשִׁים מִצֵּידָם וְאֶת־פִּי יְהוָה לֹא שָׁאָלוּ:

15 *Yehoshua* established friendship with them; he made a pact with them to spare their lives, and the chieftains of the community gave them their oath.

טו וַיַּעַשׂ לָהֶם יְהוֹשֻׁעַ שָׁלוֹם וַיִּכְרֹת לָהֶם בְּרִית לְחַיּוֹתָם וַיִּשָּׁבְעוּ לָהֶם נְשִׂיאֵי הָעֵדָה:

16 But when three days had passed after they made this pact with them, they learned that they were neighbors, living among them.

טז וַיְהִי מִקְצֵה שְׁלֹשֶׁת יָמִים אַחֲרֵי אֲשֶׁר־כָּרְתוּ לָהֶם בְּרִית וַיִּשְׁמְעוּ כִּי־קְרֹבִים הֵם אֵלָיו וּבְקִרְבּוֹ הֵם יֹשְׁבִים:

17 So the Israelites set out, and on the third day they came to their towns; these towns were *Givon*, Chephirah, Beeroth, and *Kiryat Ye'arim*.

יז וַיִּסְעוּ בְנֵי־יִשְׂרָאֵל וַיָּבֹאוּ אֶל־עָרֵיהֶם בַּיּוֹם הַשְּׁלִישִׁי וְעָרֵיהֶם גִּבְעוֹן וְהַכְּפִירָה וּבְאֵרוֹת וְקִרְיַת יְעָרִים:

18 But the Israelites did not attack them, since the chieftains of the community had sworn to them by *Hashem*, the God of *Yisrael*. The whole community muttered against the chieftains,

יח וְלֹא הִכּוּם בְּנֵי יִשְׂרָאֵל כִּי־נִשְׁבְּעוּ לָהֶם נְשִׂיאֵי הָעֵדָה בַּיהוָה אֱלֹהֵי יִשְׂרָאֵל וַיִּלֹּנוּ כָל־הָעֵדָה עַל־הַנְּשִׂיאִים:

19 but all the chieftains answered the whole community, "We swore to them by *Hashem*, the God of *Yisrael*; therefore we cannot touch them.

יט וַיֹּאמְרוּ כָל־הַנְּשִׂיאִים אֶל־כָּל־הָעֵדָה אֲנַחְנוּ נִשְׁבַּעְנוּ לָהֶם בַּיהוָה אֱלֹהֵי יִשְׂרָאֵל וְעַתָּה לֹא נוּכַל לִנְגֹּעַ בָּהֶם:

²⁰ This is what we will do to them: We will spare their lives, so that there may be no wrath against us because of the oath that we swore to them."

כ זֹאת נַעֲשֶׂה לָהֶם וְהַחֲיֵה אוֹתָם וְלֹא־יִהְיֶה עָלֵינוּ קֶצֶף עַל־הַשְּׁבוּעָה אֲשֶׁר־נִשְׁבַּעְנוּ לָהֶם:

²¹ And the chieftains declared concerning them, "They shall live!" And they became hewers of wood and drawers of water for the whole community, as the chieftains had decreed concerning them.

כא וַיֹּאמְרוּ אֲלֵיהֶם הַנְּשִׂיאִים יִחְיוּ וַיִּהְיוּ חֹטְבֵי עֵצִים וְשֹׁאֲבֵי־מַיִם לְכָל־הָעֵדָה כַּאֲשֶׁר דִּבְּרוּ לָהֶם הַנְּשִׂיאִים:

²² *Yehoshua* summoned them and spoke to them thus: "Why did you deceive us and tell us you lived very far from us, when in fact you live among us?

כב וַיִּקְרָא לָהֶם יְהוֹשֻׁעַ וַיְדַבֵּר אֲלֵיהֶם לֵאמֹר לָמָה רִמִּיתֶם אֹתָנוּ לֵאמֹר רְחוֹקִים אֲנַחְנוּ מִכֶּם מְאֹד וְאַתֶּם בְּקִרְבֵּנוּ יֹשְׁבִים:

²³ Therefore, be accursed! Never shall your descendants cease to be slaves, hewers of wood and drawers of water for the House of my God."

כג וְעַתָּה אֲרוּרִים אַתֶּם וְלֹא־יִכָּרֵת מִכֶּם עֶבֶד וְחֹטְבֵי עֵצִים וְשֹׁאֲבֵי־מַיִם לְבֵית אֱלֹהָי:

²⁴ But they replied to *Yehoshua*, "You see, your servants had heard that *Hashem* your God had promised His servant *Moshe* to give you the whole land and to wipe out all the inhabitants of the country on your account; so we were in great fear for our lives on your account. That is why we did this thing.

כד וַיַּעֲנוּ אֶת־יְהוֹשֻׁעַ וַיֹּאמְרוּ כִּי הֻגֵּד הֻגַּד לַעֲבָדֶיךָ אֵת אֲשֶׁר צִוָּה יְהוָה אֱלֹהֶיךָ אֶת־מֹשֶׁה עַבְדּוֹ לָתֵת לָכֶם אֶת־כָּל־הָאָרֶץ וּלְהַשְׁמִיד אֶת־כָּל־יֹשְׁבֵי הָאָרֶץ מִפְּנֵיכֶם וַנִּירָא מְאֹד לְנַפְשֹׁתֵינוּ מִפְּנֵיכֶם וַנַּעֲשֶׂה אֶת־הַדָּבָר הַזֶּה:

²⁵ And now we are at your mercy; do with us what you consider right and proper."

כה וְעַתָּה הִנְנוּ בְיָדֶךָ כַּטּוֹב וְכַיָּשָׁר בְּעֵינֶיךָ לַעֲשׂוֹת לָנוּ עֲשֵׂה:

²⁶ And he did so; he saved them from being killed by the Israelites.

כו וַיַּעַשׂ לָהֶם כֵּן וַיַּצֵּל אוֹתָם מִיַּד בְּנֵי־יִשְׂרָאֵל וְלֹא הֲרָגוּם:

²⁷ That day *Yehoshua* made them hewers of wood and drawers of water – as they still are – for the community and for the *Mizbayach* of *Hashem*, in the place that He would choose.

כז וַיִּתְּנֵם יְהוֹשֻׁעַ בַּיּוֹם הַהוּא חֹטְבֵי עֵצִים וְשֹׁאֲבֵי מַיִם לָעֵדָה וּלְמִזְבַּח יְהוָה עַד־הַיּוֹם הַזֶּה אֶל־הַמָּקוֹם אֲשֶׁר יִבְחָר:

*va-yi-t'-NAYM y'-ho-SHU-a ba-YOM ha-HU kho-t'-VAY ay-TZEEM
v'-SHO-a-vay MA-yim la-ay-DAH ul-miz-BAKH a-do-NAI ad
ha-YOM ha-ZEH el ha-ma-KOM a-SHER yiv-KHAR*

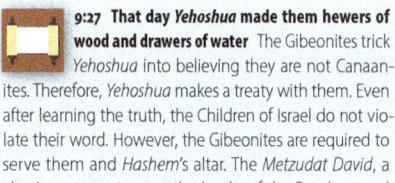

9:27 That day *Yehoshua* made them hewers of wood and drawers of water The Gibeonites trick *Yehoshua* into believing they are not Canaanites. Therefore, *Yehoshua* makes a treaty with them. Even after learning the truth, the Children of Israel do not violate their word. However, the Gibeonites are required to serve them and *Hashem*'s altar. The *Metzudat David*, a classic commentary on the books of the Prophets and Writings written in the late 17th and early 18th centuries, explains that this means they are to support the soldiers of Israel during war and to labor in the *Mishkan* in *Shilo*, and later in the *Beit Hamikdash* in *Yerushalayim*. Their service in the *Beit Hamikdash* would be important, as it would become the place for both Jews and non-Jews to direct their service of the one God.

Ancient well in *Givon*

Joshua

10 **¹** When King Adoni-zedek of *Yerushalayim* learned that *Yehoshua* had captured Ai and proscribed it, treating Ai and its king as he had treated *Yericho* and its king, and that, moreover, the people of *Givon* had come to terms with *Yisrael* and remained among them,

א וַיְהִי כִשְׁמֹעַ אֲדֹנִי־צֶדֶק מֶלֶךְ יְרוּשָׁלַם כִּי־לָכַד יְהוֹשֻׁעַ אֶת־הָעַי וַיַּחֲרִימָהּ כַּאֲשֶׁר עָשָׂה לִירִיחוֹ וּלְמַלְכָּהּ כֵּן־עָשָׂה לָעַי וּלְמַלְכָּהּ וְכִי הִשְׁלִימוּ יֹשְׁבֵי גִבְעוֹן אֶת־יִשְׂרָאֵל וַיִּהְיוּ בְּקִרְבָּם:

vai-HEE khish-MO-a a-do-nee TZE-dek ME-lekh y'-ru-sha-LA-yim kee la-KHAD y'-ho-SHU-a et ha-AI va-ya-kha-ree-MAH ka-a-SHER a-SAH lee-ree-KHO ul-mal-KAH kayn a-SAH la-AI ul-mal-KAH v'-KHEE hish-LEE-mu yo-sh'-VAY giv-ON et yis-ra-AYL va-yih-YU b'-kir-BAM

² he was very frightened. For *Givon* was a large city, like one of the royal cities – in fact, larger than Ai – and all its men were warriors.

ב וַיִּירְאוּ מְאֹד כִּי עִיר גְּדוֹלָה גִּבְעוֹן כְּאַחַת עָרֵי הַמַּמְלָכָה וְכִי הִיא גְדוֹלָה מִן־הָעַי וְכָל־אֲנָשֶׁיהָ גִּבֹּרִים:

³ So King Adoni-zedek of *Yerushalayim* sent this message to King Hoham of *Chevron*, King Piram of *Yarmut*, King Japhia of *Lachish*, and King Debir of Eglon:

ג וַיִּשְׁלַח אֲדֹנִי־צֶדֶק מֶלֶךְ יְרוּשָׁלַם אֶל־הוֹהָם מֶלֶךְ־חֶבְרוֹן וְאֶל־פִּרְאָם מֶלֶךְ־יַרְמוּת וְאֶל־יָפִיעַ מֶלֶךְ־לָכִישׁ וְאֶל־דְּבִיר מֶלֶךְ־עֶגְלוֹן לֵאמֹר:

⁴ "Come up and help me defeat *Givon*; for it has come to terms with *Yehoshua* and the Israelites."

ד עֲלוּ־אֵלַי וְעִזְרֻנִי וְנַכֶּה אֶת־גִּבְעוֹן כִּי־הִשְׁלִימָה אֶת־יְהוֹשֻׁעַ וְאֶת־בְּנֵי יִשְׂרָאֵל:

⁵ The five Amorite kings – the king of *Yerushalayim*, the king of *Chevron*, the king of *Yarmut*, the king of *Lachish*, and the king of Eglon, with all their armies – joined forces and marched on *Givon*, and encamped against it and attacked it.

ה וַיֵּאָסְפוּ וַיַּעֲלוּ חֲמֵשֶׁת מַלְכֵי הָאֱמֹרִי מֶלֶךְ יְרוּשָׁלַם מֶלֶךְ־חֶבְרוֹן מֶלֶךְ־יַרְמוּת מֶלֶךְ־לָכִישׁ מֶלֶךְ־עֶגְלוֹן הֵם וְכָל־מַחֲנֵיהֶם וַיַּחֲנוּ עַל־גִּבְעוֹן וַיִּלָּחֲמוּ עָלֶיהָ:

⁶ The people of *Givon* thereupon sent this message to *Yehoshua* in the camp at *Gilgal*: "Do not fail your servants; come up quickly and aid us and deliver us, for all the Amorite kings of the hill country have gathered against us."

ו וַיִּשְׁלְחוּ אַנְשֵׁי גִבְעוֹן אֶל־יְהוֹשֻׁעַ אֶל־הַמַּחֲנֶה הַגִּלְגָּלָה לֵאמֹר אַל־תֶּרֶף יָדֶיךָ מֵעֲבָדֶיךָ עֲלֵה אֵלֵינוּ מְהֵרָה וְהוֹשִׁיעָה לָּנוּ וְעָזְרֵנוּ כִּי נִקְבְּצוּ אֵלֵינוּ כָּל־מַלְכֵי הָאֱמֹרִי יֹשְׁבֵי הָהָר:

⁷ So *Yehoshua* marched up from *Gilgal* with his whole fighting force, all the trained warriors.

ז וַיַּעַל יְהוֹשֻׁעַ מִן־הַגִּלְגָּל הוּא וְכָל־עַם הַמִּלְחָמָה עִמּוֹ וְכֹל גִּבּוֹרֵי הֶחָיִל:

Yerushalayim

צדק

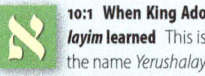

10:1 When King Adoni-zedek of *Yerusha-layim* learned This is the first mention of the name *Yerushalayim* in the Bible. King Adoni-zedek, like Melchizedek King of *Shalem* (Genesis 14:18), gets his name *tzedek* (צדק), 'righteousness,' because he resides in *Yerushalayim*, the city of righteousness, as it says "righteousness lodged in her" (Isaiah 1:21). *Yerushalayim* is not only filled with righteousness, it even causes its residents to be righteous and just. Adoni-zedek uses this virtue to stand up for moral justice by attacking the *Givonim* who had violated the Canaanite pact not to surrender to the Israelites. The *Ramban*, in his commentary (Genesis 14:18), points out that from time immemorial, the nations of the world have recognized the uniqueness of *Yerushalayim*. Physically, *Yerushalayim* is in a prime location at the center of the country. Spiritually, they knew it is aligned with the heavenly Temple where God's spirit dwells on high, and is the site He selected for the *Beit Hamikdash*.

8 *Hashem* said to *Yehoshua*, "Do not be afraid of them, for I will deliver them into your hands; not one of them shall withstand you."

ח וַיֹּ֨אמֶר יְהֹוָ֤ה אֶל־יְהוֹשֻׁ֙עַ֙ אַל־תִּירָ֣א מֵהֶ֔ם כִּ֥י בְיָדְךָ֖ נְתַתִּ֑ים לֹֽא־יַעֲמֹ֥ד אִ֛ישׁ מֵהֶ֖ם בְּפָנֶֽיךָ׃

9 *Yehoshua* took them by surprise, marching all night from *Gilgal*.

ט וַיָּבֹ֧א אֲלֵיהֶ֛ם יְהוֹשֻׁ֖עַ פִּתְאֹ֑ם כׇּל־הַלַּ֕יְלָה עָלָ֖ה מִן־הַגִּלְגָּֽל׃

10 *Hashem* threw them into a panic before *Yisrael*: [*Yehoshua*] inflicted a crushing defeat on them at *Givon*, pursued them in the direction of the Beth-horon ascent, and harried them all the way to *Azeika* and Makkedah.

י וַיְהֻמֵּ֤ם יְהֹוָה֙ לִפְנֵ֣י יִשְׂרָאֵ֔ל וַיַּכֵּ֥ם מַכָּֽה־גְדוֹלָ֖ה בְּגִבְע֑וֹן וַֽיִּרְדְּפֵ֗ם דֶּ֚רֶךְ מַעֲלֵ֣ה בֵית־חוֹרֹ֔ן וַיַּכֵּ֥ם עַד־עֲזֵקָ֖ה וְעַד־מַקֵּדָֽה׃

11 While they were fleeing before *Yisrael* down the descent from Beth-horon, *Hashem* hurled huge stones on them from the sky, all the way to *Azeika*, and they perished; more perished from the hailstones than were killed by the Israelite weapons.

יא וַיְהִ֞י בְּנֻסָ֣ם ׀ מִפְּנֵ֣י יִשְׂרָאֵ֗ל הֵ֞ם בְּמוֹרַ֤ד בֵּית־חוֹרֹן֙ וַֽיהֹוָ֡ה הִשְׁלִ֣יךְ עֲלֵיהֶם֩ אֲבָנִ֨ים גְּדֹל֧וֹת מִן־הַשָּׁמַ֛יִם עַד־עֲזֵקָ֖ה וַיָּמֻ֑תוּ רַבִּ֗ים אֲשֶׁר־מֵ֙תוּ֙ בְּאַבְנֵ֣י הַבָּרָ֔ד מֵאֲשֶׁ֥ר הָרְג֛וּ בְּנֵ֥י יִשְׂרָאֵ֖ל בֶּחָֽרֶב׃

12 On that occasion, when *Hashem* routed the Amorites before the Israelites, *Yehoshua* addressed *Hashem*; he said in the presence of the Israelites: "Stand still, O sun, at *Givon*, O moon, in the Valley of Aijalon!"

יב אָ֣ז יְדַבֵּ֤ר יְהוֹשֻׁעַ֙ לַֽיהֹוָ֔ה בְּי֗וֹם תֵּ֤ת יְהֹוָה֙ אֶת־הָ֣אֱמֹרִ֔י לִפְנֵ֖י בְּנֵ֣י יִשְׂרָאֵ֑ל וַיֹּ֣אמֶר ׀ לְעֵינֵ֣י יִשְׂרָאֵ֗ל שֶׁ֚מֶשׁ בְּגִבְע֣וֹן דּ֔וֹם וְיָרֵ֖חַ בְּעֵ֥מֶק אַיָּלֽוֹן׃

13 And the sun stood still And the moon halted, While a nation wreaked judgment on its foes – as is written in the Book of Jashar. Thus the sun halted in midheaven, and did not press on to set, for a whole day;

יג וַיִּדֹּ֨ם הַשֶּׁ֜מֶשׁ וְיָרֵ֣חַ עָמָ֗ד עַד־יִקֹּ֥ם גּוֹי֙ אֹֽיְבָ֔יו הֲלֹא־הִ֥יא כְתוּבָ֖ה עַל־סֵ֣פֶר הַיָּשָׁ֑ר וַיַּעֲמֹ֤ד הַשֶּׁ֙מֶשׁ֙ בַּחֲצִ֣י הַשָּׁמַ֔יִם וְלֹא־אָ֥ץ לָב֖וֹא כְּי֥וֹם תָּמִֽים׃

14 for *Hashem* fought for *Yisrael*. Neither before nor since has there ever been such a day, when *Hashem* acted on words spoken by a man.

יד וְלֹ֨א הָיָ֜ה כַּיּ֤וֹם הַהוּא֙ לְפָנָ֣יו וְאַחֲרָ֔יו לִשְׁמֹ֥עַ יְהֹוָ֖ה בְּק֣וֹל אִ֑ישׁ כִּ֣י יְהֹוָ֔ה נִלְחָ֖ם לְיִשְׂרָאֵֽל׃

15 Then *Yehoshua* together with all *Yisrael* returned to the camp at *Gilgal*.

טו וַיָּ֤שׇׁב יְהוֹשֻׁ֙עַ֙ וְכׇל־יִשְׂרָאֵ֣ל עִמּ֔וֹ אֶל־הַֽמַּחֲנֶ֖ה הַגִּלְגָּֽלָה׃

16 Meanwhile, those five kings fled and hid in a cave at Makkedah.

טז וַיָּנֻ֕סוּ חֲמֵ֖שֶׁת הַמְּלָכִ֣ים הָאֵ֑לֶּה וַיֵּחָבְא֥וּ בַמְּעָרָ֖ה בְּמַקֵּדָֽה׃

17 When it was reported to *Yehoshua* that the five kings had been found hiding in a cave at Makkedah,

יז וַיֻּגַּ֖ד לִיהוֹשֻׁ֑עַ לֵאמֹ֗ר נִמְצְאוּ֙ חֲמֵ֣שֶׁת הַמְּלָכִ֔ים נֶחְבְּאִ֥ים בַּמְּעָרָ֖ה בְּמַקֵּדָֽה׃

18 *Yehoshua* ordered, "Roll large stones up against the mouth of the cave, and post men over it to keep guard over them.

יח וַיֹּ֣אמֶר יְהוֹשֻׁ֔עַ גֹּ֛לּוּ אֲבָנִ֥ים גְּדֹל֖וֹת אֶל־פִּ֣י הַמְּעָרָ֑ה וְהַפְקִ֧ידוּ עָלֶ֛יהָ אֲנָשִׁ֖ים לְשׇׁמְרָֽם׃

19 But as for the rest of you, don't stop, but press on the heels of your enemies and harass them from the rear. Don't let them reach their towns, for *Hashem* your God has delivered them into your hands."

יט וְאַתֶּם֙ אַֽל־תַּעֲמֹ֔דוּ רִדְפוּ֙ אַחֲרֵ֣י אֹֽיְבֵיכֶ֔ם וְזִנַּבְתֶּ֖ם אוֹתָ֑ם אַֽל־תִּתְּנ֗וּם לָבוֹא֙ אֶל־עָ֣רֵיהֶ֔ם כִּ֧י נְתָנָ֛ם יְהֹוָ֥ה אֱלֹהֵיכֶ֖ם בְּיֶדְכֶֽם׃

Joshua

24

20 When *Yehoshua* and the Israelites had finished dealing them a deadly blow, they were wiped out, except for some fugitives who escaped into the fortified towns.

כ וַיְהִי כְּכַלּוֹת יְהוֹשֻׁעַ וּבְנֵי יִשְׂרָאֵל לְהַכּוֹתָם מַכָּה גְדוֹלָה־מְאֹד עַד־תֻּמָּם וְהַשְּׂרִידִים שָׂרְדוּ מֵהֶם וַיָּבֹאוּ אֶל־עָרֵי הַמִּבְצָר:

21 The whole army returned in safety to *Yehoshua* in the camp at Makkedah; no one so much as snarled at the Israelites.

כא וַיָּשֻׁבוּ כָל־הָעָם אֶל־הַמַּחֲנֶה אֶל־יְהוֹשֻׁעַ מַקֵּדָה בְּשָׁלוֹם לֹא־חָרַץ לִבְנֵי יִשְׂרָאֵל לְאִישׁ אֶת־לְשֹׁנוֹ:

22 And now *Yehoshua* ordered, "Open the mouth of the cave, and bring those five kings out of the cave to me."

כב וַיֹּאמֶר יְהוֹשֻׁעַ פִּתְחוּ אֶת־פִּי הַמְּעָרָה וְהוֹצִיאוּ אֵלַי אֶת־חֲמֵשֶׁת הַמְּלָכִים הָאֵלֶּה מִן־הַמְּעָרָה:

23 This was done. Those five kings – the king of *Yerushalayim*, the king of *Chevron*, the king of *Yarmut*, the king of *Lachish*, and the king of Eglon – were brought out to him from the cave.

כג וַיַּעֲשׂוּ כֵן וַיֹּצִיאוּ אֵלָיו אֶת־חֲמֵשֶׁת הַמְּלָכִים הָאֵלֶּה מִן־הַמְּעָרָה אֵת מֶלֶךְ יְרוּשָׁלַ͏ִם אֶת־מֶלֶךְ חֶבְרוֹן אֶת־מֶלֶךְ יַרְמוּת אֶת־מֶלֶךְ לָכִישׁ אֶת־מֶלֶךְ עֶגְלוֹן:

24 And when the kings were brought out to *Yehoshua*, *Yehoshua* summoned all the men of *Yisrael* and ordered the army officers who had accompanied him, "Come forward and place your feet on the necks of these kings." They came forward and placed their feet on their necks.

כד וַיְהִי כְּהוֹצִיאָם אֶת־הַמְּלָכִים הָאֵלֶּה אֶל־יְהוֹשֻׁעַ וַיִּקְרָא יְהוֹשֻׁעַ אֶל־כָּל־אִישׁ יִשְׂרָאֵל וַיֹּאמֶר אֶל־קְצִינֵי אַנְשֵׁי הַמִּלְחָמָה הֶהָלְכוּא אִתּוֹ קִרְבוּ שִׂימוּ אֶת־רַגְלֵיכֶם עַל־צַוְּארֵי הַמְּלָכִים הָאֵלֶּה וַיִּקְרְבוּ וַיָּשִׂימוּ אֶת־רַגְלֵיהֶם עַל־צַוְּארֵיהֶם:

25 *Yehoshua* said to them, "Do not be frightened or dismayed; be firm and resolute. For this is what *Hashem* is going to do to all the enemies with whom you are at war."

כה וַיֹּאמֶר אֲלֵיהֶם יְהוֹשֻׁעַ אַל־תִּירְאוּ וְאַל־תֵּחַתּוּ חִזְקוּ וְאִמְצוּ כִּי כָכָה יַעֲשֶׂה יְהוָה לְכָל־אֹיְבֵיכֶם אֲשֶׁר אַתֶּם נִלְחָמִים אוֹתָם:

26 After that, *Yehoshua* had them put to death and impaled on five stakes, and they remained impaled on the stakes until evening.

כו וַיַּכֵּם יְהוֹשֻׁעַ אַחֲרֵי־כֵן וַיְמִיתֵם וַיִּתְלֵם עַל חֲמִשָּׁה עֵצִים וַיִּהְיוּ תְּלוּיִם עַל־הָעֵצִים עַד־הָעָרֶב:

27 At sunset *Yehoshua* ordered them taken down from the poles and thrown into the cave in which they had hidden. Large stones were placed over the mouth of the cave, [and there they are] to this very day.

כז וַיְהִי לְעֵת בּוֹא הַשֶּׁמֶשׁ צִוָּה יְהוֹשֻׁעַ וַיֹּרִידוּם מֵעַל הָעֵצִים וַיַּשְׁלִכֻם אֶל־הַמְּעָרָה אֲשֶׁר נֶחְבְּאוּ־שָׁם וַיָּשִׂמוּ אֲבָנִים גְּדֹלוֹת עַל־פִּי הַמְּעָרָה עַד־עֶצֶם הַיּוֹם הַזֶּה:

28 At that time *Yehoshua* captured Makkedah and put it and its king to the sword, proscribing it and every person in it and leaving none that escaped. And he treated the king of Makkedah as he had treated the king of *Yericho*.

כח וְאֶת־מַקֵּדָה לָכַד יְהוֹשֻׁעַ בַּיּוֹם הַהוּא וַיַּכֶּהָ לְפִי־חֶרֶב וְאֶת־מַלְכָּהּ הֶחֱרִם אוֹתָם וְאֶת־כָּל־הַנֶּפֶשׁ אֲשֶׁר־בָּהּ לֹא הִשְׁאִיר שָׂרִיד וַיַּעַשׂ לְמֶלֶךְ מַקֵּדָה כַּאֲשֶׁר עָשָׂה לְמֶלֶךְ יְרִיחוֹ:

29 From Makkedah, *Yehoshua* proceeded with all *Yisrael* to Libnah, and he attacked it.

כט וַיַּעֲבֹר יְהוֹשֻׁעַ וְכָל־יִשְׂרָאֵל עִמּוֹ מִמַּקֵּדָה לִבְנָה וַיִּלָּחֶם עִם־לִבְנָה:

30 *Hashem* delivered it and its king into the hands of *Yisrael*; they put it and all the people in it to the sword, letting none escape. And he treated its king as he had treated the king of *Yericho*.

ל וַיִּתֵּן יְהֹוָה גַּם־אוֹתָהּ בְּיַד יִשְׂרָאֵל וְאֶת־מַלְכָּהּ וַיַּכֶּהָ לְפִי־חֶרֶב וְאֶת־כָּל־הַנֶּפֶשׁ אֲשֶׁר־בָּהּ לֹא־הִשְׁאִיר בָּהּ שָׂרִיד וַיַּעַשׂ לְמַלְכָּהּ כַּאֲשֶׁר עָשָׂה לְמֶלֶךְ יְרִיחוֹ:

31 From Libnah, *Yehoshua* proceeded with all *Yisrael* to *Lachish*; he encamped against it and attacked it.

לא וַיַּעֲבֹר יְהוֹשֻׁעַ וְכָל־יִשְׂרָאֵל עִמּוֹ מִלִּבְנָה לָכִישָׁה וַיִּחַן עָלֶיהָ וַיִּלָּחֶם בָּהּ:

32 *Hashem* delivered *Lachish* into the hands of *Yisrael*. They captured it on the second day and put it and all the people in it to the sword, just as they had done to Libnah.

לב וַיִּתֵּן יְהֹוָה אֶת־לָכִישׁ בְּיַד יִשְׂרָאֵל וַיִּלְכְּדָהּ בַּיּוֹם הַשֵּׁנִי וַיַּכֶּהָ לְפִי־חֶרֶב וְאֶת־כָּל־הַנֶּפֶשׁ אֲשֶׁר־בָּהּ כְּכֹל אֲשֶׁר־עָשָׂה לְלִבְנָה:

33 At that time King Horam of Gezer marched to the help of *Lachish*; but *Yehoshua* defeated him and his army, letting none of them escape.

לג אָז עָלָה הֹרָם מֶלֶךְ גֶּזֶר לַעְזֹר אֶת־לָכִישׁ וַיַּכֵּהוּ יְהוֹשֻׁעַ וְאֶת־עַמּוֹ עַד־בִּלְתִּי הִשְׁאִיר־לוֹ שָׂרִיד:

34 From *Lachish*, *Yehoshua* proceeded with all *Yisrael* to Eglon; they encamped against it and attacked it.

לד וַיַּעֲבֹר יְהוֹשֻׁעַ וְכָל־יִשְׂרָאֵל עִמּוֹ מִלָּכִישׁ עֶגְלֹנָה וַיַּחֲנוּ עָלֶיהָ וַיִּלָּחֲמוּ עָלֶיהָ:

35 They captured it on the same day and put it to the sword, proscribing all the people that were in it, as they had done to *Lachish*.

לה וַיִּלְכְּדוּהָ בַּיּוֹם הַהוּא וַיַּכּוּהָ לְפִי־חֶרֶב וְאֵת כָּל־הַנֶּפֶשׁ אֲשֶׁר־בָּהּ בַּיּוֹם הַהוּא הֶחֱרִים כְּכֹל אֲשֶׁר־עָשָׂה לְלָכִישׁ:

36 From Eglon, *Yehoshua* marched with all *Yisrael* to *Chevron* and attacked it.

לו וַיַּעַל יְהוֹשֻׁעַ וְכָל־יִשְׂרָאֵל עִמּוֹ מֵעֶגְלוֹנָה חֶבְרוֹנָה וַיִּלָּחֲמוּ עָלֶיהָ:

37 They captured it and put it, its king, and all its towns, and all the people that were in it, to the sword. He let none escape, proscribing it and all the people in it, just as he had done in the case of Eglon.

לז וַיִּלְכְּדוּהָ וַיַּכּוּהָ לְפִי־חֶרֶב וְאֶת־מַלְכָּהּ וְאֶת־כָּל־עָרֶיהָ וְאֶת־כָּל־הַנֶּפֶשׁ אֲשֶׁר־בָּהּ לֹא־הִשְׁאִיר שָׂרִיד כְּכֹל אֲשֶׁר־עָשָׂה לְעֶגְלוֹן וַיַּחֲרֵם אוֹתָהּ וְאֶת־כָּל־הַנֶּפֶשׁ אֲשֶׁר־בָּהּ:

38 *Yehoshua* and all *Yisrael* with him then turned back to Debir and attacked it.

לח וַיָּשָׁב יְהוֹשֻׁעַ וְכָל־יִשְׂרָאֵל עִמּוֹ דְּבִרָה וַיִּלָּחֶם עָלֶיהָ:

39 He captured it and its king and all its towns. They put them to the sword and proscribed all the people in it. They let none escape; just as they had done to *Chevron*, and as they had done to Libnah and its king, so they did to Debir and its king.

לט וַיִּלְכְּדָהּ וְאֶת־מַלְכָּהּ וְאֶת־כָּל־עָרֶיהָ וַיַּכּוּם לְפִי־חֶרֶב וַיַּחֲרִימוּ אֶת־כָּל־נֶפֶשׁ אֲשֶׁר־בָּהּ לֹא הִשְׁאִיר שָׂרִיד כַּאֲשֶׁר עָשָׂה לְחֶבְרוֹן כֵּן־עָשָׂה לִדְבִרָה וּלְמַלְכָּהּ וְכַאֲשֶׁר עָשָׂה לְלִבְנָה וּלְמַלְכָּהּ:

40 Thus *Yehoshua* conquered the whole country: the hill country, the *Negev*, the Shephelah, and the slopes, with all their kings; he let none escape, but proscribed everything that breathed – as *Hashem*, the God of *Yisrael*, had commanded.

מ וַיַּכֶּה יְהוֹשֻׁעַ אֶת־כָּל־הָאָרֶץ הָהָר וְהַנֶּגֶב וְהַשְּׁפֵלָה וְהָאֲשֵׁדוֹת וְאֵת כָּל־מַלְכֵיהֶם לֹא הִשְׁאִיר שָׂרִיד וְאֵת כָּל־הַנְּשָׁמָה הֶחֱרִים כַּאֲשֶׁר צִוָּה יְהֹוָה אֱלֹהֵי יִשְׂרָאֵל:

41 *Yehoshua* conquered them from Kadesh-barnea to *Azza*, all the land of Goshen, and up to *Givon*.

מא וַיַּכֵּם יְהוֹשֻׁעַ מִקָּדֵשׁ בַּרְנֵעַ וְעַד־עַזָּה וְאֵת כָּל־אֶרֶץ גֹּשֶׁן וְעַד־גִּבְעוֹן:

⁴² All those kings and their lands were conquered by *Yehoshua* at a single stroke, for *Hashem*, the God of *Yisrael*, fought for *Yisrael*.

מב וְאֵת כָּל־הַמְּלָכִים הָאֵלֶּה וְאֶת־אַרְצָם לָכַד יְהוֹשֻׁעַ פַּעַם אֶחָת כִּי יְהוָֹה אֱלֹהֵי יִשְׂרָאֵל נִלְחָם לְיִשְׂרָאֵל:

⁴³ Then *Yehoshua*, with all *Yisrael*, returned to the camp at *Gilgal*.

מג וַיָּשָׁב יְהוֹשֻׁעַ וְכָל־יִשְׂרָאֵל עִמּוֹ אֶל־הַמַּחֲנֶה הַגִּלְגָּלָה:

11 ¹ When the news reached King Jabin of Hazor, he sent messages to King Jobab of Madon, to the king of Shimron, to the king of Achshaph,

יא א וַיְהִי כִּשְׁמֹעַ יָבִין מֶלֶךְ־חָצוֹר וַיִּשְׁלַח אֶל־יוֹבָב מֶלֶךְ מָדוֹן וְאֶל־מֶלֶךְ שִׁמְרוֹן וְאֶל־מֶלֶךְ אַכְשָׁף:

² and to the other kings in the north – in the hill country, in the Arabah south of Chinnereth, in the lowlands, and in the district of Dor on the west;

ב וְאֶל־הַמְּלָכִים אֲשֶׁר מִצְּפוֹן בָּהָר וּבָעֲרָבָה נֶגֶב כִּנְרוֹת וּבַשְּׁפֵלָה וּבְנָפוֹת דּוֹר מִיָּם:

³ to the Canaanites in the east and in the west; to the Amorites, Hittites, Perizzites, and Jebusites in the hill country; and to the Hivites at the foot of *Chermon*, in the land of *Mitzpa*.

ג הַכְּנַעֲנִי מִמִּזְרָח וּמִיָּם וְהָאֱמֹרִי וְהַחִתִּי וְהַפְּרִזִּי וְהַיְבוּסִי בָּהָר וְהַחִוִּי תַּחַת חֶרְמוֹן בְּאֶרֶץ הַמִּצְפָּה:

⁴ They took the field with all their armies – an enormous host, as numerous as the sands on the seashore – and a vast multitude of horses and chariots.

ד וַיֵּצְאוּ הֵם וְכָל־מַחֲנֵיהֶם עִמָּם עַם־רָב כַּחוֹל אֲשֶׁר עַל־שְׂפַת־הַיָּם לָרֹב וְסוּס וָרֶכֶב רַב־מְאֹד:

⁵ All these kings joined forces; they came and encamped together at the Waters of Merom to give battle to *Yisrael*.

ה וַיִּוָּעֲדוּ כֹּל הַמְּלָכִים הָאֵלֶּה וַיָּבֹאוּ וַיַּחֲנוּ יַחְדָּו אֶל־מֵי מֵרוֹם לְהִלָּחֵם עִם־יִשְׂרָאֵל:

⁶ But *Hashem* said to *Yehoshua*, "Do not be afraid of them; tomorrow at this time I will have them all lying slain before *Yisrael*. You shall hamstring their horses and burn their chariots."

ו וַיֹּאמֶר יְהוָֹה אֶל־יְהוֹשֻׁעַ אַל־תִּירָא מִפְּנֵיהֶם כִּי־מָחָר כָּעֵת הַזֹּאת אָנֹכִי נֹתֵן אֶת־כֻּלָּם חֲלָלִים לִפְנֵי יִשְׂרָאֵל אֶת־סוּסֵיהֶם תְּעַקֵּר וְאֶת־מַרְכְּבֹתֵיהֶם תִּשְׂרֹף בָּאֵשׁ:

⁷ So *Yehoshua*, with all his fighting men, came upon them suddenly at the Waters of Merom, and pounced upon them.

ז וַיָּבֹא יְהוֹשֻׁעַ וְכָל־עַם הַמִּלְחָמָה עִמּוֹ עֲלֵיהֶם עַל־מֵי מֵרוֹם פִּתְאֹם וַיִּפְּלוּ בָּהֶם:

⁸ *Hashem* delivered them into the hands of *Yisrael*, and they defeated them and pursued them all the way to Great Sidon and Misrephothmaim, and all the way to the Valley of Mizpeh on the east; they crushed them, letting none escape.

ח וַיִּתְּנֵם יְהוָֹה בְּיַד־יִשְׂרָאֵל וַיַּכּוּם וַיִּרְדְּפוּם עַד־צִידוֹן רַבָּה וְעַד מִשְׂרְפוֹת מַיִם וְעַד־בִּקְעַת מִצְפֶּה מִזְרָחָה וַיַּכֻּם עַד־בִּלְתִּי הִשְׁאִיר־לָהֶם שָׂרִיד:

⁹ And *Yehoshua* dealt with them as *Hashem* had ordered him; he hamstrung their horses and burned their chariots.

ט וַיַּעַשׂ לָהֶם יְהוֹשֻׁעַ כַּאֲשֶׁר אָמַר־לוֹ יְהוָֹה אֶת־סוּסֵיהֶם עִקֵּר וְאֶת־מַרְכְּבֹתֵיהֶם שָׂרַף בָּאֵשׁ:

¹⁰ *Yehoshua* then turned back and captured Hazor and put her king to the sword. – Hazor was formerly the head of all those kingdoms.

י וַיָּשָׁב יְהוֹשֻׁעַ בָּעֵת הַהִיא וַיִּלְכֹּד אֶת־חָצוֹר וְאֶת־מַלְכָּהּ הִכָּה בֶחָרֶב כִּי־חָצוֹר לְפָנִים הִיא רֹאשׁ כָּל־הַמַּמְלָכוֹת הָאֵלֶּה:

11 They proscribed and put to the sword every person in it. Not a soul survived, and Hazor itself was burned down.

יא וַיַּכּוּ אֶת־כָּל־הַנֶּפֶשׁ אֲשֶׁר־בָּהּ לְפִי־חֶרֶב הַחֲרֵם לֹא נוֹתַר כָּל־נְשָׁמָה וְאֶת־חָצוֹר שָׂרַף בָּאֵשׁ׃

12 *Yehoshua* captured all those royal cities and their kings. He put them to the sword; he proscribed them in accordance with the charge of *Moshe*, the servant of *Hashem*.

יב וְאֶת־כָּל־עָרֵי הַמְּלָכִים־הָאֵלֶּה וְאֶת־כָּל־מַלְכֵיהֶם לָכַד יְהוֹשֻׁעַ וַיַּכֵּם לְפִי־חֶרֶב הֶחֱרִים אוֹתָם כַּאֲשֶׁר צִוָּה מֹשֶׁה עֶבֶד יְהוָה׃

v'-et kol a-RAY ha-m'-la-kheem ha-AY-leh v'-et kol mal-khay-HEM la-KHAD y'-ho-SHU-a va-ya-KAYM l'-fee KHE-rev he-khe-REEM o-TAM ka-a-SHER tzi-VAH mo-SHEH E-ved a-do-NAI

13 However, all those towns that are still standing on their mounds were not burned down by *Yisrael*; it was Hazor alone that *Yehoshua* burned down.

יג רַק כָּל־הֶעָרִים הָעֹמְדוֹת עַל־תִּלָּם לֹא שְׂרָפָם יִשְׂרָאֵל זוּלָתִי אֶת־חָצוֹר לְבַדָּהּ שָׂרַף יְהוֹשֻׁעַ׃

14 The Israelites kept all the spoil and cattle of the rest of those cities as booty. But they cut down their populations with the sword until they exterminated them; they did not spare a soul.

יד וְכֹל שְׁלַל הֶעָרִים הָאֵלֶּה וְהַבְּהֵמָה בָּזְזוּ לָהֶם בְּנֵי יִשְׂרָאֵל רַק אֶת־כָּל־הָאָדָם הִכּוּ לְפִי־חֶרֶב עַד־הִשְׁמִדָם אוֹתָם לֹא הִשְׁאִירוּ כָּל־נְשָׁמָה׃

15 Just as *Hashem* had commanded His servant *Moshe*, so *Moshe* had charged *Yehoshua*, and so *Yehoshua* did; he left nothing undone of all that *Hashem* had commanded *Moshe*.

טו כַּאֲשֶׁר צִוָּה יְהוָה אֶת־מֹשֶׁה עַבְדּוֹ כֵּן־צִוָּה מֹשֶׁה אֶת־יְהוֹשֻׁעַ וְכֵן עָשָׂה יְהוֹשֻׁעַ לֹא־הֵסִיר דָּבָר מִכֹּל אֲשֶׁר־צִוָּה יְהוָה אֶת־מֹשֶׁה׃

16 *Yehoshua* conquered the whole of this region: the hill country [of *Yehuda*], the *Negev*, the whole land of Goshen, the Shephelah, the Arabah, and the hill country and coastal plain of *Yisrael*

טז וַיִּקַּח יְהוֹשֻׁעַ אֶת־כָּל־הָאָרֶץ הַזֹּאת הָהָר וְאֶת־כָּל־הַנֶּגֶב וְאֵת כָּל־אֶרֶץ הַגֹּשֶׁן וְאֶת־הַשְּׁפֵלָה וְאֶת־הָעֲרָבָה וְאֶת־הַר יִשְׂרָאֵל וּשְׁפֵלָתֹה׃

17 [everything] from Mount Halak, which ascends to Seir, all the way to Baal-gad in the Valley of the Lebanon at the foot of Mount *Chermon*; and he captured all the kings there and executed them.

יז מִן־הָהָר הֶחָלָק הָעוֹלֶה שֵׂעִיר וְעַד־בַּעַל גָּד בְּבִקְעַת הַלְּבָנוֹן תַּחַת הַר־חֶרְמוֹן וְאֵת כָּל־מַלְכֵיהֶם לָכַד וַיַּכֵּם וַיְמִיתֵם׃

18 *Yehoshua* waged war with all those kings over a long period.

יח יָמִים רַבִּים עָשָׂה יְהוֹשֻׁעַ אֶת־כָּל־הַמְּלָכִים הָאֵלֶּה מִלְחָמָה׃

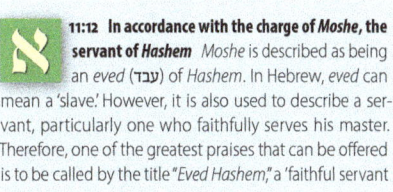

11:12 In accordance with the charge of *Moshe*, the servant of *Hashem* *Moshe* is described as being an *eved* (עבד) of *Hashem*. In Hebrew, *eved* can mean a 'slave.' However, it is also used to describe a servant, particularly one who faithfully serves his master. Therefore, one of the greatest praises that can be offered is to be called by the title "*Eved Hashem*," a 'faithful servant of God,' who always strives to fulfill His will. *Moshe* is the greatest example of this, but all human beings are to strive to achieve this high level of being a faithful servant to God.

עבד

Woman praying at the Western Wall

19 Apart from the Hivites who dwelt in *Givon*, not a single city made terms with the Israelites; all were taken in battle.

יט לֹא־הָיְתָה עִיר אֲשֶׁר הִשְׁלִימָה אֶל־בְּנֵי יִשְׂרָאֵל בִּלְתִּי הַחִוִּי יֹשְׁבֵי גִבְעוֹן אֶת־הַכֹּל לָקְחוּ בַמִּלְחָמָה:

20 For it was *Hashem*'s doing to stiffen their hearts to give battle to *Yisrael*, in order that they might be proscribed without quarter and wiped out, as *Hashem* had commanded *Moshe*.

כ כִּי מֵאֵת יְהֹוָה הָיְתָה לְחַזֵּק אֶת־לִבָּם לִקְרַאת הַמִּלְחָמָה אֶת־יִשְׂרָאֵל לְמַעַן הַחֲרִימָם לְבִלְתִּי הֱיוֹת־לָהֶם תְּחִנָּה כִּי לְמַעַן הַשְׁמִידָם כַּאֲשֶׁר צִוָּה יְהֹוָה אֶת־מֹשֶׁה:

21 At that time, *Yehoshua* went and wiped out the Anakites from the hill country, from *Chevron*, Debir, and Anab, from the entire hill country of *Yehuda*, and from the entire hill country of *Yisrael*; *Yehoshua* proscribed them and their towns.

כא וַיָּבֹא יְהוֹשֻׁעַ בָּעֵת הַהִיא וַיַּכְרֵת אֶת־הָעֲנָקִים מִן־הָהָר מִן־חֶבְרוֹן מִן־דְּבִר מִן־עֲנָב וּמִכֹּל הַר יְהוּדָה וּמִכֹּל הַר יִשְׂרָאֵל עִם־עָרֵיהֶם הֶחֱרִימָם יְהוֹשֻׁעַ:

22 No Anakites remained in the land of the Israelites; but some remained in *Azza*, Gath, and *Ashdod*.

כב לֹא־נוֹתַר עֲנָקִים בְּאֶרֶץ בְּנֵי יִשְׂרָאֵל רַק בְּעַזָּה בְּגַת וּבְאַשְׁדּוֹד נִשְׁאָרוּ:

23 Thus *Yehoshua* conquered the whole country, just as *Hashem* had promised *Moshe*; and *Yehoshua* assigned it to *Yisrael* to share according to their tribal divisions. And the land had rest from war.

כג וַיִּקַּח יְהוֹשֻׁעַ אֶת־כָּל־הָאָרֶץ כְּכֹל אֲשֶׁר דִּבֶּר יְהֹוָה אֶל־מֹשֶׁה וַיִּתְּנָהּ יְהוֹשֻׁעַ לְנַחֲלָה לְיִשְׂרָאֵל כְּמַחְלְקֹתָם לְשִׁבְטֵיהֶם וְהָאָרֶץ שָׁקְטָה מִמִּלְחָמָה:

12 1 The following are the local kings whom the Israelites defeated and whose territories they took possession of: East of the *Yarden*, from the Wadi Arnon to Mount *Chermon*, including the eastern half of the Arabah:

יב א וְאֵלֶּה מַלְכֵי הָאָרֶץ אֲשֶׁר הִכּוּ בְנֵי־יִשְׂרָאֵל וַיִּרְשׁוּ אֶת־אַרְצָם בְּעֵבֶר הַיַּרְדֵּן מִזְרְחָה הַשָּׁמֶשׁ מִנַּחַל אַרְנוֹן עַד־הַר חֶרְמוֹן וְכָל־הָעֲרָבָה מִזְרָחָה:

2 King Sihon of the Amorites, who resided in Heshbon and ruled over part of *Gilad* – from Aroer on the bank of the Wadi Arnon and the wadi proper up to the Wadi Jabbok [and] the border of the Ammonites

ב סִיחוֹן מֶלֶךְ הָאֱמֹרִי הַיּוֹשֵׁב בְּחֶשְׁבּוֹן מֹשֵׁל מֵעֲרוֹעֵר אֲשֶׁר עַל־שְׂפַת־נַחַל אַרְנוֹן וְתוֹךְ הַנַּחַל וַחֲצִי הַגִּלְעָד וְעַד יַבֹּק הַנַּחַל גְּבוּל בְּנֵי עַמּוֹן:

3 and over the eastern Arabah up to the Sea of Chinnereth and, southward by way of Beth-jeshimoth at the foot of the slopes of Pisgah on the east, down to the Sea of the Arabah, that is, the Dead Sea.

ג וְהָעֲרָבָה עַד־יָם כִּנְרוֹת מִזְרָחָה וְעַד יָם הָעֲרָבָה יָם־הַמֶּלַח מִזְרָחָה דֶּרֶךְ בֵּית הַיְשִׁמוֹת וּמִתֵּימָן תַּחַת אַשְׁדּוֹת הַפִּסְגָּה:

4 Also the territory of King Og of Bashan – one of the last of the Rephaim – who resided in Ashtaroth and in Edrei

ד וּגְבוּל עוֹג מֶלֶךְ הַבָּשָׁן מִיֶּתֶר הָרְפָאִים הַיּוֹשֵׁב בְּעַשְׁתָּרוֹת וּבְאֶדְרֶעִי:

5 and ruled over Mount *Chermon*, Salcah, and all of Bashan up to the border of the Geshurites and the Maacathites, as also over part of *Gilad* [down to] the border of King Sihon of Heshbon.

ה וּמֹשֵׁל בְּהַר חֶרְמוֹן וּבְסַלְכָה וּבְכָל־הַבָּשָׁן עַד־גְּבוּל הַגְּשׁוּרִי וְהַמַּעֲכָתִי וַחֲצִי הַגִּלְעָד גְּבוּל סִיחוֹן מֶלֶךְ־חֶשְׁבּוֹן:

Joshua

6 These were vanquished by *Moshe*, the servant of *Hashem*, and the Israelites; and *Moshe*, the servant of *Hashem*, assigned that territory as a possession to the Reubenites, the Gadites, and the half-tribe of *Menashe*.

א מֹשֶׁה עֶבֶד־יְהוָה וּבְנֵי יִשְׂרָאֵל הִכּוּם וַיִּתְּנָהּ מֹשֶׁה עֶבֶד־יְהוָה יְרֻשָּׁה לָרֻאוּבֵנִי וְלַגָּדִי וְלַחֲצִי שֵׁבֶט הַמְנַשֶּׁה:

> mo-SHEH e-ved a-do-NAI uv-NAY yis-ra-AYL hi-KUM
> va-yi-t'-NAH mo-SHEH e-ved a-do-NAI y'-ru-SHAH la-ru-vay-NEE
> v'-la-ga-DEE v'-la-kha-TZEE SHAY-vet ham-na-SHEH

7 And the following are the local kings whom *Yehoshua* and the Israelites defeated on the west side of the *Yarden* – from Baal-gad in the Valley of the Lebanon to Mount Halak, which ascends to Seir – which *Yehoshua* assigned as a possession to the tribal divisions of *Yisrael*:

ז וְאֵלֶּה מַלְכֵי הָאָרֶץ אֲשֶׁר הִכָּה יְהוֹשֻׁעַ וּבְנֵי יִשְׂרָאֵל בְּעֵבֶר הַיַּרְדֵּן יָמָּה מִבַּעַל גָּד בְּבִקְעַת הַלְּבָנוֹן וְעַד־הָהָר הֶחָלָק הָעֹלֶה שֵׂעִירָה וַיִּתְּנָהּ יְהוֹשֻׁעַ לְשִׁבְטֵי יִשְׂרָאֵל יְרֻשָּׁה כְּמַחְלְקֹתָם:

8 in the hill country, in the lowlands, in the Arabah, in the slopes, in the wilderness, and in the *Negev* – [in the land of] the Hittites, the Amorites, the Canaanites, the Perizzites, the Hivites, and the Jebusites.

ח בָּהָר וּבַשְּׁפֵלָה וּבָעֲרָבָה וּבָאֲשֵׁדוֹת וּבַמִּדְבָּר וּבַנֶּגֶב הַחִתִּי הָאֱמֹרִי וְהַכְּנַעֲנִי הַפְּרִזִּי הַחִוִּי וְהַיְבוּסִי:

9 They were: the king of *Yericho* 1. the king of Ai, near *Beit El*, 1.

ט מֶלֶךְ יְרִיחוֹ אֶחָד מֶלֶךְ הָעַי אֲשֶׁר־מִצַּד בֵּית־אֵל אֶחָד:

10 the king of *Yerushalayim* 1. the king of *Chevron* 1.

י מֶלֶךְ יְרוּשָׁלַם אֶחָד מֶלֶךְ חֶבְרוֹן אֶחָד:

11 the king of *Yarmut* 1. the king of *Lachish* 1.

יא מֶלֶךְ יַרְמוּת אֶחָד מֶלֶךְ לָכִישׁ אֶחָד:

12 the king of Eglon 1. the king of Gezer 1.

יב מֶלֶךְ עֶגְלוֹן אֶחָד מֶלֶךְ גֶּזֶר אֶחָד:

13 the king of Debir 1. the king of Geder 1.

יג מֶלֶךְ דְּבִר אֶחָד מֶלֶךְ גֶּדֶר אֶחָד:

14 the king of Hormah 1. the king of Arad 1.

יד מֶלֶךְ חָרְמָה אֶחָד מֶלֶךְ עֲרָד אֶחָד:

15 the king of Libnah 1.the king of *Adulam* 1.

טו מֶלֶךְ לִבְנָה אֶחָד מֶלֶךְ עֲדֻלָּם אֶחָד:

16 the king of Makkedah 1. the king of *Beit El* 1.

טז מֶלֶךְ מַקֵּדָה אֶחָד מֶלֶךְ בֵּית־אֵל אֶחָד:

17 the king of *Tapuach* 1. the king of Hepher 1.

יז מֶלֶךְ תַּפּוּחַ אֶחָד מֶלֶךְ חֵפֶר אֶחָד:

18 the king of Aphek 1. the king of Sharon 1.

יח מֶלֶךְ אֲפֵק אֶחָד מֶלֶךְ לַשָּׁרוֹן אֶחָד:

19 the king of Madon 1. the king of Hazor 1.

יט מֶלֶךְ מָדוֹן אֶחָד מֶלֶךְ חָצוֹר אֶחָד:

12:6 *Moshe*, the servant of *Hashem*, assigned that territory as a possession In this chapter, which summarizes the wars fought by the Children of Israel to take possession of the Promised Land, we are also reminded of the wars *Moshe* fought. *Moshe* led the people against Sihon and Og, and captured the Gilead and the Bashan. This area became the inheritance of the tribes of *Gad*, *Reuven* and half of *Menashe* (see Numbers 32:33). The Bashan is now known as the Golan Heights, which Israel conquered in the Six Day War from Syria. Towering over the north of the country, the Golan Heights provides an essential strategic perch that is vital for Israel's security. Coupled with its biblical significance, the Golan Heights remain an important part of the State of Israel. In his final interview before suffering a massive stroke in 2006, Prime Minister Ariel Sharon told Japanese reporters, "I am a Jew, and that is the most important thing for me. Therefore when it comes to the security of Israel I will not make any compromises…I don't see any situation where Israel will not be sitting on the Golan Heights."

Prime Minister Ariel Sharon (1928–2014)

Joshua

20 the king of Shimron-meron 1. the king of Achshaph 1.

כ מֶלֶךְ שִׁמְרוֹן מְראוֹן אֶחָד מֶלֶךְ אַכְשָׁף אֶחָד:

21 the king of Taanach 1. the king of Megiddo 1.

כא מֶלֶךְ תַּעְנַךְ אֶחָד מֶלֶךְ מְגִדּוֹ אֶחָד:

22 the king of Kedesh 1. the king of Jokneam in the *Carmel* 1.

כב מֶלֶךְ קֶדֶשׁ אֶחָד מֶלֶךְ־יׇקְנְעָם לַכַּרְמֶל אֶחָד:

23 the king of Dor in the district of Dor 1. the king of Goiim in *Gilgal* 1.

כג מֶלֶךְ דּוֹר לְנָפַת דּוֹר אֶחָד מֶלֶךְ־גּוֹיִם לְגִלְגָּל אֶחָד:

24 the king of *Tirtza* 1. Total number of kings 31.

כד מֶלֶךְ תִּרְצָה אֶחָד כׇּל־מְלָכִים שְׁלֹשִׁים וְאֶחָד:

13 1 *Yehoshua* was now old, advanced in years. *Hashem* said to him, "You have grown old, you are advanced in years; and very much of the land still remains to be taken possession of.

יג א וִיהוֹשֻׁעַ זָקֵן בָּא בַּיָּמִים וַיֹּאמֶר יְהֹוָה אֵלָיו אַתָּה זָקַנְתָּה בָּאתָ בַיָּמִים וְהָאָרֶץ נִשְׁאֲרָה הַרְבֵּה־מְאֹד לְרִשְׁתָּהּ:

2 This is the territory that remains: all the districts of the Philistines and all [those of] the Geshurites,

ב זֹאת הָאָרֶץ הַנִּשְׁאָרֶת כׇּל־גְּלִילוֹת הַפְּלִשְׁתִּים וְכׇל־הַגְּשׁוּרִי:

3 from the Shihor, which is close to Egypt, to the territory of Ekron on the north, are accounted Canaanite, namely, those of the five lords of the Philistines – the Gazites, the Ashdodites, the Ashkelonites, the Gittites, and the Ekronites – and those of the Avvim

ג מִן־הַשִּׁיחוֹר אֲשֶׁר עַל־פְּנֵי מִצְרַיִם וְעַד גְּבוּל עֶקְרוֹן צָפוֹנָה לַכְּנַעֲנִי תֵּחָשֵׁב חֲמֵשֶׁת סַרְנֵי פְלִשְׁתִּים הָעַזָּתִי וְהָאַשְׁדּוֹדִי הָאֶשְׁקְלוֹנִי הַגִּתִּי וְהָעֶקְרוֹנִי וְהָעַוִּים:

4 on the south; further, all the Canaanite country from Mearah of the Sidonians to Aphek at the Amorite border

ד מִתֵּימָן כׇּל־אֶרֶץ הַכְּנַעֲנִי וּמְעָרָה אֲשֶׁר לַצִּידֹנִים עַד־אֲפֵקָה עַד גְּבוּל הָאֱמֹרִי:

5 and the land of the Gebalites, with the whole [Valley of the] Lebanon, from Baal-gad at the foot of Mount *Chermon* to Lebo-hamath on the east,

ה וְהָאָרֶץ הַגִּבְלִי וְכׇל־הַלְּבָנוֹן מִזְרַח הַשֶּׁמֶשׁ מִבַּעַל גָּד תַּחַת הַר־חֶרְמוֹן עַד לְבוֹא חֲמָת:

6 with all the inhabitants of the hill country from the [Valley of the] Lebanon to Misrephoth-maim, namely, all the Sidonians. I Myself will dispossess those nations for the Israelites; you have only to apportion their lands by lot among *Yisrael*, as I have commanded you.

ו כׇּל־יֹשְׁבֵי הָהָר מִן־הַלְּבָנוֹן עַד־מִשְׂרְפֹת מַיִם כׇּל־צִידֹנִים אָנֹכִי אוֹרִישֵׁם מִפְּנֵי בְּנֵי יִשְׂרָאֵל רַק הַפִּלֶהָ לְיִשְׂרָאֵל בְּנַחֲלָה כַּאֲשֶׁר צִוִּיתִיךָ:

7 Therefore, divide this territory into hereditary portions for the nine tribes and the half-tribe of *Menashe*."

ז וְעַתָּה חַלֵּק אֶת־הָאָרֶץ הַזֹּאת בְּנַחֲלָה לְתִשְׁעַת הַשְּׁבָטִים וַחֲצִי הַשֵּׁבֶט הַמְנַשֶּׁה:

8 Now the Reubenites and the Gadites, along with the other half-tribe, had already received the shares which *Moshe* assigned to them on the east side of the *Yarden* – as assigned to them by *Moshe* the servant of *Hashem*:

ח עִמּוֹ הָראוּבֵנִי וְהַגָּדִי לָקְחוּ נַחֲלָתָם אֲשֶׁר נָתַן לָהֶם מֹשֶׁה בְּעֵבֶר הַיַּרְדֵּן מִזְרָחָה כַּאֲשֶׁר נָתַן לָהֶם מֹשֶׁה עֶבֶד יְהֹוָה:

9 from Aroer on the edge of the Wadi Arnon and the town in the middle of the wadi, the entire Tableland [from] Medeba to Dibon,

ט מֵעֲרוֹעֵר אֲשֶׁר עַל־שְׂפַת־נַחַל אַרְנוֹן וְהָעִיר אֲשֶׁר בְּתוֹךְ־הַנַּחַל וְכָל־הַמִּישֹׁר מֵידְבָא עַד־דִּיבוֹן:

10 embracing all the towns of King Sihon of the Amorites, who had reigned in Heshbon, up to the border of the Ammonites;

י וְכֹל עָרֵי סִיחוֹן מֶלֶךְ הָאֱמֹרִי אֲשֶׁר מָלַךְ בְּחֶשְׁבּוֹן עַד־גְּבוּל בְּנֵי עַמּוֹן:

11 further, *Gilad*, the territories of the Geshurites and the Maacathites, and all of Mount *Chermon*, and the whole of Bashan up to Salcah

יא וְהַגִּלְעָד וּגְבוּל הַגְּשׁוּרִי וְהַמַּעֲכָתִי וְכֹל הַר חֶרְמוֹן וְכָל־הַבָּשָׁן עַד־סַלְכָה:

12 the entire kingdom of Og, who had reigned over Bashan at Ashtaroth and at Edrei. (He was the last of the remaining Rephaim.) These were defeated and dispossessed by *Moshe*;

יב כָּל־מַמְלְכוּת עוֹג בַּבָּשָׁן אֲשֶׁר־מָלַךְ בְּעַשְׁתָּרוֹת וּבְאֶדְרֶעִי הוּא נִשְׁאַר מִיֶּתֶר הָרְפָאִים וַיַּכֵּם מֹשֶׁה וַיֹּרִשֵׁם:

13 but the Israelites failed to dispossess the Geshurites and the Maacathites, and Geshur and Maacath remain among *Yisrael* to this day.

יג וְלֹא הוֹרִישׁוּ בְּנֵי יִשְׂרָאֵל אֶת־הַגְּשׁוּרִי וְאֶת־הַמַּעֲכָתִי וַיֵּשֶׁב גְּשׁוּר וּמַעֲכָת בְּקֶרֶב יִשְׂרָאֵל עַד הַיּוֹם הַזֶּה:

14 No hereditary portion, however, was assigned to the tribe of *Levi*, their portion being the fire offerings of *Hashem*, the God of *Yisrael*, as He spoke concerning them.

יד רַק לְשֵׁבֶט הַלֵּוִי לֹא נָתַן נַחֲלָה אִשֵּׁי יְהוָה אֱלֹהֵי יִשְׂרָאֵל הוּא נַחֲלָתוֹ כַּאֲשֶׁר דִּבֶּר־לוֹ:

15 And so *Moshe* assigned [the following] to the tribe of the Reubenites, for their various clans,

טו וַיִּתֵּן מֹשֶׁה לְמַטֵּה בְנֵי־רְאוּבֵן לְמִשְׁפְּחֹתָם:

16 and it became theirs: The territory from Aroer, on the edge of the Wadi Arnon and the town in the middle of the wadi, up to Medeba – the entire Tableland

טז וַיְהִי לָהֶם הַגְּבוּל מֵעֲרוֹעֵר אֲשֶׁר עַל־שְׂפַת־נַחַל אַרְנוֹן וְהָעִיר אֲשֶׁר בְּתוֹךְ־הַנַּחַל וְכָל־הַמִּישֹׁר עַל־מֵידְבָא:

17 Heshbon and all its towns in the Tableland: Dibon, Bamoth-baal, Beth-baal-meon,

יז חֶשְׁבּוֹן וְכָל־עָרֶיהָ אֲשֶׁר בַּמִּישֹׁר דִּיבוֹן וּבָמוֹת בַּעַל וּבֵית בַּעַל מְעוֹן:

18 Jahaz, Kedemoth, Mephaath,

יח וְיַהְצָה וּקְדֵמֹת וּמֵפָעַת:

19 Kiriathaim, Sibmah, and Zereth-shahar in the hill of the valley,

יט וְקִרְיָתַיִם וְשִׂבְמָה וְצֶרֶת הַשַּׁחַר בְּהַר הָעֵמֶק:

20 Beth-peor, the slopes of Pisgah, and Beth-jeshimoth,

כ וּבֵית פְּעוֹר וְאַשְׁדּוֹת הַפִּסְגָּה וּבֵית הַיְשִׁמוֹת:

21 all the towns of the Tableland and the entire kingdom of Sihon, the king of the Amorites, who had reigned in Heshbon. (For *Moshe* defeated him and the Midianite chiefs Evi, Rekem, Zur, Hur, and Reba, who had dwelt in the land as princes of Sihon.

כא וְכֹל עָרֵי הַמִּישֹׁר וְכָל־מַמְלְכוּת סִיחוֹן מֶלֶךְ הָאֱמֹרִי אֲשֶׁר מָלַךְ בְּחֶשְׁבּוֹן אֲשֶׁר הִכָּה מֹשֶׁה אֹתוֹ וְאֶת־נְשִׂיאֵי מִדְיָן אֶת־אֱוִי וְאֶת־רֶקֶם וְאֶת־צוּר וְאֶת־חוּר וְאֶת־רֶבַע נְסִיכֵי סִיחוֹן יֹשְׁבֵי הָאָרֶץ:

22 Together with the others that they slew, the Israelites put Balaam son of Beor, the augur, to the sword.)

כב וְאֶת־בִּלְעָם בֶּן־בְּעוֹר הַקּוֹסֵם הָרְגוּ בְנֵי־יִשְׂרָאֵל בַּחֶרֶב אֶל־חַלְלֵיהֶם:

23 The boundary of the Reubenites was the edge of the *Yarden*. That was the portion of the Reubenites for their various clans – those towns with their villages.

כג וַיְהִי גְּבוּל בְּנֵי רְאוּבֵן הַיַּרְדֵּן וּגְבוּל זֹאת נַחֲלַת בְּנֵי־רְאוּבֵן לְמִשְׁפְּחֹתָם הֶעָרִים וְחַצְרֵיהֶן:

24 To the tribe of *Gad*, for the various Gadite clans, *Moshe* assigned [the following],

כד וַיִּתֵּן מֹשֶׁה לְמַטֵּה־גָד לִבְנֵי־גָד לְמִשְׁפְּחֹתָם:

25 and it became their territory: Jazer, all the towns of *Gilad*, part of the country of the Ammonites up to Aroer, which is close to Rabbah,

כה וַיְהִי לָהֶם הַגְּבוּל יַעְזֵר וְכָל־עָרֵי הַגִּלְעָד וַחֲצִי אֶרֶץ בְּנֵי עַמּוֹן עַד־עֲרוֹעֵר אֲשֶׁר עַל־פְּנֵי רַבָּה:

26 and from Heshbon to Ramath-mizpeh and Betonim, and from Mahanaim to the border of Lidbir;

כו וּמֵחֶשְׁבּוֹן עַד־רָמַת הַמִּצְפֶּה וּבְטֹנִים וּמִמַּחֲנַיִם עַד־גְּבוּל לִדְבִר:

27 and in the Valley, Beth-haram, Beth-nimrah, Succoth, and Zaphon – the rest of the kingdom of Sihon, the king of Heshbon – down to the edge of the *Yarden* and up to the tip of the Sea of Chinnereth on the east side of the *Yarden*.

כז וּבָעֵמֶק בֵּית הָרָם וּבֵית נִמְרָה וְסֻכּוֹת וְצָפוֹן יֶתֶר מַמְלְכוּת סִיחוֹן מֶלֶךְ חֶשְׁבּוֹן הַיַּרְדֵּן וּגְבֻל עַד־קְצֵה יָם־כִּנֶּרֶת עֵבֶר הַיַּרְדֵּן מִזְרָחָה:

28 That was the portion of the Gadites, for their various clans – those towns with their villages.

כח זֹאת נַחֲלַת בְּנֵי־גָד לְמִשְׁפְּחֹתָם הֶעָרִים וְחַצְרֵיהֶם:

29 And to the half-tribe of *Menashe Moshe* assigned [the following], so that it went to the half-tribe of *Menashe*, for its various clans,

כט וַיִּתֵּן מֹשֶׁה לַחֲצִי שֵׁבֶט מְנַשֶּׁה וַיְהִי לַחֲצִי מַטֵּה בְנֵי־מְנַשֶּׁה לְמִשְׁפְּחוֹתָם:

30 and became their territory: Mahanaim, all of Bashan, the entire kingdom of Og, king of Bashan, and all of Havvoth-jair in Bashan, sixty towns;

ל וַיְהִי גְבוּלָם מִמַּחֲנַיִם כָּל־הַבָּשָׁן כָּל־מַמְלְכוּת עוֹג מֶלֶךְ־הַבָּשָׁן וְכָל־חַוֺּת יָאִיר אֲשֶׁר בַּבָּשָׁן שִׁשִּׁים עִיר:

31 and part of *Gilad*, and Ashtaroth and Edrei, the royal cities of Og in Bashan, were assigned to the descendants of Machir son of *Menashe* – to a part of the descendants of Machir – for their various clans.

לא וַחֲצִי הַגִּלְעָד וְעַשְׁתָּרוֹת וְאֶדְרֶעִי עָרֵי מַמְלְכוּת עוֹג בַּבָּשָׁן לִבְנֵי מָכִיר בֶּן־מְנַשֶּׁה לַחֲצִי בְנֵי־מָכִיר לְמִשְׁפְּחוֹתָם:

32 Those, then, were the portions that *Moshe* assigned in the steppes of Moab, on the east side of the *Yarden*.

לב אֵלֶּה אֲשֶׁר־נִחַל מֹשֶׁה בְּעַרְבוֹת מוֹאָב מֵעֵבֶר לְיַרְדֵּן יְרִיחוֹ מִזְרָחָה:

33 But no portion was assigned by *Moshe* to the tribe of *Levi*; *Hashem*, the God of *Yisrael*, is their portion, as He spoke concerning them.

לג וּלְשֵׁבֶט הַלֵּוִי לֹא־נָתַן מֹשֶׁה נַחֲלָה יְהֹוָה אֱלֹהֵי יִשְׂרָאֵל הוּא נַחֲלָתָם כַּאֲשֶׁר דִּבֶּר לָהֶם:

*ul-SHAY-vet ha-lay-VEE lo na-TAN mo-SHEH na-kha-LAH a-do-NAI
e-lo-HAY yis-ra-AYL HU na-kha-la-TAM ka-a-SHER di-BER la-HEM*

13:33 But no portion was assigned by *Moshe* to the tribe of *Levi* The tribe of *Levi* is the only one who was not assigned a portion of land. Instead of land, *Hashem* is to be their inheritance: The *Kohanim* (Priests) and the *Leviim*

Variety of Israel-grown cherry tomatoes

14 ¹ And these are the allotments of the Israelites in the land of Canaan, that were apportioned to them by the *Kohen Elazar*, by *Yehoshua* son of *Nun*, and by the heads of the ancestral houses of the Israelite tribes,

² the portions that fell to them by lot, as *Hashem* had commanded through *Moshe* for the nine and a half tribes.

³ For the portion of the other two and a half tribes had been assigned to them by *Moshe* on the other side of the *Yarden*. He had not assigned any portion among them to the *Leviim*;

⁴ for whereas the descendants of *Yosef* constituted two tribes, *Menashe* and *Efraim*, the *Leviim* were assigned no share in the land, but only some towns to live in, with the pastures for their livestock and cattle.

⁵ Just as *Hashem* had commanded *Moshe*, so the Israelites did when they apportioned the land.

⁶ The Judites approached *Yehoshua* at *Gilgal*, and *Kalev* son of Jephunneh the Kenizzite said to him: "You know what instructions *Hashem* gave at Kadesh-barnea to *Moshe*, the man of *Hashem*, concerning you and me.

⁷ I was forty years old when *Moshe* the servant of *Hashem* sent me from Kadesh-barnea to spy out the land, and I gave him a forthright report.

⁸ While my companions who went up with me took the heart out of the people, I was loyal to *Hashem* my God.

⁹ On that day, *Moshe* promised on oath, 'The land on which your foot trod shall be a portion for you and your descendants forever, because you were loyal to *Hashem* my God.'

יד א וְאֵ֣לֶּה אֲשֶׁ֧ר נָחֲל֛וּ בְנֵֽי־יִשְׂרָאֵ֖ל בְּאֶ֣רֶץ כְּנָ֑עַן אֲשֶׁ֨ר נִחֲל֜וּ אוֹתָ֗ם אֶלְעָזָ֣ר הַכֹּהֵ֗ן וִיהוֹשֻׁ֙עַ֙ בִּן־נ֔וּן וְרָאשֵׁ֛י אֲב֥וֹת הַמַּטּ֖וֹת לִבְנֵ֥י יִשְׂרָאֵֽל:

ב בְּגוֹרַ֖ל נַחֲלָתָ֑ם כַּאֲשֶׁ֨ר צִוָּ֤ה יְהוָה֙ בְּיַד־מֹשֶׁ֔ה לְתִשְׁעַ֥ת הַמַּטּ֖וֹת וַחֲצִ֥י הַמַּטֶּֽה:

ג כִּֽי־נָתַ֨ן מֹשֶׁ֜ה נַחֲלַ֗ת שְׁנֵ֤י הַמַּטּוֹת֙ וַחֲצִ֣י הַמַּטֶּ֔ה מֵעֵ֖בֶר לַיַּרְדֵּ֑ן וְלַ֨לְוִיִּ֔ם לֹֽא־נָתַ֥ן נַחֲלָ֖ה בְּתוֹכָֽם:

ד כִּֽי־הָי֤וּ בְנֵֽי־יוֹסֵף֙ שְׁנֵ֣י מַטּ֔וֹת מְנַשֶּׁ֖ה וְאֶפְרָ֑יִם וְלֹֽא־נָתְנוּ֩ חֵ֨לֶק לַלְוִיִּ֜ם בָּאָ֗רֶץ כִּ֣י אִם־עָרִים֙ לָשֶׁ֔בֶת וּמִ֨גְרְשֵׁיהֶ֔ם לְמִקְנֵיהֶ֖ם וּלְקִנְיָנָֽם:

ה כַּאֲשֶׁ֨ר צִוָּ֤ה יְהוָה֙ אֶת־מֹשֶׁ֔ה כֵּ֥ן עָשׂ֖וּ בְּנֵ֣י יִשְׂרָאֵ֑ל וַֽיַּחְלְק֖וּ אֶת־הָאָֽרֶץ:

ו וַיִּגְּשׁ֨וּ בְנֵֽי־יְהוּדָ֤ה אֶל־יְהוֹשֻׁ֙עַ֙ בַּגִּלְגָּ֔ל וַיֹּ֣אמֶר אֵלָ֗יו כָּלֵ֤ב בֶּן־יְפֻנֶּה֙ הַקְּנִזִּ֔י אַתָּ֣ה יָדַ֗עְתָּ אֶֽת־הַדָּבָ֞ר אֲשֶׁר־דִּבֶּ֣ר יְהוָ֗ה אֶל־מֹשֶׁ֤ה אִישׁ־הָאֱלֹהִים֙ עַ֣ל אֹדוֹתַ֔י וְעַ֖ל אֹדוֹתֶ֑יךָ בְּקָדֵ֖שׁ בַּרְנֵֽעַ:

ז בֶּן־אַרְבָּעִ֨ים שָׁנָ֜ה אָֽנֹכִ֗י בִּ֠שְׁלֹ֠חַ מֹשֶׁ֨ה עֶֽבֶד־יְהוָ֥ה אֹתִ֛י מִקָּדֵ֥שׁ בַּרְנֵ֖עַ לְרַגֵּ֣ל אֶת־הָאָ֑רֶץ וָאָשֵׁ֤ב אֹתוֹ֙ דָּבָ֔ר כַּאֲשֶׁ֖ר עִם־לְבָבִֽי:

ח וְאַחַי֙ אֲשֶׁ֣ר עָל֣וּ עִמִּ֔י הִמְסִ֖יו אֶת־לֵ֣ב הָעָ֑ם וְאָ֣נֹכִ֔י מִלֵּ֕אתִי אַחֲרֵ֖י יְהוָ֥ה אֱלֹהָֽי:

ט וַיִּשָּׁבַ֣ע מֹשֶׁ֗ה בַּיּ֣וֹם הַהוּא֮ לֵאמֹר֒ אִם־לֹ֣א הָאָ֗רֶץ אֲשֶׁ֨ר דָּרְכָ֤ה רַגְלְךָ֙ בָּ֔הּ לְךָ֨ תִֽהְיֶ֧ה לְנַחֲלָ֛ה וּלְבָנֶ֖יךָ עַד־עוֹלָ֑ם כִּ֣י מִלֵּ֔אתָ אַחֲרֵ֖י יְהוָ֥ה אֱלֹהָֽי:

(Levites) are to perform the special task of serving in the Holy Temple and teaching *Hashem*'s *Torah* to the people. In return, the people, as a whole, are obligated to support them financially, by giving them special gifts from produce grown in *Eretz Yisrael*, as commanded in the *Torah*. In the case of the *Kohanim*, they are also to receive portions of certain sacrifices. Although in our era these gifts are not given, Jews still separate a small amount of all produce grown in Israel. The continuation of this practice is a constant reminder of the sacred obligation to make sure that all members of society are provided with a sufficient livelihood.

Joshua

¹⁰ Now *Hashem* has preserved me, as He promised. It is forty-five years since *Hashem* made this promise to *Moshe*, when *Yisrael* was journeying through the wilderness; and here I am today, eighty-five years old.

י וְעַתָּה הִנֵּה הֶחֱיָה יְהֹוָה אוֹתִי כַּאֲשֶׁר דִּבֵּר זֶה אַרְבָּעִים וְחָמֵשׁ שָׁנָה מֵאָז דִּבֶּר יְהֹוָה אֶת־הַדָּבָר הַזֶּה אֶל־מֹשֶׁה אֲשֶׁר־הָלַךְ יִשְׂרָאֵל בַּמִּדְבָּר וְעַתָּה הִנֵּה אָנֹכִי הַיּוֹם בֶּן־חָמֵשׁ וּשְׁמוֹנִים שָׁנָה:

¹¹ I am still as strong today as on the day that *Moshe* sent me; my strength is the same now as it was then, for battle and for activity.

יא עוֹדֶנִּי הַיּוֹם חָזָק כַּאֲשֶׁר בְּיוֹם שְׁלֹחַ אוֹתִי מֹשֶׁה כְּכֹחִי אָז וּכְכֹחִי עָתָּה לַמִּלְחָמָה וְלָצֵאת וְלָבוֹא:

¹² So assign to me this hill country as *Hashem* promised on that day. Though you too heard on that day that Anakites are there and great fortified cities, if only *Hashem* is with me, I will dispossess them, as *Hashem* promised."

יב וְעַתָּה תְּנָה־לִּי אֶת־הָהָר הַזֶּה אֲשֶׁר־דִּבֶּר יְהֹוָה בַּיּוֹם הַהוּא כִּי אַתָּה־שָׁמַעְתָּ בַיּוֹם הַהוּא כִּי־עֲנָקִים שָׁם וְעָרִים גְּדֹלוֹת בְּצֻרוֹת אוּלַי יְהֹוָה אוֹתִי וְהוֹרַשְׁתִּים כַּאֲשֶׁר דִּבֶּר יְהֹוָה:

¹³ So *Yehoshua* blessed *Kalev* son of Jephunneh and assigned *Chevron* to him as his portion.

יג וַיְבָרֲכֵהוּ יְהוֹשֻׁעַ וַיִּתֵּן אֶת־חֶבְרוֹן לְכָלֵב בֶּן־יְפֻנֶּה לְנַחֲלָה:

vai-va-r'-KHAY-hu y'-ho-SHU-a va-yi-TAYN et khev-RON
l'-kha-LAYV ben y'-fu-NEH l'-na-kha-LAH

¹⁴ Thus *Chevron* became the portion of *Kalev* son of Jephunneh the Kenizzite, as it still is, because he was loyal to *Hashem*, the God of *Yisrael*.

יד עַל־כֵּן הָיְתָה־חֶבְרוֹן לְכָלֵב בֶּן־יְפֻנֶּה הַקְּנִזִּי לְנַחֲלָה עַד הַיּוֹם הַזֶּה יַעַן אֲשֶׁר מִלֵּא אַחֲרֵי יְהֹוָה אֱלֹהֵי יִשְׂרָאֵל:

¹⁵ The name of *Chevron* was formerly *Kiryat Arba*: [Arba] was the great man among the Anakites. And the land had rest from war.

טו וְשֵׁם חֶבְרוֹן לְפָנִים קִרְיַת אַרְבַּע הָאָדָם הַגָּדוֹל בָּעֲנָקִים הוּא וְהָאָרֶץ שָׁקְטָה מִמִּלְחָמָה:

15 ¹ The portion that fell by lot to the various clans of the tribe of *Yehuda* lay farthest south, down to the border of Edom, which is the Wilderness of Zin.

טו א וַיְהִי הַגּוֹרָל לְמַטֵּה בְּנֵי יְהוּדָה לְמִשְׁפְּחֹתָם אֶל־גְּבוּל אֱדוֹם מִדְבַּר־צִן נֶגְבָּה מִקְצֵה תֵימָן:

² Their southern boundary began from the tip of the Dead Sea, from the tongue that projects southward.

ב וַיְהִי לָהֶם גְּבוּל נֶגֶב מִקְצֵה יָם הַמֶּלַח מִן־הַלָּשֹׁן הַפֹּנֶה נֶגְבָּה:

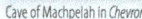

14:13 So *Yehoshua* blessed *Kalev* son of Jephunneh The ancient city of *Chevron* is also known as *Kiryat Arba* (although today, the name *Kiryat Arba* is used for a modern suburb next to the ancient holy city). There, *Avraham* bought the Cave of Machpelah to serve as the burial site of his wife, *Sara* (Genesis 23). This cave then became the burial site of all of the Patriarchs and three of the Matriarchs (*Rachel* is buried in *Beit Lechem*). *Yehoshua* gave this city, located within the territory of the tribe of *Yehuda*, as a special inheritance to *Kalev*, son of *Jephunneh*. *Rashi* (Numbers 13:22) explains that when *Kalev* was sent by *Moshe* to scout out the land, he

Cave of Machpelah in *Chevron*

prayed at the Cave Machpelah, asking God to help him avoid being influenced by the evil spies. Indeed, he remained loyal to *Hashem* and to His promise to give the Land of Israel to the Children of Israel. It is therefore fitting that he is rewarded with *Chevron* as his inheritance, and he bravely fights to claim it. Today, the Jewish residents of *Chevron* follow in *Kalev*'s footsteps. Despite many violent threats to their existence in the city – such as a brutal massacre in 1929 and many more recent terrorist attacks – they bravely preserve both their own community and the rights of the entire Jewish People to pray in the holy Cave of Machpelah.

3 It proceeded to the south of the Ascent of Akrabbim, passed on to Zin, ascended to the south of Kadesh-barnea, passed on to *Chetzron*, ascended to Addar, and made a turn to Karka.

ג וְיָצָא אֶל־מִנֶּגֶב לְמַעֲלֵה עַקְרַבִּים וְעָבַר צִנָה וְעָלָה מִנֶּגֶב לְקָדֵשׁ בַּרְנֵעַ וְעָבַר חֶצְרוֹן וְעָלָה אַדָּרָה וְנָסַב הַקַּרְקָעָה:

4 From there it passed on to Azmon and proceeded to the Wadi of Egypt; and the boundary ran on to the Sea. That shall be your southern boundary.

ד וְעָבַר עַצְמוֹנָה וְיָצָא נַחַל מִצְרַיִם וְהָיָה [וְהָיוּ] תֹצְאוֹת הַגְּבוּל יָמָּה זֶה־יִהְיֶה לָכֶם גְּבוּל נֶגֶב:

5 The boundary on the east was the Dead Sea up to the mouth of the *Yarden*. On the northern side, the boundary began at the tongue of the Sea at the mouth of the *Yarden*.

ה וּגְבוּל קֵדְמָה יָם הַמֶּלַח עַד־קְצֵה הַיַּרְדֵּן וּגְבוּל לִפְאַת צָפוֹנָה מִלְּשׁוֹן הַיָּם מִקְצֵה הַיַּרְדֵּן:

6 The boundary ascended to Beth-hoglah and passed north of Beth-arabah; then the boundary ascended to the Stone of Bohan son of *Reuven*.

ו וְעָלָה הַגְּבוּל בֵּית חָגְלָה וְעָבַר מִצְּפוֹן לְבֵית הָעֲרָבָה וְעָלָה הַגְּבוּל אֶבֶן בֹּהַן בֶּן־רְאוּבֵן:

7 The boundary ascended from the Valley of Achor to Debir and turned north to *Gilgal*, facing the Ascent of Adummim which is south of the wadi; from there the boundary continued to the waters of En-shemesh and ran on to En-rogel.

ז וְעָלָה הַגְּבוּל דְּבִרָה מֵעֵמֶק עָכוֹר וְצָפוֹנָה פֹּנֶה אֶל־הַגִּלְגָּל אֲשֶׁר־נֹכַח לְמַעֲלֵה אֲדֻמִּים אֲשֶׁר מִנֶּגֶב לַנָּחַל וְעָבַר הַגְּבוּל אֶל־מֵי־עֵין שֶׁמֶשׁ וְהָיוּ תֹצְאֹתָיו אֶל־עֵין רֹגֵל:

8 Then the boundary ascended into the Valley of Ben-hinnom, along the southern flank of the Jebusites – that is, *Yerushalayim*. The boundary then ran up to the top of the hill which flanks the Valley of Hinnom on the west, at the northern end of the Valley of Rephaim.

ח וְעָלָה הַגְּבוּל גֵּי בֶן־הִנֹּם אֶל־כֶּתֶף הַיְבוּסִי מִנֶּגֶב הִיא יְרוּשָׁלָ͏ִם וְעָלָה הַגְּבוּל אֶל־רֹאשׁ הָהָר אֲשֶׁר עַל־פְּנֵי גֵי־הִנֹּם יָמָּה אֲשֶׁר בִּקְצֵה עֵמֶק־רְפָאִים צָפֹנָה:

9 From that hilltop the boundary curved to the fountain of the Waters of Nephtoah and ran on to the towns of Mount Ephron; then the boundary curved to Baalah – that is, *Kiryat Ye'arim*.

ט וְתָאַר הַגְּבוּל מֵרֹאשׁ הָהָר אֶל־מַעְיַן מֵי נֶפְתּוֹחַ וְיָצָא אֶל־עָרֵי הַר־עֶפְרוֹן וְתָאַר הַגְּבוּל בַּעֲלָה הִיא קִרְיַת יְעָרִים:

10 From Baalah the boundary turned westward to Mount Seir, passed north of the slope of Mount Jearim – that is, Chesalon – descended to *Beit Shemesh*, and passed on to Timnah.

י וְנָסַב הַגְּבוּל מִבַּעֲלָה יָמָּה אֶל־הַר שֵׂעִיר וְעָבַר אֶל־כֶּתֶף הַר־יְעָרִים מִצָּפוֹנָה הִיא כְסָלוֹן וְיָרַד בֵּית־שֶׁמֶשׁ וְעָבַר תִּמְנָה:

11 The boundary then proceeded to the northern flank of Ekron; the boundary curved to Shikkeron, passed on to Mount Baalah, and proceeded to Jabneel; and the boundary ran on to the Sea.

יא וְיָצָא הַגְּבוּל אֶל־כֶּתֶף עֶקְרוֹן צָפוֹנָה וְתָאַר הַגְּבוּל שִׁכְּרוֹנָה וְעָבַר הַר־הַבַּעֲלָה וְיָצָא יַבְנְאֵל וְהָיוּ תֹּצְאוֹת הַגְּבוּל יָמָּה:

12 And the western boundary was the edge of the Mediterranean Sea. Those were the boundaries of the various clans of the Judites on all sides.

יב וּגְבוּל יָם הַיָּמָּה הַגָּדוֹל וּגְבוּל זֶה גְּבוּל בְּנֵי־יְהוּדָה סָבִיב לְמִשְׁפְּחֹתָם:

13 In accordance with *Hashem*'s command to *Yehoshua*, *Kalev* son of Jephunneh was given a portion among the Judites, namely, *Kiryat Arba* – that is, *Chevron*. ([Arba] was the father of Anak.)

יג וּלְכָלֵב בֶּן־יְפֻנֶּה נָתַן חֵלֶק בְּתוֹךְ בְּנֵי־יְהוּדָה אֶל־פִּי יְהֹוָה לִיהוֹשֻׁעַ אֶת־קִרְיַת אַרְבַּע אֲבִי הָעֲנָק הִיא חֶבְרוֹן:

ul-kha-LAYV ben y'-fu-NEH na-TAN KHAY-lek b'-TOKH b'-nay y'-hu-DAH el PEE a-do-NAI lee-ho-SHU-a et kir-YAT ar-BA a-VEE ha-a-NAK HEE khev-RON

14 *Kalev* dislodged from there the three Anakites: Sheshai, Ahiman, and Talmai, descendants of Anak.

יד וַיֹּרֶשׁ מִשָּׁם כָּלֵב אֶת־שְׁלוֹשָׁה בְּנֵי הָעֲנָק אֶת־שֵׁשַׁי וְאֶת־אֲחִימַן וְאֶת־תַּלְמַי יְלִידֵי הָעֲנָק:

15 From there he marched against the inhabitants of Debir – the name of Debir was formerly *Kiryat Sefer*

טו וַיַּעַל מִשָּׁם אֶל־יֹשְׁבֵי דְּבִר וְשֵׁם־דְּבִר לְפָנִים קִרְיַת־סֵפֶר:

16 and *Kalev* announced, "I will give my daughter Achsah in marriage to the man who attacks and captures *Kiryat Sefer*."

טז וַיֹּאמֶר כָּלֵב אֲשֶׁר־יַכֶּה אֶת־קִרְיַת־סֵפֶר וּלְכָדָהּ וְנָתַתִּי לוֹ אֶת־עַכְסָה בִתִּי לְאִשָּׁה:

17 His kinsman *Otniel* the Kenizzite captured it; and *Kalev* gave him his daughter Achsah in marriage.

יז וַיִּלְכְּדָהּ עָתְנִיאֵל בֶּן־קְנַז אֲחִי כָלֵב וַיִּתֶּן־לוֹ אֶת־עַכְסָה בִתּוֹ לְאִשָּׁה:

18 When she came [to him], she induced him to ask her father for some property. She dismounted from her donkey, and *Kalev* asked her, "What is the matter?"

יח וַיְהִי בְּבוֹאָהּ וַתְּסִיתֵהוּ לִשְׁאוֹל מֵאֵת־אָבִיהָ שָׂדֶה וַתִּצְנַח מֵעַל הַחֲמוֹר וַיֹּאמֶר־לָהּ כָּלֵב מַה־לָּךְ:

19 She replied, "Give me a present; for you have given me away as *Negev*-land; so give me springs of water." And he gave her Upper and Lower Gulloth.

יט וַתֹּאמֶר תְּנָה־לִּי בְרָכָה כִּי אֶרֶץ הַנֶּגֶב נְתַתָּנִי וְנָתַתָּה לִי גֻּלֹּת מָיִם וַיִּתֶּן־לָהּ אֵת גֻּלֹּת עִלִּיּוֹת וְאֵת גֻּלֹּת תַּחְתִּיּוֹת:

20 This was the portion of the tribe of the Judites by their clans:

כ זֹאת נַחֲלַת מַטֵּה בְנֵי־יְהוּדָה לְמִשְׁפְּחֹתָם:

21 The towns at the far end of the tribe of *Yehuda*, near the border of Edom, in the *Negev*, were: Kabzeel, Eder, Jagur,

כא וַיִּהְיוּ הֶעָרִים מִקְצֵה לְמַטֵּה בְנֵי־יְהוּדָה אֶל־גְּבוּל אֱדוֹם בַּנֶּגְבָּה קַבְצְאֵל וְעֵדֶר וְיָגוּר:

22 Kinah, Dimonah, Adadah,

כב וְקִינָה וְדִימוֹנָה וְעַדְעָדָה:

23 Kedesh, Hazor, Ithnan,

כג וְקֶדֶשׁ וְחָצוֹר וְיִתְנָן:

24 Ziph, Telem, Bealoth,

כד זִיף וָטֶלֶם וּבְעָלוֹת:

25 Hazor-hadattah, Kerioth-hezron – that is, Hazor

כה וְחָצוֹר חֲדַתָּה וּקְרִיּוֹת חֶצְרוֹן הִיא חָצוֹר:

 **15:13** *Kalev* son of *Jephunneh* **was given** Although *Eretz Yisrael* is divided among the tribes by divinely-directed lots, *Kalev* asks for, and receives, *Chevron*. He and *Yehoshua* had been the only scouts sent by *Moshe* who stayed loyal to God and promised the people that they could succeed in entering the land (Numbers

Inside the *Avraham Avinu* synagogue in *Chevron*

13:30). Therefore, he receives this reward. As Rabbi Shlomo Aviner writes, "He had something even greater than the determination of the divine lots – he had self-sacrifice." *Kalev* had risked his safety by speaking against the ten evil spies, and was also willing to risk his life by fighting the Canaanites for *Chevron*. Self-sacrifice for *Eretz Yisrael* is greatly rewarded.

26 Amam, Shema, Moladah,

אָמָם וּשְׁמַע וּמוֹלָדָה: כו

27 Hazar-gaddah, Heshmon, Beth-pelet,

וַחֲצַר גַּדָּה וְחֶשְׁמוֹן וּבֵית פָּלֶט: כז

28 Hazar-shual, *Be'er Sheva*, Biziothiah,

וַחֲצַר שׁוּעָל וּבְאֵר שֶׁבַע וּבִזְיוֹתְיָה: כח

29 Baalah, Iim, Ezem,

בַּעֲלָה וְעִיִּים וָעָצֶם: כט

30 Eltolad, Chesil, Hormah,

וְאֶלְתּוֹלַד וּכְסִיל וְחָרְמָה: ל

31 *Tziklag*, Madmannah, Sansannah,

וְצִקְלַג וּמַדְמַנָּה וְסַנְסַנָּה: לא

32 Lebaoth, Shilhim, Ain and Rimmon. Total: 29 towns, with their villages.

וּלְבָאוֹת וְשִׁלְחִים וְעַיִן וְרִמּוֹן כָּל־עָרִים לב
עֶשְׂרִים וָתֵשַׁע וְחַצְרֵיהֶן:

33 In the Lowland: *Eshtaol, Tzora*, Ashnah,

בַּשְּׁפֵלָה אֶשְׁתָּאוֹל וְצָרְעָה וְאַשְׁנָה: לג

34 Zanoach, En-gannim, *Tapuach*, Enam,

וְזָנוֹחַ וְעֵין גַּנִּים תַּפּוּחַ וְהָעֵינָם: לד

35 Yarmut, *Adulam*, Socoh, *Azeika*,

יַרְמוּת וַעֲדֻלָּם שׂוֹכֹה וַעֲזֵקָה: לה

36 *Shaarayim*, Adithaim, *Gedera*, and Gederothaim – 14 towns, with their villages.

וְשַׁעֲרַיִם וַעֲדִיתַיִם וְהַגְּדֵרָה וּגְדֵרֹתָיִם לו
עָרִים אַרְבַּע־עֶשְׂרֵה וְחַצְרֵיהֶן:

37 Zenan, Hadashah, Migdal-gad,

צְנָן וַחֲדָשָׁה וּמִגְדַּל־גָּד: לז

38 Dilan, Mizpeh, Joktheel,

וְדִלְעָן וְהַמִּצְפֶּה וְיָקְתְאֵל: לח

39 *Lachish*, Bozkath, Eglon,

לָכִישׁ וּבָצְקַת וְעֶגְלוֹן: לט

40 Cabbon, Lahmas, Chithlish,

וְכַבּוֹן וְלַחְמָס וְכִתְלִישׁ: מ

41 Gederoth, Beth-dagon, Naamah, and Makkedah: 16 towns, with their villages.

וּגְדֵרוֹת בֵּית־דָּגוֹן וְנַעֲמָה וּמַקֵּדָה עָרִים מא
שֵׁשׁ־עֶשְׂרֵה וְחַצְרֵיהֶן:

42 Libnah, Ether, Ashan,

לִבְנָה וָעֶתֶר וְעָשָׁן: מב

43 Iphtah, Ashnah, Nezib,

וְיִפְתָּח וְאַשְׁנָה וּנְצִיב: מג

44 Keilah, Achzib, and Mareshah: 9 towns, with their villages.

וּקְעִילָה וְאַכְזִיב וּמָרֵאשָׁה עָרִים תֵּשַׁע מד
וְחַצְרֵיהֶן:

45 Ekron, with its dependencies and villages.

עֶקְרוֹן וּבְנֹתֶיהָ וַחֲצֵרֶיהָ: מה

46 From Ekron westward, all the towns in the vicinity of *Ashdod*, with their villages

מֵעֶקְרוֹן וָיָמָּה כֹּל אֲשֶׁר־עַל־יַד אַשְׁדּוֹד מו
וְחַצְרֵיהֶן:

47 *Ashdod*, its dependencies and its villages – *Azza*, its dependencies and its villages, all the way to the Wadi of Egypt and the edge of the Mediterranean Sea.

אַשְׁדּוֹד בְּנוֹתֶיהָ וַחֲצֵרֶיהָ עַזָּה בְּנוֹתֶיהָ מז
וַחֲצֵרֶיהָ עַד־נַחַל מִצְרָיִם וְהַיָּם הַגְּבוּל
[הַגָּדוֹל] וּגְבוּל:

48 And in the hill country: Shamir, Jattir, Socoh,

וּבָהָר שָׁמִיר וְיַתִּיר וְשׂוֹכֹה: מח

49 Dannah, Kiriath-sannah – that is, Debir

וְדַנָּה וְקִרְיַת־סַנָּה הִיא דְבִר: מט

50 Anab, Eshtemoh, Anim,

וַעֲנָב וְאֶשְׁתְּמֹה וְעָנִים: נ

51 Goshen, Holon, and Giloh: 11 towns, with their villages.

וְגֹשֶׁן וְחֹלֹן וְגִלֹה עָרִים אַחַת־עֶשְׂרֵה נא
וְחַצְרֵיהֶן:

52 Arab, Dumah, Eshan,

נב אֲרַב וְרוּמָה וְאֶשְׁעָן:

53 Janum, Beth-tappuah, Aphekah,

נג וְיָנִים [וְיָנוּם] וּבֵית־תַּפּוּחַ וַאֲפֵקָה:

54 Humtah, *Kiryat Arba* – that is, *Chevron* – and Zior: 9 towns, with their villages.

נד וְחֻמְטָה וְקִרְיַת אַרְבַּע הִיא חֶבְרוֹן וְצִיעֹר עָרִים תֵּשַׁע וְחַצְרֵיהֶן:

55 Maon, *Carmel*, Ziph, Juttah,

נה מָעוֹן כַּרְמֶל וָזִיף וְיוּטָּה:

56 *Yizrael*, Jokdeam, *Zanoach*,

נו וְיִזְרְעֶאל וְיָקְדְעָם וְזָנוֹחַ:

57 Kain, *Giva*, and Timnah: 10 towns, with their villages.

נז הַקַּיִן גִּבְעָה וְתִמְנָה עָרִים עֶשֶׂר וְחַצְרֵיהֶן:

58 Halhul, Beth-zur, Gedor,

נח חַלְחוּל בֵּית־צוּר וּגְדוֹר:

59 Maarath, Beth-anoth, and Eltekon: 6 towns, with their villages.

נט וּמַעֲרָת וּבֵית־עֲנוֹת וְאֶלְתְּקֹן עָרִים שֵׁשׁ וְחַצְרֵיהֶן:

60 Kiriath-baal – that is, *Kiryat Ye'arim* – and Rabbah: 2 towns, with their villages.

ס קִרְיַת־בַּעַל הִיא קִרְיַת יְעָרִים וְהָרַבָּה עָרִים שְׁתַּיִם וְחַצְרֵיהֶן:

61 In the wilderness: Beth-arabah, Middin, Secacah,

סא בַּמִּדְבָּר בֵּית הָעֲרָבָה מִדִּין וּסְכָכָה:

62 Nibshan, Ir-melah, and *Ein Gedi*: 6 towns, with their villages.

סב וְהַנִּבְשָׁן וְעִיר־הַמֶּלַח וְעֵין גֶּדִי עָרִים שֵׁשׁ וְחַצְרֵיהֶן:

63 But the Judites could not dispossess the Jebusites, the inhabitants of *Yerushalayim*; so the Judites dwell with the Jebusites in *Yerushalayim* to this day.

סג וְאֶת־הַיְבוּסִי יוֹשְׁבֵי יְרוּשָׁלַםִ לֹא־יוכְלוּ [יָכְלוּ] בְנֵי־יְהוּדָה לְהוֹרִישָׁם וַיֵּשֶׁב הַיְבוּסִי אֶת־בְּנֵי יְהוּדָה בִּירוּשָׁלַםִ עַד הַיּוֹם הַזֶּה:

16 1 The portion that fell by lot to the Josephites ran from the *Yarden* at *Yericho* – from the waters of *Yericho* east of the wilderness. From *Yericho* it ascended through the hill country to *Beit El*.

טז א וַיֵּצֵא הַגּוֹרָל לִבְנֵי יוֹסֵף מִיַּרְדֵּן יְרִיחוֹ לְמֵי יְרִיחוֹ מִזְרָחָה הַמִּדְבָּר עֹלֶה מִירִיחוֹ בָּהָר בֵּית־אֵל:

2 From *Beit El* it ran to Luz and passed on to the territory of the Archites at Ataroth,

ב וְיָצָא מִבֵּית־אֵל לוּזָה וְעָבַר אֶל־גְּבוּל הָאַרְכִּי עֲטָרוֹת:

v'-ya-TZA mi-bayt EL LU-zah v'-a-VAR el g'-VUL ha-ar-KEE a-ta-ROT

3 descended westward to the territory of the Japhletites as far as the border of Lower Beth-horon and Gezer, and ran on to the Sea.

ג וְיָרַד־יָמָּה אֶל־גְּבוּל הַיַּפְלֵטִי עַד גְּבוּל בֵּית־חוֹרֹן תַּחְתּוֹן וְעַד־גָּזֶר וְהָיוּ תֹצְאֹתָו [תֹצְאֹתָיו] יָמָּה:

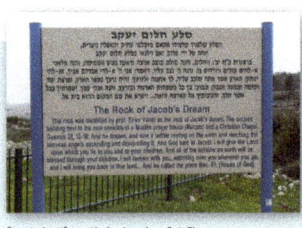

Sign Indentifying *Yaakov's* rock at *Beit El*

16:2 From *Beit El* it ran

Beit El, located in the territory of the tribe of *Binyamin*, near the border with *Efraim*, has an important place in Jewish history. It is near the site where *Avraham* built an altar and called out in *Hashem's* name (Genesis 12:8). It is where *Yaakov* prayed, and dreamt about the angels ascending and descending a ladder that reached to the heavens (Genesis 28:12). It was also there that *Yaakov* received the promise that his children would inherit the Land of Israel (28:14). In 1838, the famous biblical archaeologist Edward Robinson identified the ancient site of *Beit El*. Following the Six Day War, a modern Jewish community was founded adjacent to the ancient site, and given the same name. Contemporary *Beit El* is the home of hundreds of Jewish families who are raising their children in the city of their forefathers.

4 Thus the Josephites – that is, *Menashe* and *Efraim* – received their portion.

ד וַיִּנְחֲלוּ בְנֵי־יוֹסֵף מְנַשֶּׁה וְאֶפְרָיִם:

5 The territory of the Ephraimites, by their clans, was as follows: The boundary of their portion ran from Atroth-addar on the east to Upper Beth-horon,

ה וַיְהִי גְּבוּל בְּנֵי־אֶפְרַיִם לְמִשְׁפְּחֹתָם וַיְהִי גְּבוּל נַחֲלָתָם מִזְרָחָה עַטְרוֹת אַדָּר עַד־בֵּית חוֹרֹן עֶלְיוֹן:

6 and the boundary ran on to the Sea. And on the north, the boundary proceeded from Michmethath to the east of Taanath-shiloh and passed beyond it up to the east of Janoah;

ו וְיָצָא הַגְּבוּל הַיָּמָּה הַמִּכְמְתָת מִצָּפוֹן וְנָסַב הַגְּבוּל מִזְרָחָה תַּאֲנַת שִׁלֹה וְעָבַר אוֹתוֹ מִמִּזְרַח יָנוֹחָה:

7 from Janoah it descended to Ataroth and Naarath, touched on *Yericho*, and ran on to the *Yarden*.

ז וְיָרַד מִיָּנוֹחָה עֲטָרוֹת וְנַעֲרָתָה וּפָגַע בִּירִיחוֹ וְיָצָא הַיַּרְדֵּן:

8 Westward, the boundary proceeded from *Tapuach* to the Wadi Kanah and ran on to the Sea. This was the portion of the tribe of the Ephraimites, by their clans,

ח מִתַּפּוּחַ יֵלֵךְ הַגְּבוּל יָמָּה נַחַל קָנָה וְהָיוּ תֹצְאֹתָיו הַיָּמָּה זֹאת נַחֲלַת מַטֵּה בְנֵי־אֶפְרַיִם לְמִשְׁפְּחֹתָם:

9 together with the towns marked off for the Ephraimites within the territory of the Manassites – all those towns with their villages.

ט וְהֶעָרִים הַמִּבְדָּלוֹת לִבְנֵי אֶפְרַיִם בְּתוֹךְ נַחֲלַת בְּנֵי־מְנַשֶּׁה כָּל־הֶעָרִים וְחַצְרֵיהֶן:

10 However, they failed to dispossess the Canaanites who dwelt in Gezer; so the Canaanites remained in the midst of *Efraim*, as is still the case. But they had to perform forced labor.

י וְלֹא הוֹרִישׁוּ אֶת־הַכְּנַעֲנִי הַיּוֹשֵׁב בְּגָזֶר וַיֵּשֶׁב הַכְּנַעֲנִי בְּקֶרֶב אֶפְרַיִם עַד־הַיּוֹם הַזֶּה וַיְהִי לְמַס־עֹבֵד:

17 1 And this is the portion that fell by lot to the tribe of *Menashe* – for he was *Yosef*'s first-born. Since Machir, the first-born of *Menashe* and the father of *Gilad*, was a valiant warrior, *Gilad* and Bashan were assigned to him.

יז א וַיְהִי הַגּוֹרָל לְמַטֵּה מְנַשֶּׁה כִּי־הוּא בְּכוֹר יוֹסֵף לְמָכִיר בְּכוֹר מְנַשֶּׁה אֲבִי הַגִּלְעָד כִּי הוּא הָיָה אִישׁ מִלְחָמָה וַיְהִי־לוֹ הַגִּלְעָד וְהַבָּשָׁן:

2 And now assignments were made to the remaining Manassites, by their clans: the descendants of Abiezer, Helek, Asriel, *Shechem*, Hepher, and Shemida. Those were the male descendants of *Menashe* son of *Yosef*, by their clans.

ב וַיְהִי לִבְנֵי מְנַשֶּׁה הַנּוֹתָרִים לְמִשְׁפְּחֹתָם לִבְנֵי אֲבִיעֶזֶר וְלִבְנֵי־חֵלֶק וְלִבְנֵי אַשְׂרִיאֵל וְלִבְנֵי־שֶׁכֶם וְלִבְנֵי־חֵפֶר וְלִבְנֵי שְׁמִידָע אֵלֶּה בְּנֵי מְנַשֶּׁה בֶּן־יוֹסֵף הַזְּכָרִים לְמִשְׁפְּחֹתָם:

3 Now *Tzelofchad* son of Hepher son of *Gilad* son of Machir son of *Menashe* had no sons, but only daughters. The names of his daughters were *Machla, Noa, Chagla, Milka,* and *Tirtza.*

ג וְלִצְלָפְחָד בֶּן־חֵפֶר בֶּן־גִּלְעָד בֶּן־מָכִיר בֶּן־מְנַשֶּׁה לֹא־הָיוּ לוֹ בָּנִים כִּי אִם־בָּנוֹת וְאֵלֶּה שְׁמוֹת בְּנֹתָיו מַחְלָה וְנֹעָה חָגְלָה מִלְכָּה וְתִרְצָה:

4 They appeared before the *Kohen Elazar, Yehoshua* son of *Nun,* and the chieftains, saying: "*Hashem* commanded *Moshe* to grant us a portion among our male kinsmen." So, in accordance with *Hashem*'s instructions, they were granted a portion among their father's kinsmen.

ד וַתִּקְרַבְנָה לִפְנֵי אֶלְעָזָר הַכֹּהֵן וְלִפְנֵי יְהוֹשֻׁעַ בִּן־נוּן וְלִפְנֵי הַנְּשִׂיאִים לֵאמֹר יְהֹוָה צִוָּה אֶת־מֹשֶׁה לָתֶת־לָנוּ נַחֲלָה בְּתוֹךְ אַחֵינוּ וַיִּתֵּן לָהֶם אֶל־פִּי יְהֹוָה נַחֲלָה בְּתוֹךְ אֲחֵי אֲבִיהֶן:

*va-tik-RAV-nah lif-NAY el-a-ZAR ha-ko-HAYN v'-lif-NAY y'-ho-SHU-a
bin NUN v'-lif-NAY ha-n'-see-EEM lay-MOR a-do-NAI tzi-VAH et
mo-SHEH la-tet LA-nu na-kha-LAH b'-TOKH a-KHAY-nu va-yi-TAYN
la-HEM el PEE a-do-NAI na-kha-LAH b'-TOKH a-KHAY a-vee-HEN*

⁵ Ten districts fell to *Menashe*, apart from the lands of *Gilad* and Bashan, which are across the *Yarden*.

ה וַיִּפְּלוּ חַבְלֵי־מְנַשֶּׁה עֲשָׂרָה לְבַד מֵאֶרֶץ הַגִּלְעָד וְהַבָּשָׁן אֲשֶׁר מֵעֵבֶר לַיַּרְדֵּן:

⁶ *Menashe*'s daughters inherited a portion in these together with his sons, while the land of *Gilad* was assigned to the rest of *Menashe*'s descendants.

ו כִּי בְּנוֹת מְנַשֶּׁה נָחֲלוּ נַחֲלָה בְּתוֹךְ בָּנָיו וְאֶרֶץ הַגִּלְעָד הָיְתָה לִבְנֵי־מְנַשֶּׁה הַנּוֹתָרִים:

⁷ The boundary of *Menashe* ran from *Asher* to Michmethath, which lies near *Shechem*. The boundary continued to the right, toward the inhabitants of En-tappuah.

ז וַיְהִי גְבוּל־מְנַשֶּׁה מֵאָשֵׁר הַמִּכְמְתָת אֲשֶׁר עַל־פְּנֵי שְׁכֶם וְהָלַךְ הַגְּבוּל אֶל־הַיָּמִין אֶל־יֹשְׁבֵי עֵין תַּפּוּחַ:

⁸ The region of *Tapuach* belonged to *Menashe*; but *Tapuach*, on the border of *Menashe*, belonged to the Ephraimites.

ח לִמְנַשֶּׁה הָיְתָה אֶרֶץ תַּפּוּחַ וְתַפּוּחַ אֶל־גְּבוּל מְנַשֶּׁה לִבְנֵי אֶפְרָיִם:

⁹ Then the boundary descended to the Wadi Kanah. Those towns to the south of the wadi belonged to *Efraim* as an enclave among the towns of *Menashe*. The boundary of *Menashe* lay north of the wadi and ran on to the Sea.

ט וְיָרַד הַגְּבוּל נַחַל קָנָה נֶגְבָּה לַנַּחַל עָרִים הָאֵלֶּה לְאֶפְרַיִם בְּתוֹךְ עָרֵי מְנַשֶּׁה וּגְבוּל מְנַשֶּׁה מִצְּפוֹן לַנַּחַל וַיְהִי תֹצְאֹתָיו הַיָּמָּה:

¹⁰ What lay to the south belonged to *Efraim*, and what lay to the north belonged to *Menashe*, with the Sea as its boundary. [This territory] was contiguous with *Asher* on the north and with *Yissachar* on the east.

י נֶגְבָּה לְאֶפְרַיִם וְצָפוֹנָה לִמְנַשֶּׁה וַיְהִי הַיָּם גְּבוּלוֹ וּבְאָשֵׁר יִפְגְּעוּן מִצָּפוֹן וּבְיִשָּׂשכָר מִמִּזְרָח:

¹¹ Within *Yissachar* and *Asher*, *Menashe* possessed *Beit-Shean* and its dependencies, Ibleam and its dependencies, the inhabitants of Dor and its dependencies, the inhabitants of En-dor and its dependencies, the inhabitants of Taanach and its dependencies, and the inhabitants of Megiddo and its dependencies: these constituted three regions.

יא וַיְהִי לִמְנַשֶּׁה בְּיִשָּׂשכָר וּבְאָשֵׁר בֵּית־שְׁאָן וּבְנוֹתֶיהָ וְיִבְלְעָם וּבְנוֹתֶיהָ וְאֶת־יֹשְׁבֵי דֹאר וּבְנוֹתֶיהָ וְיֹשְׁבֵי עֵין־דֹּר וּבְנֹתֶיהָ וְיֹשְׁבֵי תַעְנַךְ וּבְנֹתֶיהָ וְיֹשְׁבֵי מְגִדּוֹ וּבְנוֹתֶיהָ שְׁלֹשֶׁת הַנָּפֶת:

17:4 *Eleazer, Yehoshua son of Nun, and the chieftains* During the division of the land, the daughters of *Tzelofchad* remind *Yehoshua* and *Elazar* the priest that since their father had no sons to inherit his portion in the Land of Israel, God had told *Moshe* that they, his daughters, were to receive his inheritance (Numbers 22:2–7). *Tzelofchad*'s daughters are exemplars of women in every generation who have had a special love for *Eretz Yisrael*. Two prominent twentieth-century women to epitomize the same characteristics of love and dedication to the Holy Land were Golda Meir and Sarah Herzog. Meir was Israel's first female Prime Minister, and Herzog, who was the wife of former Chief Rabbi Yitzchak Herzog, helped found the leading hospital for geriatrics and psychiatry in the Middle East, as well as the Jewish women's organization Emunah, one of the largest social service providers in Israel. Their great impact on Israeli society is still evident today, decades after their passing.

Sarah Herzog
(1898–1979)

12 The Manassites could not dispossess [the inhabitants of] these towns, and the Canaanites stubbornly remained in this region.

יב וְלֹא יָכְלוּ בְּנֵי מְנַשֶּׁה לְהוֹרִישׁ אֶת־הֶעָרִים הָאֵלֶּה וַיּוֹאֶל הַכְּנַעֲנִי לָשֶׁבֶת בָּאָרֶץ הַזֹּאת:

13 When the Israelites became stronger, they imposed tribute on the Canaanites; but they did not dispossess them.

יג וַיְהִי כִּי חָזְקוּ בְּנֵי יִשְׂרָאֵל וַיִּתְּנוּ אֶת־הַכְּנַעֲנִי לָמַס וְהוֹרֵשׁ לֹא הוֹרִישׁוֹ:

14 The Josephites complained to *Yehoshua*, saying, "Why have you assigned as our portion a single allotment and a single district, seeing that we are a numerous people whom *Hashem* has blessed so greatly?"

יד וַיְדַבְּרוּ בְּנֵי יוֹסֵף אֶת־יְהוֹשֻׁעַ לֵאמֹר מַדּוּעַ נָתַתָּה לִּי נַחֲלָה גּוֹרָל אֶחָד וְחֶבֶל אֶחָד וַאֲנִי עַם־רָב עַד אֲשֶׁר־עַד־כֹּה בֵּרְכַנִי יְהֹוָה:

15 "If you are a numerous people," *Yehoshua* answered them, "go up to the forest country and clear an area for yourselves there, in the territory of the Perizzites and the Rephaim, seeing that you are cramped in the hill country of *Efraim*."

טו וַיֹּאמֶר אֲלֵיהֶם יְהוֹשֻׁעַ אִם־עַם־רָב אַתָּה עֲלֵה לְךָ הַיַּעְרָה וּבֵרֵאתָ לְךָ שָׁם בְּאֶרֶץ הַפְּרִזִּי וְהָרְפָאִים כִּי־אָץ לְךָ הַר־אֶפְרָיִם:

16 "The hill country is not enough for us," the Josephites replied, "and all the Canaanites who live in the valley area have iron chariots, both those in *Beit-Shean* and its dependencies and those in the Valley of *Yizrael*."

טז וַיֹּאמְרוּ בְּנֵי יוֹסֵף לֹא־יִמָּצֵא לָנוּ הָהָר וְרֶכֶב בַּרְזֶל בְּכָל־הַכְּנַעֲנִי הַיֹּשֵׁב בְּאֶרֶץ־הָעֵמֶק לַאֲשֶׁר בְּבֵית־שְׁאָן וּבְנוֹתֶיהָ וְלַאֲשֶׁר בְּעֵמֶק יִזְרְעֶאל:

17 But *Yehoshua* declared to the House of *Yosef*, to *Efraim* and *Menashe*, "You are indeed a numerous people, possessed of great strength; you shall not have one allotment only.

יז וַיֹּאמֶר יְהוֹשֻׁעַ אֶל־בֵּית יוֹסֵף לְאֶפְרַיִם וְלִמְנַשֶּׁה לֵאמֹר עַם־רָב אַתָּה וְכֹחַ גָּדוֹל לָךְ לֹא־יִהְיֶה לְךָ גּוֹרָל אֶחָד:

18 The hill country shall be yours as well; true, it is forest land, but you will clear it and possess it to its farthest limits. And you shall also dispossess the Canaanites, even though they have iron chariots and even though they are strong."

יח כִּי הַר יִהְיֶה־לָּךְ כִּי־יַעַר הוּא וּבֵרֵאתוֹ וְהָיָה לְךָ תֹּצְאֹתָיו כִּי־תוֹרִישׁ אֶת־הַכְּנַעֲנִי כִּי רֶכֶב בַּרְזֶל לוֹ כִּי חָזָק הוּא:

18

1 The whole community of *B'nei Yisrael* assembled at *Shilo*, and set up the Tent of Meeting there. The land was now under their control;

יח א וַיִּקָּהֲלוּ כָּל־עֲדַת בְּנֵי־יִשְׂרָאֵל שִׁלֹה וַיַּשְׁכִּינוּ שָׁם אֶת־אֹהֶל מוֹעֵד וְהָאָרֶץ נִכְבְּשָׁה לִפְנֵיהֶם:

va-yi-ka-ha-LU kol a-DAT b'-nay yis-ra-AYL shi-LOH va-yash-KEE-nu SHAM et O-hel mo-AYD v'-ha-A-retz nikh-b'-SHAH lif-nay-HEM

18:1 The whole community of *B'nei Yisrael* assembled at *Shilo* The Jewish People bring the *Mishkan* to *Shilo*. This is meant to be its temporary location, until the *Beit Hamikdash* would be built in *Yerushalayim*. The *Mishkan* remains in *Shilo* for 369 years, serving as the central point for Israelite service to *Hashem* during that period, as is evident in the opening chapters of *Sefer Shmuel*. Like many biblical cities, the site of ancient *Shilo* has been identified and excavated, and a new Jewish community with the same name has been established adjacent to it. Today, hundreds of Jewish families live in the flourishing town of *Shilo*.

Ruins at *Tel Shilo*

Joshua

² but there remained seven tribes of the Israelites which had not yet received their portions.

³ So *Yehoshua* said to the Israelites, "How long will you be slack about going and taking possession of the land which *Hashem*, the God of your fathers, has assigned to you?

⁴ Appoint three men of each tribe; I will send them out to go through the country and write down a description of it for purposes of apportionment, and then come back to me.

⁵ They shall divide it into seven parts – *Yehuda* shall remain by its territory in the south, and the house of *Yosef* shall remain by its territory in the north.

⁶ When you have written down the description of the land in seven parts, bring it here to me. Then I will cast lots for you here before *Hashem* our God.

⁷ For the *Leviim* have no share among you, since the priesthood of *Hashem* is their portion; and *Gad* and *Reuven* and the half-tribe of *Menashe* have received the portions which were assigned to them by *Moshe* the servant of *Hashem*, on the eastern side of the *Yarden*."

⁸ The men set out on their journeys. *Yehoshua* ordered the men who were leaving to write down a description of the land – "Go, traverse the country and write down a description of it. Then return to me, and I will cast lots for you here at *Shilo* before *Hashem*."

⁹ So the men went and traversed the land; they described it in a document, town by town, in seven parts, and they returned to *Yehoshua* in the camp at *Shilo*.

¹⁰ *Yehoshua* cast lots for them at *Shilo* before *Hashem*, and there *Yehoshua* apportioned the land among the Israelites according to their divisions.

¹¹ The lot of the tribe of the Benjaminites, by their clans, came out first. The territory which fell to their lot lay between the Judites and the Josephites.

¹² The boundary on their northern rim began at the *Yarden*; the boundary ascended to the northern flank of *Yericho*, ascended westward into the hill country and ran on to the Wilderness of *Beit Aven*.

ב וַיִּוָּתְרוּ בִּבְנֵי יִשְׂרָאֵל אֲשֶׁר לֹא־חָלְקוּ אֶת־נַחֲלָתָם שִׁבְעָה שְׁבָטִים:

ג וַיֹּאמֶר יְהוֹשֻׁעַ אֶל־בְּנֵי יִשְׂרָאֵל עַד־אָנָה אַתֶּם מִתְרַפִּים לָבוֹא לָרֶשֶׁת אֶת־הָאָרֶץ אֲשֶׁר נָתַן לָכֶם יְהוָה אֱלֹהֵי אֲבוֹתֵיכֶם:

ד הָבוּ לָכֶם שְׁלֹשָׁה אֲנָשִׁים לַשָּׁבֶט וְאֶשְׁלָחֵם וְיָקֻמוּ וְיִתְהַלְּכוּ בָאָרֶץ וְיִכְתְּבוּ אוֹתָהּ לְפִי נַחֲלָתָם וְיָבֹאוּ אֵלָי:

ה וְהִתְחַלְּקוּ אֹתָהּ לְשִׁבְעָה חֲלָקִים יְהוּדָה יַעֲמֹד עַל־גְּבוּלוֹ מִנֶּגֶב וּבֵית יוֹסֵף יַעַמְדוּ עַל־גְּבוּלָם מִצָּפוֹן:

ו וְאַתֶּם תִּכְתְּבוּ אֶת־הָאָרֶץ שִׁבְעָה חֲלָקִים וַהֲבֵאתֶם אֵלַי הֵנָּה וְיָרִיתִי לָכֶם גּוֹרָל פֹּה לִפְנֵי יְהוָה אֱלֹהֵינוּ:

ז כִּי אֵין־חֵלֶק לַלְוִיִּם בְּקִרְבְּכֶם כִּי־כְהֻנַּת יְהוָה נַחֲלָתוֹ וְגָד וּרְאוּבֵן וַחֲצִי שֵׁבֶט הַמְנַשֶּׁה לָקְחוּ נַחֲלָתָם מֵעֵבֶר לַיַּרְדֵּן מִזְרָחָה אֲשֶׁר נָתַן לָהֶם מֹשֶׁה עֶבֶד יְהוָה:

ח וַיָּקֻמוּ הָאֲנָשִׁים וַיֵּלֵכוּ וַיְצַו יְהוֹשֻׁעַ אֶת־הַהֹלְכִים לִכְתֹּב אֶת־הָאָרֶץ לֵאמֹר לְכוּ וְהִתְהַלְּכוּ בָאָרֶץ וְכִתְבוּ אוֹתָהּ וְשׁוּבוּ אֵלַי וּפֹה אַשְׁלִיךְ לָכֶם גּוֹרָל לִפְנֵי יְהוָה בְּשִׁלֹה:

ט וַיֵּלְכוּ הָאֲנָשִׁים וַיַּעַבְרוּ בָאָרֶץ וַיִּכְתְּבוּהָ לֶעָרִים לְשִׁבְעָה חֲלָקִים עַל־סֵפֶר וַיָּבֹאוּ אֶל־יְהוֹשֻׁעַ אֶל־הַמַּחֲנֶה שִׁלֹה:

י וַיַּשְׁלֵךְ לָהֶם יְהוֹשֻׁעַ גּוֹרָל בְּשִׁלֹה לִפְנֵי יְהוָה וַיְחַלֶּק־שָׁם יְהוֹשֻׁעַ אֶת־הָאָרֶץ לִבְנֵי יִשְׂרָאֵל כְּמַחְלְקֹתָם:

יא וַיַּעַל גּוֹרַל מַטֵּה בְנֵי־בִנְיָמִן לְמִשְׁפְּחֹתָם וַיֵּצֵא גְּבוּל גּוֹרָלָם בֵּין בְּנֵי יְהוּדָה וּבֵין בְּנֵי יוֹסֵף:

יב וַיְהִי לָהֶם הַגְּבוּל לִפְאַת צָפוֹנָה מִן־הַיַּרְדֵּן וְעָלָה הַגְּבוּל אֶל־כֶּתֶף יְרִיחוֹ מִצָּפוֹן וְעָלָה בָהָר יָמָּה והיה [וְהָיוּ] תֹּצְאֹתָיו מִדְבַּרָה בֵּית אָוֶן:

13 From there the boundary passed on southward to Luz, to the flank of Luz – that is, *Beit El*; then the boundary descended to Atroth-addar [and] to the hill south of Lower Beth-horon.

יג וְעָבַר מִשָּׁם הַגְּבוּל לוּזָה אֶל־כֶּתֶף לוּזָה נֶגְבָּה הִיא בֵּית־אֵל וְיָרַד הַגְּבוּל עַטְרוֹת אַדָּר עַל־הָהָר אֲשֶׁר מִנֶּגֶב לְבֵית־חוֹרוֹן תַּחְתּוֹן:

14 The boundary now turned and curved onto the western rim; and the boundary ran southward from the hill on the south side of Beth-horon till it ended at Kiriath-baal – that is, *Kiryat Ye'arim* – a town of the Judites. That was the western rim.

יד וְתָאַר הַגְּבוּל וְנָסַב לִפְאַת־יָם נֶגְבָּה מִן־הָהָר אֲשֶׁר עַל־פְּנֵי בֵית־חוֹרוֹן נֶגְבָּה וְהָיָה [וְהָיוּ] תֹצְאֹתָיו אֶל־קִרְיַת־בַּעַל הִיא קִרְיַת יְעָרִים עִיר בְּנֵי יְהוּדָה זֹאת פְּאַת־יָם:

15 The southern rim: From the outskirts of *Kiryat Ye'arim*, the boundary passed westward and ran on to the fountain of the Waters of Nephtoah.

טו וּפְאַת־נֶגְבָּה מִקְצֵה קִרְיַת יְעָרִים וְיָצָא הַגְּבוּל יָמָּה וְיָצָא אֶל־מַעְיַן מֵי נֶפְתּוֹחַ:

16 Then the boundary descended to the foot of the hill by the Valley of Ben-hinnom at the northern end of the Valley of Rephaim; then it ran down the Valley of Hinnom along the southern flank of the Jebusites to En-rogel.

טז וְיָרַד הַגְּבוּל אֶל־קְצֵה הָהָר אֲשֶׁר עַל־פְּנֵי גֵּי בֶן־הִנֹּם אֲשֶׁר בְּעֵמֶק רְפָאִים צָפוֹנָה וְיָרַד גֵּי הִנֹּם אֶל־כֶּתֶף הַיְבוּסִי נֶגְבָּה וְיָרַד עֵין רֹגֵל:

17 Curving northward, it ran on to En-shemesh and ran on to Geliloth, facing the Ascent of Adummim, and descended to the Stone of Bohan son of *Reuven*.

יז וְתָאַר מִצָּפוֹן וְיָצָא עֵין שֶׁמֶשׁ וְיָצָא אֶל־גְּלִילוֹת אֲשֶׁר־נֹכַח מַעֲלֵה אֲדֻמִּים וְיָרַד אֶבֶן בֹּהַן בֶּן־רְאוּבֵן:

18 It continued northward to the edge of the Arabah and descended into the Arabah.

יח וְעָבַר אֶל־כֶּתֶף מוּל־הָעֲרָבָה צָפוֹנָה וְיָרַד הָעֲרָבָתָה:

19 The boundary passed on to the northern flank of Beth-hoglah, and the boundary ended at the northern tongue of the Dead Sea, at the southern end of the *Yarden*. That was the southern boundary.

יט וְעָבַר הַגְּבוּל אֶל־כֶּתֶף בֵּית־חָגְלָה צָפוֹנָה וְהָיָה [וְהָיוּ] תֹצְאוֹתָיו [תֹצְאוֹת] הַגְּבוּל אֶל־לְשׁוֹן יָם־הַמֶּלַח צָפוֹנָה אֶל־קְצֵה הַיַּרְדֵּן נֶגְבָּה זֶה גְּבוּל נֶגֶב:

20 On their eastern rim, finally, the *Yarden* was their boundary. That was the portion of the Benjaminites, by their clans, according to its boundaries on all sides.

כ וְהַיַּרְדֵּן יִגְבֹּל־אֹתוֹ לִפְאַת־קֵדְמָה זֹאת נַחֲלַת בְּנֵי בִנְיָמִן לִגְבוּלֹתֶיהָ סָבִיב לְמִשְׁפְּחֹתָם:

21 And the towns of the tribe of the Benjaminites, by its clans, were: *Yericho*, Beth-hoglah, Emek-keziz,

כא וְהָיוּ הֶעָרִים לְמַטֵּה בְּנֵי בִנְיָמִן לְמִשְׁפְּחוֹתֵיהֶם יְרִיחוֹ וּבֵית־חָגְלָה וְעֵמֶק קְצִיץ:

22 Beth-arabah, Zemaraim, *Beit El*,

כב וּבֵית הָעֲרָבָה וּצְמָרַיִם וּבֵית־אֵל:

23 Avvim, Parah, Ophrah,

כג וְהָעַוִּים וְהַפָּרָה וְעָפְרָה:

24 Chephar-ammonah, Ophni, and Geba – 12 towns, with their villages.

כד וּכְפַר הָעַמֹּנִי [הָעַמֹּנָה] וְהָעָפְנִי וָגָבַע עָרִים שְׁתֵּים־עֶשְׂרֵה וְחַצְרֵיהֶן:

25 Also *Givon*, *Rama*, Beeroth,

כה גִּבְעוֹן וְהָרָמָה וּבְאֵרוֹת:

26 Mizpeh, Chephirah, Mozah,

כו וְהַמִּצְפֶּה וְהַכְּפִירָה וְהַמֹּצָה:

27 Rekem, Irpeel, Taralah,

כז וְרֶקֶם וְיִרְפְּאֵל וְתַרְאֲלָה:

28 Zela, Eleph, and Jebus – that is, *Yerushalayim* – Gibeath [and] Kiriath: 14 towns, with their villages. That was the portion of the Benjaminites, by their clans.

כח וְצֵלַע הָאֶלֶף וְהַיְבוּסִי הִיא יְרוּשָׁלַם גִּבְעַת קִרְיַת עָרִים אַרְבַּע־עֶשְׂרֵה וְחַצְרֵיהֶן זֹאת נַחֲלַת בְּנֵי־בִנְיָמִן לְמִשְׁפְּחֹתָם:

19 1 The second lot fell to *Shimon*. The portion of the tribe of the Simeonites, by their clans, lay inside the portion of the Judites.

יט א וַיֵּצֵא הַגּוֹרָל הַשֵּׁנִי לְשִׁמְעוֹן לְמַטֵּה בְנֵי־שִׁמְעוֹן לְמִשְׁפְּחוֹתָם וַיְהִי נַחֲלָתָם בְּתוֹךְ נַחֲלַת בְּנֵי־יְהוּדָה:

2 Their portion comprised: *Be'er Sheva* – or Sheba – Moladah,

ב וַיְהִי לָהֶם בְּנַחֲלָתָם בְּאֵר־שֶׁבַע וְשֶׁבַע וּמוֹלָדָה:

3 Hazar-shual, Balah, Ezem,

ג וַחֲצַר שׁוּעָל וּבָלָה וָעָצֶם:

4 Eltolad, Bethul, Hormah,

ד וְאֶלְתּוֹלַד וּבְתוּל וְחָרְמָה:

5 *Tziklag*, Beth-marcaboth, Hazar-susah,

ה וְצִקְלַג וּבֵית־הַמַּרְכָּבוֹת וַחֲצַר סוּסָה:

6 Beth-lebaoth, and Sharuhen – 13 towns, with their villages.

ו וּבֵית לְבָאוֹת וְשָׁרוּחֶן עָרִים שְׁלֹשׁ־עֶשְׂרֵה וְחַצְרֵיהֶן:

7 Ain, Rimmon, Ether, and Ashan: 4 towns, with their villages

ז עַיִן רִמּוֹן וָעֶתֶר וְעָשָׁן עָרִים אַרְבַּע וְחַצְרֵיהֶן:

8 together with all the villages in the vicinity of those towns, down to Baalath-beer [and] Ramath-negeb. That was the portion of the tribe of the Simeonites, by their clans.

ח וְכָל־הַחֲצֵרִים אֲשֶׁר סְבִיבוֹת הֶעָרִים הָאֵלֶּה עַד־בַּעֲלַת בְּאֵר רָאמַת נֶגֶב זֹאת נַחֲלַת מַטֵּה בְנֵי־שִׁמְעוֹן לְמִשְׁפְּחֹתָם:

9 The portion of the Simeonites was part of the territory of the Judites; since the share of the Judites was larger than they needed, the Simeonites received a portion inside their portion.

ט מֵחֶבֶל בְּנֵי יְהוּדָה נַחֲלַת בְּנֵי שִׁמְעוֹן כִּי־הָיָה חֵלֶק בְּנֵי־יְהוּדָה רַב מֵהֶם וַיִּנְחֲלוּ בְנֵי־שִׁמְעוֹן בְּתוֹךְ נַחֲלָתָם:

10 The third lot emerged for the Zebulunites, by their clans. The boundary of their portion: Starting at Sarid,

י וַיַּעַל הַגּוֹרָל הַשְּׁלִישִׁי לִבְנֵי זְבוּלֻן לְמִשְׁפְּחֹתָם וַיְהִי גְּבוּל נַחֲלָתָם עַד־שָׂרִיד:

11 their boundary ascended westward to Maralah, touching Dabbesheth and touching the wadi alongside Jokneam.

יא וְעָלָה גְבוּלָם לַיָּמָּה וּמַרְעֲלָה וּפָגַע בְּדַבָּשֶׁת וּפָגַע אֶל־הַנַּחַל אֲשֶׁר עַל־פְּנֵי יָקְנְעָם:

12 And it also ran from Sarid along the eastern side, where the sun rises, past the territory of Chisloth-tabor and on to Daberath and ascended to Japhia.

יב וְשָׁב מִשָּׂרִיד קֵדְמָה מִזְרַח הַשֶּׁמֶשׁ עַל־גְּבוּל כִּסְלֹת תָּבֹר וְיָצָא אֶל־הַדָּבְרַת וְעָלָה יָפִיעַ:

13 From there it ran [back] to the east, toward the sunrise, to Gath-hepher, to Eth-kazin, and on to Rimmon, where it curved to Neah.

יג וּמִשָּׁם עָבַר קֵדְמָה מִזְרָחָה גִּתָּה חֵפֶר עִתָּה קָצִין וְיָצָא רִמּוֹן הַמְּתֹאָר הַנֵּעָה:

14 Then it turned – that is, the boundary on the north – to Hannathon. Its extreme limits were the Valley of Iphtah-el,

יד וְנָסַב אֹתוֹ הַגְּבוּל מִצְּפוֹן חַנָּתֹן וְהָיוּ תֹּצְאֹתָיו גֵּי יִפְתַּח־אֵל:

Joshua

15 Kattath, Nahalal, Shimron, Idalah, and *Beit Lechem*: 12 towns, with their villages.

טו וְקַטָּת וְנַהֲלָל וְשִׁמְרוֹן וְיִדְאֲלָה וּבֵית לָחֶם עָרִים שְׁתֵּים־עֶשְׂרֵה וְחַצְרֵיהֶן׃

16 That was the portion of the Zebulunites by their clans – those towns, with their villages.

טז זֹאת נַחֲלַת בְּנֵי־זְבוּלֻן לְמִשְׁפְּחוֹתָם הֶעָרִים הָאֵלֶּה וְחַצְרֵיהֶן׃

17 The fourth lot fell to *Yissachar*, the Issacharites by their clans.

יז לְיִשָּׂשכָר יָצָא הַגּוֹרָל הָרְבִיעִי לִבְנֵי יִשָּׂשכָר לְמִשְׁפְּחוֹתָם׃

18 Their territory comprised: *Yizrael*, Chesulloth, Shunem,

יח וַיְהִי גְּבוּלָם יִזְרְעֶאלָה וְהַכְּסֻלֹּת וְשׁוּנֵם׃

19 Hapharaim, Shion, Anaharath,

יט וַחֲפָרַיִם וְשִׁיאֹן וַאֲנָחֲרַת׃

20 Rabbith, Kishion, Ebez,

כ וְהָרַבִּית וְקִשְׁיוֹן וָאָבֶץ׃

21 Remeth, En-gannim, En-haddah, and Beth-pazzez.

כא וְרֶמֶת וְעֵין־גַּנִּים וְעֵין חַדָּה וּבֵית פַּצֵּץ׃

22 The boundary touched *Tavor*, Shahazimah, and *Beit Shemesh*; and their boundary ran to the *Yarden*: 16 towns, with their villages.

כב וּפָגַע הַגְּבוּל בְּתָבוֹר וְשַׁחֲצוֹמָה [וְשַׁחֲצִימָה] וּבֵית שֶׁמֶשׁ וְהָיוּ תֹּצְאוֹת גְּבוּלָם הַיַּרְדֵּן עָרִים שֵׁשׁ־עֶשְׂרֵה וְחַצְרֵיהֶן׃

23 That was the portion of the tribe of the Issacharites, by their clans – the towns with their villages.

כג זֹאת נַחֲלַת מַטֵּה בְנֵי־יִשָּׂשכָר לְמִשְׁפְּחֹתָם הֶעָרִים וְחַצְרֵיהֶן׃

24 The fifth lot fell to the tribe of the Asherites, by their clans.

כד וַיֵּצֵא הַגּוֹרָל הַחֲמִישִׁי לְמַטֵּה בְנֵי־אָשֵׁר לְמִשְׁפְּחוֹתָם׃

25 Their boundary ran along Helkath, Hali, Beten, Achshaph,

כה וַיְהִי גְּבוּלָם חֶלְקַת וַחֲלִי וָבֶטֶן וְאַכְשָׁף׃

26 Allammelech, Amad, and Mishal; and it touched *Carmel* on the west, and Shihor-libnath.

כו וְאַלַמֶּלֶךְ וְעַמְעָד וּמִשְׁאָל וּפָגַע בְּכַרְמֶל הַיָּמָּה וּבְשִׁיחוֹר לִבְנָת׃

27 It also ran along the east side to Beth-dagon, and touched *Zevulun* and the Valley of Iphtah-el to the north, [as also] Beth-emek and Neiel; then it ran to Cabul on the north,

כז וְשָׁב מִזְרַח הַשֶּׁמֶשׁ בֵּית דָּגֹן וּפָגַע בִּזְבֻלוּן וּבְגֵי יִפְתַּח־אֵל צָפוֹנָה בֵּית הָעֵמֶק וּנְעִיאֵל וְיָצָא אֶל־כָּבוּל מִשְּׂמֹאל׃

28 Ebron, Rehob, Hammon, and Kanah, up to Great Sidon.

כח וְעֶבְרֹן וּרְחֹב וְחַמּוֹן וְקָנָה עַד צִידוֹן רַבָּה׃

29 The boundary turned to *Rama* and on to the fortified city of Tyre; then the boundary turned to Hosah and it ran on westward to Mehebel, Achzib,

כט וְשָׁב הַגְּבוּל הָרָמָה וְעַד־עִיר מִבְצַר־צֹר וְשָׁב הַגְּבוּל חֹסָה ויהיו [וְהָיוּ] תֹצְאֹתָיו הַיָּמָּה מֵחֶבֶל אַכְזִיבָה׃

30 Ummah, Aphek, and Rehob: 22 towns, with their villages.

ל וְעֻמָה וַאֲפֵק וּרְחֹב עָרִים עֶשְׂרִים וּשְׁתַּיִם וְחַצְרֵיהֶן׃

31 That was the portion of the tribe of the Asherites, by their clans – those towns, with their villages.

לא זֹאת נַחֲלַת מַטֵּה בְנֵי־אָשֵׁר לְמִשְׁפְּחֹתָם הֶעָרִים הָאֵלֶּה וְחַצְרֵיהֶן׃

32 The sixth lot fell to the Naphtalites, the Naphtalites by their clans.

לב לִבְנֵי נַפְתָּלִי יָצָא הַגּוֹרָל הַשִּׁשִּׁי לִבְנֵי נַפְתָּלִי לְמִשְׁפְּחֹתָם׃

Joshua

33 Their boundary ran from Heleph, Elon-bezaanannim, Adaminekeb, and Jabneel to Lakkum, and it ended at the *Yarden*.

לג וַיְהִי גְבוּלָם מֵחֵלֶף מֵאֵלוֹן בְּצַעֲנַנִּים וַאֲדָמִי הַנֶּקֶב וְיַבְנְאֵל עַד־לַקּוּם וַיְהִי תֹצְאֹתָיו הַיַּרְדֵּן׃

34 The boundary then turned westward to Aznoth-tabor and ran from there to Hukok. It touched *Zevulun* on the south, and it touched *Asher* on the west, and *Yehuda* at the *Yarden* on the east.

לד וְשָׁב הַגְּבוּל יָמָּה אַזְנוֹת תָּבוֹר וְיָצָא מִשָּׁם חוּקֹקָה וּפָגַע בִּזְבֻלוּן מִנֶּגֶב וּבְאָשֵׁר פָּגַע מִיָּם וּבִיהוּדָה הַיַּרְדֵּן מִזְרַח הַשָּׁמֶשׁ׃

35 Its fortified towns were Ziddim, Zer, Hammath, Rakkath, Chinnereth,

לה וְעָרֵי מִבְצָר הַצִּדִּים צֵר וְחַמַּת רַקַּת וְכִנָּרֶת׃

36 Adamah, *Rama*, Hazor,

לו וַאֲדָמָה וְהָרָמָה וְחָצוֹר׃

37 Kedesh, Edrei, En-hazor,

לז וְקֶדֶשׁ וְאֶדְרֶעִי וְעֵין חָצוֹר׃

38 Iron, Migdal-el, Horem, Beth-anath, and *Beit Shemesh*: 19 towns, with their villages.

לח וְיִרְאוֹן וּמִגְדַּל־אֵל חֳרֵם וּבֵית־עֲנָת וּבֵית שָׁמֶשׁ עָרִים תְּשַׁע־עֶשְׂרֵה וְחַצְרֵיהֶן׃

39 That was the portion of the tribe of the Naphtalites, by their clans – the towns, with their villages.

לט זֹאת נַחֲלַת מַטֵּה בְנֵי־נַפְתָּלִי לְמִשְׁפְּחֹתָם הֶעָרִים וְחַצְרֵיהֶן׃

40 The seventh lot fell to the tribe of the Danites, by their clans.

מ לְמַטֵּה בְנֵי־דָן לְמִשְׁפְּחֹתָם יָצָא הַגּוֹרָל הַשְּׁבִיעִי׃

41 Their allotted territory comprised: *Tzora, Eshtaol*, Ir-shemesh,

מא וַיְהִי גְּבוּל נַחֲלָתָם צָרְעָה וְאֶשְׁתָּאוֹל וְעִיר שָׁמֶשׁ׃

42 Shaalabbin, Aijalon, Ithlah,

מב וְשַׁעֲלַבִּין וְאַיָּלוֹן וְיִתְלָה׃

43 Elon, Timnah, Ekron,

מג וְאֵילוֹן וְתִמְנָתָה וְעֶקְרוֹן׃

44 Eltekeh, Gibbethon, Baalath,

מד וְאֶלְתְּקֵה וְגִבְּתוֹן וּבַעֲלָת׃

45 Jehud, Bene-berak, Gath-rimmon,

מה וִיהֻד וּבְנֵי־בְרַק וְגַת־רִמּוֹן׃

46 Me-jarkon, and Rakkon, at the border near *Yaffo*.

מו וּמֵי הַיַּרְקוֹן וְהָרַקּוֹן עִם־הַגְּבוּל מוּל יָפוֹ׃

47 But the territory of the Danites slipped from their grasp. So the Danites migrated and made war on Leshem. They captured it and put it to the sword; they took possession of it and settled in it. And they changed the name of Leshem to *Dan*, after their ancestor *Dan*.

מז וַיֵּצֵא גְבוּל־בְּנֵי־דָן מֵהֶם וַיַּעֲלוּ בְנֵי־דָן וַיִּלָּחֲמוּ עִם־לֶשֶׁם וַיִּלְכְּדוּ אוֹתָהּ וַיַּכּוּ אוֹתָהּ לְפִי־חֶרֶב וַיִּרְשׁוּ אוֹתָהּ וַיֵּשְׁבוּ בָהּ וַיִּקְרְאוּ לְלֶשֶׁם דָּן כְּשֵׁם דָּן אֲבִיהֶם׃

48 That was the portion of the tribe of the Danites, by their clans – those towns, with their villages.

מח זֹאת נַחֲלַת מַטֵּה בְנֵי־דָן לְמִשְׁפְּחֹתָם הֶעָרִים הָאֵלֶּה וְחַצְרֵיהֶן׃

49 When they had finished allotting the land by its boundaries, the Israelites gave a portion in their midst to *Yehoshua* son of Nun.

מט וַיְכַלּוּ לִנְחֹל־אֶת־הָאָרֶץ לִגְבוּלֹתֶיהָ וַיִּתְּנוּ בְנֵי־יִשְׂרָאֵל נַחֲלָה לִיהוֹשֻׁעַ בִּן־נוּן בְּתוֹכָם׃

Joshua

50 At the command of *Hashem* they gave him the town that he asked for, Timnath-serah in the hill country of *Efraim*; he fortified the town and settled in it.

נ עַל־פִּי יְהֹוָה נָתְנוּ לוֹ אֶת־הָעִיר אֲשֶׁר שָׁאָל אֶת־תִּמְנַת־סֶרַח בְּהַר אֶפְרָיִם וַיִּבְנֶה אֶת־הָעִיר וַיֵּשֶׁב בָּהּ:

al PEE a-do-NAI na-t'-NU LO et ha-EER a-SHER sha-AL et tim-nat SE-rakh b'-HAR ef-RA-yim va-yiv-NEH va-ha-EER va-YAY-shev bah

51 These are the portions assigned by lot to the tribes of *Yisrael* by the *Kohen Elazar, Yehoshua* son of *Nun,* and the heads of the ancestral houses, before *Hashem* at *Shilo,* at the entrance of the Tent of Meeting.

נא אֵלֶּה הַנְּחָלֹת אֲשֶׁר נִחֲלוּ אֶלְעָזָר הַכֹּהֵן וִיהוֹשֻׁעַ בִּן־נוּן וְרָאשֵׁי הָאָבוֹת לְמַטּוֹת בְּנֵי־יִשְׂרָאֵל בְּגוֹרָל בְּשִׁלֹה לִפְנֵי יְהֹוָה פֶּתַח אֹהֶל מוֹעֵד וַיְכַלּוּ מֵחַלֵּק אֶת־הָאָרֶץ:

20 1 When they had finished dividing the land, *Hashem* said to *Yehoshua:*

כ א וַיְדַבֵּר יְהֹוָה אֶל־יְהוֹשֻׁעַ לֵאמֹר:

2 "Speak to the Israelites: Designate the cities of refuge – about which I commanded you through *Moshe*

ב דַּבֵּר אֶל־בְּנֵי יִשְׂרָאֵל לֵאמֹר תְּנוּ לָכֶם אֶת־עָרֵי הַמִּקְלָט אֲשֶׁר־דִּבַּרְתִּי אֲלֵיכֶם בְּיַד־מֹשֶׁה:

da-BAYR el b'-NAY yis-ra-AYL lay-MOR t'-NU la-KHEM et a-RAY ha-mik-LAT a-sher di-BAR-tee a-lay-KHEM b'-yad mo-SHEH

3 to which a manslayer who kills a person by mistake, unintentionally, may flee. They shall serve you as a refuge from the blood avenger.

ג לָנוּס שָׁמָּה רוֹצֵחַ מַכֵּה־נֶפֶשׁ בִּשְׁגָגָה בִּבְלִי־דָעַת וְהָיוּ לָכֶם לְמִקְלָט מִגֹּאֵל הַדָּם:

Tomb of *Yehoshua* in Kifl Hares, biblical *Timnat Serach*

 19:50 They gave him the town that he asked for As the leader of the people, *Yehoshua* waits until the end of the process of dividing the land before receiving his own inheritance. He asks for *Timnat Serach* (Timnath-serah), in the mountains of *Efraim,* and through the lots, *Hashem* grants his request. However, unlike others who inherited existing towns built by the Canaanites, *Yehoshua* would not be able to simply move in; first, he needs to build the city. This is the task of leaders – to build something where nothing currently exists. In contemporary in Israel, many modern religious, political and business leaders have followed this model, and like *Yehoshua,* have been blessed by *Hashem* with success. In the context of the miraculous growth of the State of Israel, many communities, schools, organizations and institutions, as well as fertile farmland and stunning landscapes, have risen out of nothingness.

20:2 Designate the cities of refuge The cities of refuge are places where people who are guilty of unintentional manslaughter must flee for protection from the relatives of their victims. The accidental killer must remain in the city of refuge until the death of the *Kohen Gadol.* This law, which subjects the unwitting murderer to exile from his home, teaches a powerful lesson. The section of the *Torah* which details these laws ends with the words, "You shall not pollute the land in which you live; for blood pollutes the land … You shall not defile the land in which you live, in which I Myself abide, for I *Hashem* abide among *B'nei Yisrael*" (Numbers 35:33–34). Bloodshed, even unintentional, defiles the sanctity of the land. Therefore, the perpetrator must undergo a symbolic exile from the land which he has defiled. He can return only once atonement is achieved through the death of the *Kohen Gadol.* Similarly, the Jewish people were exiled from the Land of Israel because of their collective desecration of the land. And just as the unwitting murderer eventually returns home from the city of refuge, the People of Israel are now also returning home from their long and painful exile, to *Eretz Yisrael.*

⁴ He shall flee to one of those cities, present himself at the entrance to the city gate, and plead his case before the elders of that city; and they shall admit him into the city and give him a place in which to live among them.

ד וְנָס אֶל־אַחַת מֵהֶעָרִים הָאֵלֶּה וְעָמַד פֶּתַח שַׁעַר הָעִיר וְדִבֶּר בְּאָזְנֵי זִקְנֵי־הָעִיר הַהִיא אֶת־דְּבָרָיו וְאָסְפוּ אֹתוֹ הָעִירָה אֲלֵיהֶם וְנָתְנוּ־לוֹ מָקוֹם וְיָשַׁב עִמָּם:

⁵ Should the blood avenger pursue him, they shall not hand the manslayer over to him, since he killed the other person without intent and had not been his enemy in the past.

ה וְכִי יִרְדֹּף גֹּאֵל הַדָּם אַחֲרָיו וְלֹא־יַסְגִּרוּ אֶת־הָרֹצֵחַ בְּיָדוֹ כִּי בִבְלִי־דַעַת הִכָּה אֶת־רֵעֵהוּ וְלֹא־שֹׂנֵא הוּא לוֹ מִתְּמוֹל שִׁלְשׁוֹם:

⁶ He shall live in that city until he can stand trial before the assembly, [and remain there] until the death of the *Kohen Gadol* who is in office at that time. Thereafter, the manslayer may go back to his home in his own town, to the town from which he fled."

ו וְיָשַׁב בָּעִיר הַהִיא עַד־עָמְדוֹ לִפְנֵי הָעֵדָה לַמִּשְׁפָּט עַד־מוֹת הַכֹּהֵן הַגָּדוֹל אֲשֶׁר יִהְיֶה בַּיָּמִים הָהֵם אָז יָשׁוּב הָרוֹצֵחַ וּבָא אֶל־עִירוֹ וְאֶל־בֵּיתוֹ אֶל־הָעִיר אֲשֶׁר־נָס מִשָּׁם:

⁷ So they set aside Kedesh in the hill country of *Naftali* in Galilee, *Shechem* in the hill country of *Efraim*, and *Kiryat Arba* – that is, *Chevron* – in the hill country of *Yehuda*.

ז וַיַּקְדִּשׁוּ אֶת־קֶדֶשׁ בַּגָּלִיל בְּהַר נַפְתָּלִי וְאֶת־שְׁכֶם בְּהַר אֶפְרָיִם וְאֶת־קִרְיַת אַרְבַּע הִיא חֶבְרוֹן בְּהַר יְהוּדָה:

⁸ And across the *Yarden*, east of *Yericho*, they assigned Bezer in the wilderness, in the Tableland, from the tribe of *Reuven*; Ramoth in *Gilad* from the tribe of *Gad*; and Golan in Bashan from the tribe of *Menashe*.

ח וּמֵעֵבֶר לְיַרְדֵּן יְרִיחוֹ מִזְרָחָה נָתְנוּ אֶת־בֶּצֶר בַּמִּדְבָּר בַּמִּישֹׁר מִמַּטֵּה רְאוּבֵן וְאֶת־רָאמֹת בַּגִּלְעָד מִמַּטֵּה־גָד וְאֶת־גֹּלָן [גּוֹלָן] בַּבָּשָׁן מִמַּטֵּה מְנַשֶּׁה:

⁹ Those were the towns designated for all the Israelites and for aliens residing among them, to which anyone who killed a person unintentionally might flee, and not die by the hand of the blood avenger before standing trial by the assembly.

ט אֵלֶּה הָיוּ עָרֵי הַמּוּעָדָה לְכֹל בְּנֵי יִשְׂרָאֵל וְלַגֵּר הַגָּר בְּתוֹכָם לָנוּס שָׁמָּה כָּל־מַכֵּה־נֶפֶשׁ בִּשְׁגָגָה וְלֹא יָמוּת בְּיַד גֹּאֵל הַדָּם עַד־עָמְדוֹ לִפְנֵי הָעֵדָה:

21 ¹ The heads of the ancestral houses of the *Leviim* approached the *Kohen Elazar, Yehoshua* son of *Nun*, and the heads of the ancestral houses of the Israelite tribes,

כא א וַיִּגְּשׁוּ רָאשֵׁי אֲבוֹת הַלְוִיִּם אֶל־אֶלְעָזָר הַכֹּהֵן וְאֶל־יְהוֹשֻׁעַ בִּן־נוּן וְאֶל־רָאשֵׁי אֲבוֹת הַמַּטּוֹת לִבְנֵי יִשְׂרָאֵל:

² and spoke to them at *Shilo* in the land of Canaan, as follows: "*Hashem* commanded through *Moshe* that we be given towns to live in, along with their pastures for our livestock."

ב וַיְדַבְּרוּ אֲלֵיהֶם בְּשִׁלֹה בְּאֶרֶץ כְּנַעַן לֵאמֹר יְהֹוָה צִוָּה בְיַד־מֹשֶׁה לָתֶת־לָנוּ עָרִים לָשָׁבֶת וּמִגְרְשֵׁיהֶן לִבְהֶמְתֵּנוּ:

³ So the Israelites, in accordance with *Hashem's* command, assigned to the *Leviim*, out of their own portions, the following towns with their pastures:

ג וַיִּתְּנוּ בְנֵי־יִשְׂרָאֵל לַלְוִיִּם מִנַּחֲלָתָם אֶל־פִּי יְהֹוָה אֶת־הֶעָרִים הָאֵלֶּה וְאֶת־מִגְרְשֵׁיהֶן:

⁴ The [first] lot among the *Leviim* fell to the Kehatite clans. To the descendants of the *Kohen Aharon*, there fell by lot 13 towns from the tribe of *Yehuda*, the tribe of *Shimon*, and the tribe of *Binyamin*;

ד וַיֵּצֵא הַגּוֹרָל לְמִשְׁפְּחֹת הַקְּהָתִי וַיְהִי לִבְנֵי אַהֲרֹן הַכֹּהֵן מִן־הַלְוִיִּם מִמַּטֵּה יְהוּדָה וּמִמַּטֵּה הַשִּׁמְעֹנִי וּמִמַּטֵּה בִנְיָמִן בַּגּוֹרָל עָרִים שְׁלֹשׁ עֶשְׂרֵה:

5 and to the remaining Kehatites [there fell] by lot 10 towns from the clans of the tribe of *Efraim*, the tribe of *Dan*, and the half-tribe of *Menashe*.

ה וְלִבְנֵי קְהָת הַנּוֹתָרִים מִמִּשְׁפַּחַת מַטֵּה־אֶפְרַיִם וּמִמַּטֵּה־דָן וּמֵחֲצִי מַטֵּה מְנַשֶּׁה בַּגּוֹרָל עָרִים עָשֶׂר:

6 To the Gershonites [there fell] by lot 13 towns from the clans of the tribe of *Yissachar*, the tribe of *Asher*, the tribe of *Naftali*, and the half-tribe of *Menashe* in Bashan.

ו וְלִבְנֵי גֵרְשׁוֹן מִמִּשְׁפְּחוֹת מַטֵּה־יִשָּׂשכָר וּמִמַּטֵּה־אָשֵׁר וּמִמַּטֵּה נַפְתָּלִי וּמֵחֲצִי מַטֵּה מְנַשֶּׁה בַבָּשָׁן בַּגּוֹרָל עָרִים שְׁלֹשׁ עֶשְׂרֵה:

7 [And] to the Merarites, by their clans – 12 towns from the tribe of *Reuven*, the tribe of *Gad*, and the tribe of *Zevulun*.

ז לִבְנֵי מְרָרִי לְמִשְׁפְּחֹתָם מִמַּטֵּה רְאוּבֵן וּמִמַּטֵּה־גָד וּמִמַּטֵּה זְבוּלֻן עָרִים שְׁתֵּים עֶשְׂרֵה:

8 The Israelites assigned those towns with their pastures by lot to the *Leviim* – as *Hashem* had commanded through *Moshe*.

ח וַיִּתְּנוּ בְנֵי־יִשְׂרָאֵל לַלְוִיִּם אֶת־הֶעָרִים הָאֵלֶּה וְאֶת־מִגְרְשֵׁיהֶן כַּאֲשֶׁר צִוָּה יְהוָה בְּיַד־מֹשֶׁה בַּגּוֹרָל:

9 From the tribe of the Judites and the tribe of the Simeonites were assigned the following towns, which will be listed by name;

ט וַיִּתְּנוּ מִמַּטֵּה בְּנֵי יְהוּדָה וּמִמַּטֵּה בְּנֵי שִׁמְעוֹן אֵת הֶעָרִים הָאֵלֶּה אֲשֶׁר־יִקְרָא אֶתְהֶן בְּשֵׁם:

10 they went to the descendants of *Aharon* among the Kehatite clans of the *Leviim*, for the first lot had fallen to them.

י וַיְהִי לִבְנֵי אַהֲרֹן מִמִּשְׁפְּחוֹת הַקְּהָתִי מִבְּנֵי לֵוִי כִּי לָהֶם הָיָה הַגּוֹרָל רִיאשֹׁנָה:

11 To them were assigned in the hill country of *Yehuda* *Kiryat Arba* – that is, *Chevron* – together with the pastures around it. [Arba was] the father of the Anokites.

יא וַיִּתְּנוּ לָהֶם אֶת־קִרְיַת אַרְבַּע אֲבִי הָעֲנוֹק הִיא חֶבְרוֹן בְּהַר יְהוּדָה וְאֶת־מִגְרָשֶׁהָ סְבִיבֹתֶיהָ:

12 They gave the fields and the villages of the town to *Kalev* son of Jephunneh as his holding.

יב וְאֶת־שְׂדֵה הָעִיר וְאֶת־חֲצֵרֶיהָ נָתְנוּ לְכָלֵב בֶּן־יְפֻנֶּה בַּאֲחֻזָּתוֹ:

13 But to the descendants of *Aharon* the *Kohen* they assigned *Chevron* – the city of refuge for manslayers – together with its pastures, Libnah with its pastures,

יג וְלִבְנֵי אַהֲרֹן הַכֹּהֵן נָתְנוּ אֶת־עִיר מִקְלַט הָרֹצֵחַ אֶת־חֶבְרוֹן וְאֶת־מִגְרָשֶׁהָ וְאֶת־לִבְנָה וְאֶת־מִגְרָשֶׁהָ:

14 Jattir with its pastures, Eshtemoa with its pastures,

יד וְאֶת־יַתִּר וְאֶת־מִגְרָשֶׁהָ וְאֶת־אֶשְׁתְּמֹעַ וְאֶת־מִגְרָשֶׁהָ:

15 Holon with its pastures, Debir with its pastures,

טו וְאֶת־חֹלֹן וְאֶת־מִגְרָשֶׁהָ וְאֶת־דְּבִר וְאֶת־מִגְרָשֶׁהָ:

16 Ain with its pastures, Juttah with its pastures, and *Beit Shemesh* with its pastures – 9 towns from those two tribes.

טז וְאֶת־עַיִן וְאֶת־מִגְרָשֶׁהָ וְאֶת־יֻטָּה וְאֶת־מִגְרָשֶׁהָ אֶת־בֵּית שֶׁמֶשׁ וְאֶת־מִגְרָשֶׁהָ עָרִים תֵּשַׁע מֵאֵת שְׁנֵי הַשְּׁבָטִים הָאֵלֶּה:

17 And from the tribe of *Binyamin*: Givon with its pastures, Geba with its pastures,

יז וּמִמַּטֵּה בִנְיָמִן אֶת־גִּבְעוֹן וְאֶת־מִגְרָשֶׁהָ אֶת־גֶּבַע וְאֶת־מִגְרָשֶׁהָ:

18 *Anatot* with its pastures, and Almon with its pastures – 4 towns.

יח אֶת־עֲנָתוֹת וְאֶת־מִגְרָשֶׁהָ וְאֶת־עַלְמוֹן וְאֶת־מִגְרָשֶׁהָ עָרִים אַרְבַּע:

19 All the towns of the descendants of the *Kohen* Aharon, 13 towns with their pastures.

יט כָּל־עָרֵי בְנֵי־אַהֲרֹן הַכֹּהֲנִים שְׁלֹשׁ־עֶשְׂרֵה עָרִים וּמִגְרְשֵׁיהֶן:

20 As for the other clans of the Kehatites, the remaining *Leviim* descended from *Kehat,* the towns in their lot were: From the tribe of *Efraim*

כ וּלְמִשְׁפְּח֞וֹת בְּנֵי־קְהָ֣ת הַלְוִיִּ֣ם הַנּוֹתָרִ֗ים מִבְּנֵ֣י קְהָ֑ת וַיְהִי֙ עָרֵ֣י גֽוֹרָלָ֔ם מִמַּטֵּ֖ה אֶפְרָֽיִם:

21 they were given, in the hill country of *Efraim, Shechem* – the city of refuge for manslayers – with its pastures, Gezer with its pastures,

כא וַיִּתְּנ֨וּ לָהֶ֜ם אֶת־עִ֨יר מִקְלַ֤ט הָרֹצֵ֙חַ֙ אֶת־שְׁכֶ֤ם וְאֶת־מִגְרָשֶׁ֙הָ֙ בְּהַ֣ר אֶפְרָ֑יִם וְאֶת־גֶּ֖זֶר וְאֶת־מִגְרָשֶֽׁהָ:

22 Kibzaim with its pastures, and Beth-horon with its pastures – 4 towns.

כב וְאֶת־קִבְצַ֙יִם֙ וְאֶת־מִגְרָשֶׁ֔הָ וְאֶת־בֵּ֥ית חוֹרֹ֖ן וְאֶת־מִגְרָשֶׁ֑הָ עָרִ֖ים אַרְבַּֽע:

23 From the tribe of *Dan*, Elteke with its pastures, Gibbethon with its pastures,

כג וּמִֽמַּטֵּה־דָ֕ן אֶֽת־אֶלְתְּקֵ֖א וְאֶת־מִגְרָשֶׁ֑הָ אֶֽת־גִּבְּת֖וֹן וְאֶת־מִגְרָשֶֽׁהָ:

24 Aijalon with its pastures, and Gath-rimmon with its pastures – 4 towns.

כד אֶת־אַיָּלוֹן֙ וְאֶת־מִגְרָשֶׁ֔הָ אֶת־גַּת־רִמּ֖וֹן וְאֶת־מִגְרָשֶׁ֑הָ עָרִ֖ים אַרְבַּֽע:

25 And from the half-tribe of *Menashe*, Taanach with its pastures, and Gath-rimmon with its pastures – 2 towns.

כה וּמִֽמַּחֲצִ֜ית מַטֵּ֣ה מְנַשֶּׁ֗ה אֶת־תַּעְנַךְ֙ וְאֶת־מִגְרָשֶׁ֔הָ וְאֶת־גַּת־רִמּ֖וֹן וְאֶת־מִגְרָשֶׁ֑הָ עָרִ֖ים שְׁתָּֽיִם:

26 All the towns for the remaining clans of the Kehatites came to 10, with their pastures.

כו כָּל־עָרִ֥ים עֶ֛שֶׂר וּמִגְרְשֵׁיהֶ֖ן לְמִשְׁפְּח֑וֹת בְּנֵֽי־קְהָ֖ת הַנּוֹתָרִֽים:

27 To the Gershonites of the levitical clans: From the half-tribe of *Menashe*, Golan in Bashan – the city of refuge for manslayers – with its pastures, and Beeshterah with its pastures – 2 towns.

כז וְלִבְנֵ֣י גֵרְשׁ֗וֹן מִמִּשְׁפְּחֹ֣ת הַלְוִיִּם֮ מֵֽחֲצִ֣י מַטֵּ֣ה מְנַשֶּׁה֒ אֶת־עִיר֙ מִקְלַ֣ט הָרֹצֵ֔חַ אֶת־גּוֹלָ֤ן [גּוֹלָ֙ן] בַּבָּשָׁן֙ וְאֶת־מִגְרָשֶׁ֔הָ וְאֶת־בְּעֶשְׁתְּרָ֖ה וְאֶת־מִגְרָשֶׁ֑הָ עָרִ֖ים שְׁתָּֽיִם:

28 From the tribe of *Yissachar*: Kishion with its pastures, Dobrath with its pastures,

כח וּמִמַּטֵּ֣ה יִשָּׂשכָ֔ר אֶת־קִשְׁי֖וֹן וְאֶת־מִגְרָשֶׁ֑הָ אֶת־דָּֽבְרַ֖ת וְאֶת־מִגְרָשֶֽׁהָ:

29 *Yarmut* with its pastures, and Engannim with its pastures – 4 towns.

כט אֶת־יַרְמוּת֙ וְאֶת־מִגְרָשֶׁ֔הָ אֶת־עֵ֥ין גַּנִּ֖ים וְאֶת־מִגְרָשֶׁ֑הָ עָרִ֖ים אַרְבַּֽע:

30 From the tribe of *Asher*: Mishal with its pastures, *Avdon* with its pastures,

ל וּמִמַּטֵּ֣ה אָשֵׁ֔ר אֶת־מִשְׁאָ֖ל וְאֶת־מִגְרָשֶׁ֑הָ אֶת־עַבְדּ֖וֹן וְאֶת־מִגְרָשֶֽׁהָ:

31 Helkath with its pastures, and Rehob with its pastures – 4 towns.

לא אֶת־חֶלְקָת֙ וְאֶת־מִגְרָשֶׁ֔הָ וְאֶת־רְחֹ֖ב וְאֶת־מִגְרָשֶׁ֑הָ עָרִ֖ים אַרְבַּֽע:

32 From the tribe of *Naftali*, Kedesh in Galilee – the city of refuge for manslayers – with its pastures, Hammoth-dor with its pastures, and Kartan with its pastures – 3 towns.

לב וּמִמַּטֵּ֣ה נַפְתָּלִ֗י אֶת־עִ֣יר מִקְלַ֣ט הָֽרֹצֵ֧חַ אֶת־קֶ֣דֶשׁ בַּגָּלִ֛יל וְאֶת־מִגְרָשֶׁ֖הָ וְאֶת־חַמֹּ֥ת דֹּאר֙ וְאֶת־מִגְרָשֶׁ֔הָ וְאֶת־קַרְתָּ֖ן וְאֶת־מִגְרָשֶׁ֑הָ עָרִ֖ים שָׁלֹֽשׁ:

33 All the towns of the Gershonites, by their clans, came to 13 towns, with their pastures.

לג כָּל־עָרֵ֣י הַגֵּֽרְשֻׁנִּי֮ לְמִשְׁפְּחֹתָם֒ שְׁלֹשׁ־עֶשְׂרֵ֥ה עִ֖יר וּמִגְרְשֵׁיהֶֽן:

34 To the remaining *Leviim*, the clans of the Merarites: From the tribe of *Zevulun*, Jokneam with its pastures, Kartah with its pastures,

לד וּלְמִשְׁפְּח֣וֹת בְּנֵֽי־מְרָרִי֮ הַלְוִיִּ֣ם הַנּוֹתָרִים֒ מֵאֵת֙ מַטֵּ֣ה זְבוּלֻ֔ן אֶת־יָקְנְעָ֖ם וְאֶת־מִגְרָשֶׁ֑הָ אֶת־קַרְתָּ֖ה וְאֶת־מִגְרָשֶֽׁהָ:

35 Dimnah with its pastures, and Nahalal with its pastures – 4 towns.

אֶת־דִּמְנָה וְאֶת־מִגְרָשֶׁהָ אֶת־נַהֲלָל וְאֶת־מִגְרָשֶׁהָ עָרִים אַרְבַּע: לה

36 From the tribe of *Gad*, Ramoth in *Gilad* – the city of refuge for manslayers – with its pastures, Mahanaim with its pastures,

וּמִמַּטֵּה־גָד אֶת־עִיר מִקְלַט הָרֹצֵחַ אֶת־רָמֹת בַּגִּלְעָד וְאֶת־מִגְרָשֶׁהָ וְאֶת־מַחֲנַיִם וְאֶת־מִגְרָשֶׁהָ: לו

37 Heshbon with its pastures, and Jazer with its pastures – 4 towns in all.

אֶת־חֶשְׁבּוֹן וְאֶת־מִגְרָשֶׁהָ אֶת־יַעְזֵר וְאֶת־מִגְרָשֶׁהָ כָּל־עָרִים אַרְבַּע: לז

38 All the towns which went by lot to the Merarites, by their clans – the rest of the levitical clans – came to 12 towns.

כָּל־הֶעָרִים לִבְנֵי מְרָרִי לְמִשְׁפְּחֹתָם הַנּוֹתָרִים מִמִּשְׁפְּחוֹת הַלְוִיִּם וַיְהִי גּוֹרָלָם עָרִים שְׁתֵּים עֶשְׂרֵה: לח

39 All the towns of the *Leviim* within the holdings of the Israelites came to 48 towns, with their pastures.

כֹּל עָרֵי הַלְוִיִּם בְּתוֹךְ אֲחֻזַּת בְּנֵי־יִשְׂרָאֵל עָרִים אַרְבָּעִים וּשְׁמֹנֶה וּמִגְרְשֵׁיהֶן: לט

40 Thus those towns were assigned, every town with its surrounding pasture; and so it was with all those towns.

תִּהְיֶינָה הֶעָרִים הָאֵלֶּה עִיר עִיר וּמִגְרָשֶׁיהָ סְבִיבֹתֶיהָ כֵּן לְכָל־הֶעָרִים הָאֵלֶּה: מ

41 *Hashem* gave to *Yisrael* the whole country which He had sworn to their fathers that He would assign to them; they took possession of it and settled in it.

וַיִּתֵּן יְהֹוָה לְיִשְׂרָאֵל אֶת־כָּל־הָאָרֶץ אֲשֶׁר נִשְׁבַּע לָתֵת לַאֲבוֹתָם וַיִּרָשׁוּהָ וַיֵּשְׁבוּ בָהּ: מא

va-yi-TAYN a-do-NAI l'-yis-ra-AYL et kol ha-A-retz a-SHER nish-BA la-TAYT la-a-vo-TAM va-yi-ra-SHU-ha va-yay-sh'-VU VAH

42 *Hashem* gave them rest on all sides, just as He had promised to their fathers on oath. Not one man of all their enemies withstood them; *Hashem* delivered all their enemies into their hands.

וַיָּנַח יְהֹוָה לָהֶם מִסָּבִיב כְּכֹל אֲשֶׁר־נִשְׁבַּע לַאֲבוֹתָם וְלֹא־עָמַד אִישׁ בִּפְנֵיהֶם מִכָּל־אֹיְבֵיהֶם אֵת כָּל־אֹיְבֵיהֶם נָתַן יְהֹוָה בְּיָדָם: מב

43 Not one of the good things which *Hashem* had promised to the House of *Yisrael* was lacking. Everything was fulfilled.

לֹא־נָפַל דָּבָר מִכֹּל הַדָּבָר הַטּוֹב אֲשֶׁר־דִּבֶּר יְהֹוָה אֶל־בֵּית יִשְׂרָאֵל הַכֹּל בָּא: מג

22 1 Then *Yehoshua* summoned the Reubenites, the Gadites, and the half-tribe of *Menashe*,

כב אָז יִקְרָא יְהוֹשֻׁעַ לָראוּבֵנִי וְלַגָּדִי וְלַחֲצִי מַטֵּה מְנַשֶּׁה: א

2 and said to them, "You have observed all that *Moshe* the servant of *Hashem* commanded you, and have obeyed me in everything that I commanded you.

וַיֹּאמֶר אֲלֵיהֶם אַתֶּם שְׁמַרְתֶּם אֵת כָּל־אֲשֶׁר צִוָּה אֶתְכֶם מֹשֶׁה עֶבֶד יְהֹוָה וַתִּשְׁמְעוּ בְקוֹלִי לְכֹל אֲשֶׁר־צִוִּיתִי אֶתְכֶם: ב

21:41 They took possession of it and settled in it *Hashem* fulfills His promise to the People of Israel, who live in and possess the Land of Israel. The *Ramban* notes that there are three aspects to the Jewish People's obligation regarding *Eretz Yisrael*: They are commanded to live in *Eretz Yisrael*, to build up the land through strengthening its Jewish community, and to maintain a sovereign

PM Yitzchak Shamir and Rabbi Mordechai Eliyahu planting a tree on Mount Scopus in honor of Tu B'Shevat (1990)

government ruling over *Eretz Yisrael*. Thus, though it's important for individuals to live in the Land of Israel, it's also critically important that the Nation of Israel has "taken possession of it and settled in it." Former Prime Minister Yitzhak Shamir expressed how crucial it is to settle the land when he said that "the settlement of the Land of Israel is the essence of Zionism."

Joshua

3 You have not forsaken your kinsmen through the long years down to this day, but have faithfully observed the Instruction of *Hashem* your God.

ג לֹא־עֲזַבְתֶּם אֶת־אֲחֵיכֶם זֶה יָמִים רַבִּים עַד הַיּוֹם הַזֶּה וּשְׁמַרְתֶּם אֶת־מִשְׁמֶרֶת מִצְוַת יְהוָה אֱלֹהֵיכֶם:

4 Now *Hashem* your God has given your kinsmen rest, as He promised them. Therefore turn and go to your homes, to the land of your holdings beyond the *Yarden* that *Moshe* the servant of *Hashem* assigned to you.

ד וְעַתָּה הֵנִיחַ יְהוָה אֱלֹהֵיכֶם לַאֲחֵיכֶם כַּאֲשֶׁר דִּבֶּר לָהֶם וְעַתָּה פְּנוּ וּלְכוּ לָכֶם לְאָהֳלֵיכֶם אֶל־אֶרֶץ אֲחֻזַּתְכֶם אֲשֶׁר נָתַן לָכֶם מֹשֶׁה עֶבֶד יְהוָה בְּעֵבֶר הַיַּרְדֵּן:

5 But be very careful to fulfill the Instruction and the Teaching that *Moshe* the servant of *Hashem* enjoined upon you, to love *Hashem* your God and to walk in all His ways, and to keep His commandments and hold fast to Him, and to serve Him with all your heart and soul."

ה רַק שִׁמְרוּ מְאֹד לַעֲשׂוֹת אֶת־הַמִּצְוָה וְאֶת־הַתּוֹרָה אֲשֶׁר צִוָּה אֶתְכֶם מֹשֶׁה עֶבֶד־יְהוָה לְאַהֲבָה אֶת־יְהוָה אֱלֹהֵיכֶם וְלָלֶכֶת בְּכָל־דְּרָכָיו וְלִשְׁמֹר מִצְוֹתָיו וּלְדָבְקָה־בוֹ וּלְעָבְדוֹ בְּכָל־לְבַבְכֶם וּבְכָל־נַפְשְׁכֶם:

6 Then *Yehoshua* blessed them and dismissed them, and they went to their homes.

ו וַיְבָרְכֵם יְהוֹשֻׁעַ וַיְשַׁלְּחֵם וַיֵּלְכוּ אֶל־אָהֳלֵיהֶם:

7 To the one half-tribe of *Menashe Moshe* had assigned territory in Bashan, and to the other *Yehoshua* assigned [territory] on the west side of the *Yarden*, with their kinsmen. Furthermore, when *Yehoshua* sent them off to their homes, he blessed them

ז וְלַחֲצִי שֵׁבֶט הַמְנַשֶּׁה נָתַן מֹשֶׁה בַּבָּשָׁן וּלְחֶצְיוֹ נָתַן יְהוֹשֻׁעַ עִם־אֲחֵיהֶם מעבר [בְּעֵבֶר] הַיַּרְדֵּן יָמָּה וְגַם כִּי שִׁלְּחָם יְהוֹשֻׁעַ אֶל־אָהֳלֵיהֶם וַיְבָרֲכֵם:

8 and said to them, "Return to your homes with great wealth – with very much livestock, with silver and gold, with copper and iron, and with a great quantity of clothing. Share the spoil of your enemies with your kinsmen."

ח וַיֹּאמֶר אֲלֵיהֶם לֵאמֹר בִּנְכָסִים רַבִּים שׁוּבוּ אֶל־אָהֳלֵיכֶם וּבְמִקְנֶה רַב־מְאֹד בְּכֶסֶף וּבְזָהָב וּבִנְחֹשֶׁת וּבְבַרְזֶל וּבִשְׂלָמוֹת הַרְבֵּה מְאֹד חִלְקוּ שְׁלַל־אֹיְבֵיכֶם עִם־אֲחֵיכֶם:

9 So the Reubenites, the Gadites, and the half-tribe of *Menashe* left the Israelites at *Shilo*, in the land of Canaan, and made their way back to the land of *Gilad*, the land of their own holding, which they had acquired by the command of *Hashem* through *Moshe*.

ט וַיָּשֻׁבוּ וַיֵּלְכוּ בְּנֵי־רְאוּבֵן וּבְנֵי־גָד וַחֲצִי שֵׁבֶט הַמְנַשֶּׁה מֵאֵת בְּנֵי יִשְׂרָאֵל מִשִּׁלֹה אֲשֶׁר בְּאֶרֶץ־כְּנָעַן לָלֶכֶת אֶל־אֶרֶץ הַגִּלְעָד אֶל־אֶרֶץ אֲחֻזָּתָם אֲשֶׁר נֹאחֲזוּ־בָהּ עַל־פִּי יְהוָה בְּיַד־מֹשֶׁה:

10 When they came to the region of the *Yarden* in the land of Canaan, the Reubenites and the Gadites and the half-tribe of *Menashe* built a *Mizbayach* there by the *Yarden*, a great conspicuous *Mizbayach*.

י וַיָּבֹאוּ אֶל־גְּלִילוֹת הַיַּרְדֵּן אֲשֶׁר בְּאֶרֶץ כְּנָעַן וַיִּבְנוּ בְנֵי־רְאוּבֵן וּבְנֵי־גָד וַחֲצִי שֵׁבֶט הַמְנַשֶּׁה שָׁם מִזְבֵּחַ עַל־הַיַּרְדֵּן מִזְבֵּחַ גָּדוֹל לְמַרְאֶה:

11 A report reached the Israelites: "The Reubenites, the Gadites, and the half-tribe of *Menashe* have built a *Mizbayach* opposite the land of Canaan, in the region of the *Yarden*, across from the Israelites."

יא וַיִּשְׁמְעוּ בְנֵי־יִשְׂרָאֵל לֵאמֹר הִנֵּה בָנוּ בְנֵי־רְאוּבֵן וּבְנֵי־גָד וַחֲצִי שֵׁבֶט הַמְנַשֶּׁה אֶת־הַמִּזְבֵּחַ אֶל־מוּל אֶרֶץ כְּנַעַן אֶל־גְּלִילוֹת הַיַּרְדֵּן אֶל־עֵבֶר בְּנֵי יִשְׂרָאֵל:

12 When the Israelites heard this, the whole community of the Israelites assembled at *Shilo* to make war on them.

יב וַיִּשְׁמְעוּ בְּנֵי יִשְׂרָאֵל וַיִּקָּהֲלוּ כָּל־עֲדַת בְּנֵי־יִשְׂרָאֵל שִׁלֹה לַעֲלוֹת עֲלֵיהֶם לַצָּבָא:

va-yish-m'-U b'-NAY yis-ra-AYL va-yi-ka-ha-LU kol a-DAT b'-nay yis-ra-AYL shi-LOH la-a-LOT a-lay-HEM la-tza-VA

13 But [first] the Israelites sent the *Kohen Pinchas* son of *Elazar* to the Reubenites, the Gadites, and the half-tribe of *Menashe* in the land of *Gilad*,

יג וַיִּשְׁלְחוּ בְנֵי־יִשְׂרָאֵל אֶל־בְּנֵי־רְאוּבֵן וְאֶל־בְּנֵי־גָד וְאֶל־חֲצִי שֵׁבֶט־מְנַשֶּׁה אֶל־אֶרֶץ הַגִּלְעָד אֶת־פִּינְחָס בֶּן־אֶלְעָזָר הַכֹּהֵן:

14 accompanied by ten chieftains, one chieftain from each ancestral house of each of the tribes of *Yisrael*; they were every one of them heads of ancestral houses of the contingents of *Yisrael*.

יד וַעֲשָׂרָה נְשִׂאִים עִמּוֹ נָשִׂיא אֶחָד נָשִׂיא אֶחָד לְבֵית אָב לְכֹל מַטּוֹת יִשְׂרָאֵל וְאִישׁ רֹאשׁ בֵּית־אֲבוֹתָם הֵמָּה לְאַלְפֵי יִשְׂרָאֵל:

15 When they came to the Reubenites, the Gadites, and the half-tribe of *Menashe* in the land of *Gilad*, they spoke to them as follows:

טו וַיָּבֹאוּ אֶל־בְּנֵי־רְאוּבֵן וְאֶל־בְּנֵי־גָד וְאֶל־חֲצִי שֵׁבֶט־מְנַשֶּׁה אֶל־אֶרֶץ הַגִּלְעָד וַיְדַבְּרוּ אִתָּם לֵאמֹר:

16 "Thus said the whole community of *Hashem*: What is this treachery that you have committed this day against the God of *Yisrael*, turning away from *Hashem*, building yourselves a *Mizbayach* and rebelling this day against *Hashem*!

טז כֹּה אָמְרוּ כֹּל עֲדַת יְהֹוָה מָה־הַמַּעַל הַזֶּה אֲשֶׁר מְעַלְתֶּם בֵּאלֹהֵי יִשְׂרָאֵל לָשׁוּב הַיּוֹם מֵאַחֲרֵי יְהֹוָה בִּבְנוֹתְכֶם לָכֶם מִזְבֵּחַ לִמְרָדְכֶם הַיּוֹם בַּיהֹוָה:

17 Is the sin of Peor, which brought a plague upon the community of *Hashem*, such a small thing to us? We have not cleansed ourselves from it to this very day;

יז הַמְעַט־לָנוּ אֶת־עֲוֹן פְּעוֹר אֲשֶׁר לֹא־הִטַּהַרְנוּ מִמֶּנּוּ עַד הַיּוֹם הַזֶּה וַיְהִי הַנֶּגֶף בַּעֲדַת יְהֹוָה:

18 and now you would turn away from *Hashem*! If you rebel against *Hashem* today, tomorrow He will be angry with the whole community of *Yisrael*.

יח וְאַתֶּם תָּשֻׁבוּ הַיּוֹם מֵאַחֲרֵי יְהֹוָה וְהָיָה אַתֶּם תִּמְרְדוּ הַיּוֹם בַּיהֹוָה וּמָחָר אֶל־כָּל־עֲדַת יִשְׂרָאֵל יִקְצֹף:

19 If it is because the land of your holding is unclean, cross over into the land of *Hashem*'s own holding, where the *Mishkan* of *Hashem* abides, and acquire holdings among us. But do not rebel against *Hashem*, and do not rebel against us by building for yourselves altar other than the *Mizbayach* of *Hashem* our God.

יט וְאַךְ אִם־טְמֵאָה אֶרֶץ אֲחֻזַּתְכֶם עִבְרוּ לָכֶם אֶל־אֶרֶץ אֲחֻזַּת יְהֹוָה אֲשֶׁר שָׁכַן־שָׁם מִשְׁכַּן יְהֹוָה וְהֵאָחֲזוּ בְּתוֹכֵנוּ וּבַיהֹוָה אַל־תִּמְרֹדוּ וְאֹתָנוּ אַל־תִּמְרֹדוּ בִּבְנֹתְכֶם לָכֶם מִזְבֵּחַ מִבַּלְעֲדֵי מִזְבַּח יְהֹוָה אֱלֹהֵינוּ:

22:12 The whole community of the Israelites assembled at Shilo to make war on them When the 2½ tribes residing on the east bank of the *Yarden* set up an altar to *Hashem*, the other tribes react harshly and quickly. The 9½ other tribes threaten to make war if they do not put an end to this practice. Because the *Mishkan* stands, no other altars could be permitted. Similarly, once the *Beit Hamikdash* is built in *Yerushalayim*, no sacrifices are ever allowed anywhere else. Though the entire Land of Israel is holy, *Hashem* desires that His people join together to serve Him in one united center of worship, in the heart of the capital city *Yerushalayim*.

Tel Shilo, site of the Mishkan

20 When *Achan* son of *Zerach* violated the proscription, anger struck the whole community of *Yisrael*; he was not the only one who perished for that sin."

כ הֲלוֹא עָכָן בֶּן־זֶרַח מָעַל מַעַל בַּחֵרֶם וְעַל־כָּל־עֲדַת יִשְׂרָאֵל הָיָה קָצֶף וְהוּא אִישׁ אֶחָד לֹא גָוַע בַּעֲוֹנוֹ:

21 The Reubenites, the Gadites, and the half-tribe of *Menashe* replied to the heads of the contingents of *Yisrael*: They said,

כא וַיַּעֲנוּ בְּנֵי־רְאוּבֵן וּבְנֵי־גָד וַחֲצִי שֵׁבֶט הַמְנַשֶּׁה וַיְדַבְּרוּ אֶת־רָאשֵׁי אַלְפֵי יִשְׂרָאֵל:

22 "*Hashem*, the LORD *Hashem*! *Hashem*, the LORD *Hashem*! He knows, and *Yisrael* too shall know! If we acted in rebellion or in treachery against *Hashem*, do not vindicate us this day!

כב אֵל אֱלֹהִים יְהוָֹה אֵל אֱלֹהִים יְהוָֹה הוּא יֹדֵעַ וְיִשְׂרָאֵל הוּא יֵדָע אִם־בְּמֶרֶד וְאִם־בְּמַעַל בַּיהוָֹה אַל־תּוֹשִׁיעֵנוּ הַיּוֹם הַזֶּה:

23 If we built an altar to turn away from *Hashem*, if it was to offer burnt offerings or meal offerings upon it, or to present sacrifices of well-being upon it, may *Hashem* Himself demand [a reckoning]

כג לִבְנוֹת לָנוּ מִזְבֵּחַ לָשׁוּב מֵאַחֲרֵי יְהוָֹה וְאִם־לְהַעֲלוֹת עָלָיו עוֹלָה וּמִנְחָה וְאִם־לַעֲשׂוֹת עָלָיו זִבְחֵי שְׁלָמִים יְהוָֹה הוּא יְבַקֵּשׁ:

24 We did this thing only out of our concern that, in time to come, your children might say to our children, 'What have you to do with *Hashem*, the God of *Yisrael*?

כד וְאִם־לֹא מִדְּאָגָה מִדָּבָר עָשִׂינוּ אֶת־זֹאת לֵאמֹר מָחָר יֹאמְרוּ בְנֵיכֶם לְבָנֵינוּ לֵאמֹר מַה־לָּכֶם וְלַיהוָֹה אֱלֹהֵי יִשְׂרָאֵל:

25 *Hashem* has made the *Yarden* a boundary between you and us, O Reubenites and Gadites; you have no share in *Hashem*!' Thus your children might prevent our children from worshiping *Hashem*.

כה וּגְבוּל נָתַן־יְהוָֹה בֵּינֵנוּ וּבֵינֵיכֶם בְּנֵי־רְאוּבֵן וּבְנֵי־גָד אֶת־הַיַּרְדֵּן אֵין־לָכֶם חֵלֶק בַּיהוָֹה וְהִשְׁבִּיתוּ בְנֵיכֶם אֶת־בָּנֵינוּ לְבִלְתִּי יְרֹא אֶת־יְהוָֹה:

26 So we decided to provide [a witness] for ourselves by building an altar – not for burnt offerings or [other] sacrifices,

כו וַנֹּאמֶר נַעֲשֶׂה־נָּא לָנוּ לִבְנוֹת אֶת־הַמִּזְבֵּחַ לֹא לְעוֹלָה וְלֹא לְזָבַח:

27 but as a witness between you and us, and between the generations to come – that we may perform the service of *Hashem* before Him with our burnt offerings, our sacrifices, and our offerings of well-being; and that your children should not say to our children in time to come, 'You have no share in *Hashem*.'

כז כִּי עֵד הוּא בֵּינֵינוּ וּבֵינֵיכֶם וּבֵין דֹּרוֹתֵינוּ אַחֲרֵינוּ לַעֲבֹד אֶת־עֲבֹדַת יְהוָֹה לְפָנָיו בְּעֹלוֹתֵינוּ וּבִזְבָחֵינוּ וּבִשְׁלָמֵינוּ וְלֹא־יֹאמְרוּ בְנֵיכֶם מָחָר לְבָנֵינוּ אֵין־לָכֶם חֵלֶק בַּיהוָֹה:

28 We reasoned: should they speak thus to us and to our children in time to come, we would reply, 'See the replica of *Hashem*'s *Mizbayach*, which our fathers made – not for burnt offerings or sacrifices, but as a witness between you and us.'

כח וַנֹּאמֶר וְהָיָה כִּי־יֹאמְרוּ אֵלֵינוּ וְאֶל־דֹּרֹתֵינוּ מָחָר וְאָמַרְנוּ רְאוּ אֶת־תַּבְנִית מִזְבַּח יְהוָֹה אֲשֶׁר־עָשׂוּ אֲבוֹתֵינוּ לֹא לְעוֹלָה וְלֹא לְזֶבַח כִּי־עֵד הוּא בֵּינֵינוּ וּבֵינֵיכֶם:

29 Far be it from us to rebel against *Hashem*, or to turn away this day from *Hashem* and build a *Mizbayach* for burnt offerings, meal offerings, and sacrifices other than the *Mizbayach* of *Hashem* our God which stands before His *Mishkan*."

כט חָלִילָה לָּנוּ מִמֶּנּוּ לִמְרֹד בַּיהוָֹה וְלָשׁוּב הַיּוֹם מֵאַחֲרֵי יְהוָֹה לִבְנוֹת מִזְבֵּחַ לְעֹלָה לְמִנְחָה וּלְזָבַח מִלְּבַד מִזְבַּח יְהוָֹה אֱלֹהֵינוּ אֲשֶׁר לִפְנֵי מִשְׁכָּנוֹ:

30 When the *Kohen Pinchas* and the chieftains of
the community – the heads of the contingents of
Yisrael – who were with him heard the explanation
given by the Reubenites, the Gadites, and the
Manassites, they approved.

ל וַיִּשְׁמַע פִּינְחָס הַכֹּהֵן וּנְשִׂיאֵי הָעֵדָה
וְרָאשֵׁי אַלְפֵי יִשְׂרָאֵל אֲשֶׁר אִתּוֹ אֶת־
הַדְּבָרִים אֲשֶׁר דִּבְּרוּ בְּנֵי־רְאוּבֵן וּבְנֵי־גָד
וּבְנֵי מְנַשֶּׁה וַיִּיטַב בְּעֵינֵיהֶם:

31 The *Kohen Pinchas* son of *Elazar* said to the
Reubenites, the Gadites, and the Manassites,
"Now we know that *Hashem* is in our midst, since
you have not committed such treachery against
Hashem. You have indeed saved the Israelites from
punishment by *Hashem*."

לא וַיֹּאמֶר פִּינְחָס בֶּן־אֶלְעָזָר הַכֹּהֵן אֶל־
בְּנֵי־רְאוּבֵן וְאֶל־בְּנֵי־גָד וְאֶל־בְּנֵי מְנַשֶּׁה
הַיּוֹם יָדַעְנוּ כִּי־בְתוֹכֵנוּ יְהֹוָה אֲשֶׁר לֹא־
מְעַלְתֶּם בַּיהֹוָה הַמַּעַל הַזֶּה אָז הִצַּלְתֶּם
אֶת־בְּנֵי יִשְׂרָאֵל מִיַּד יְהֹוָה:

32 Then the *Kohen Pinchas* son of *Elazar* and the
chieftains returned from the Reubenites and the
Gadites in the land of *Gilad* to the Israelites in the
land of Canaan, and gave them their report.

לב וַיָּשָׁב פִּינְחָס בֶּן־אֶלְעָזָר הַכֹּהֵן
וְהַנְּשִׂיאִים מֵאֵת בְּנֵי־רְאוּבֵן וּמֵאֵת בְּנֵי־
גָד מֵאֶרֶץ הַגִּלְעָד אֶל־אֶרֶץ כְּנַעַן אֶל־
בְּנֵי יִשְׂרָאֵל וַיָּשִׁבוּ אוֹתָם דָּבָר:

33 The Israelites were pleased, and the Israelites
praised *Hashem*; and they spoke no more of going
to war against them, to ravage the land in which the
Reubenites and Gadites dwelt.

לג וַיִּיטַב הַדָּבָר בְּעֵינֵי בְּנֵי יִשְׂרָאֵל וַיְבָרְכוּ
אֱלֹהִים בְּנֵי יִשְׂרָאֵל וְלֹא אָמְרוּ לַעֲלוֹת
עֲלֵיהֶם לַצָּבָא לְשַׁחֵת אֶת־הָאָרֶץ אֲשֶׁר
בְּנֵי־רְאוּבֵן וּבְנֵי־גָד יֹשְׁבִים בָּהּ:

34 The Reubenites and the Gadites named the altar
["Witness"], meaning, "It is a witness between us
and them that *Hashem* is [our] *Hashem*."

לד וַיִּקְרְאוּ בְּנֵי־רְאוּבֵן וּבְנֵי־גָד לַמִּזְבֵּחַ כִּי
עֵד הוּא בֵּינֹתֵינוּ כִּי יְהֹוָה הָאֱלֹהִים:

23 1 Much later, after *Hashem* had given *Yisrael* rest from
all the enemies around them, and when *Yehoshua*
was old and well advanced in years,

כג א וַיְהִי מִיָּמִים רַבִּים אַחֲרֵי אֲשֶׁר־הֵנִיחַ
יְהֹוָה לְיִשְׂרָאֵל מִכָּל־אֹיְבֵיהֶם מִסָּבִיב
וִיהוֹשֻׁעַ זָקֵן בָּא בַּיָּמִים:

2 *Yehoshua* summoned all *Yisrael*, their elders and
commanders, their magistrates and officials, and
said to them: "I have grown old and am advanced
in years.

ב וַיִּקְרָא יְהוֹשֻׁעַ לְכָל־יִשְׂרָאֵל לִזְקֵנָיו
וּלְרָאשָׁיו וּלְשֹׁפְטָיו וּלְשֹׁטְרָיו וַיֹּאמֶר
אֲלֵהֶם אֲנִי זָקַנְתִּי בָּאתִי בַּיָּמִים:

3 You have seen all that *Hashem* your God has done
to all those nations on your account, for it was
Hashem your God who fought for you.

ג וְאַתֶּם רְאִיתֶם אֵת כָּל־אֲשֶׁר עָשָׂה יְהֹוָה
אֱלֹהֵיכֶם לְכָל־הַגּוֹיִם הָאֵלֶּה מִפְּנֵיכֶם כִּי
יְהֹוָה אֱלֹהֵיכֶם הוּא הַנִּלְחָם לָכֶם:

4 See, I have allotted to you, by your tribes, [the
territory of] these nations that still remain, and that
of all the nations that I have destroyed, from the
Yarden to the Mediterranean Sea in the west.

ד רְאוּ הִפַּלְתִּי לָכֶם אֶת־הַגּוֹיִם הַנִּשְׁאָרִים
הָאֵלֶּה בְּנַחֲלָה לְשִׁבְטֵיכֶם מִן־הַיַּרְדֵּן
וְכָל־הַגּוֹיִם אֲשֶׁר הִכְרַתִּי וְהַיָּם הַגָּדוֹל
מְבוֹא הַשָּׁמֶשׁ:

5 *Hashem* your God Himself will thrust them out on
your account and drive them out to make way for
you, and you shall possess their land as *Hashem*
your God promised you.

ה וַיהֹוָה אֱלֹהֵיכֶם הוּא יֶהְדְּפֵם מִפְּנֵיכֶם
וְהוֹרִישׁ אֹתָם מִלִּפְנֵיכֶם וִירִשְׁתֶּם אֶת־
אַרְצָם כַּאֲשֶׁר דִּבֶּר יְהֹוָה אֱלֹהֵיכֶם לָכֶם:

Joshua

6   "But be most resolute to observe faithfully all that is written in the Book of the Teaching of *Moshe*, without ever deviating from it to the right or to the left,

א   וַחֲזַקְתֶּם מְאֹד לִשְׁמֹר וְלַעֲשׂוֹת אֵת כָּל־הַכָּתוּב בְּסֵפֶר תּוֹרַת מֹשֶׁה לְבִלְתִּי סוּר־מִמֶּנּוּ יָמִין וּשְׂמֹאול:

*va-kha-zak-TEM m'-OD lish-MOR v'-la-a-SOT AYT kol ha-ka-TUV
b'-SAY-fer to-RAT mo-SHEH l'-vil-TEE sur mi-ME-nu ya-MEEN us-MOL*

7   and without intermingling with these nations that are left among you. Do not utter the names of their gods or swear by them; do not serve them or bow down to them.

ז   לְבִלְתִּי־בוֹא בַּגּוֹיִם הָאֵלֶּה הַנִּשְׁאָרִים הָאֵלֶּה אִתְּכֶם וּבְשֵׁם אֱלֹהֵיהֶם לֹא־תַזְכִּירוּ וְלֹא תַשְׁבִּיעוּ וְלֹא תַעַבְדוּם וְלֹא תִשְׁתַּחֲווּ לָהֶם:

8   But hold fast to *Hashem* your God as you have done to this day.

ח   כִּי אִם־בַּיהוָה אֱלֹהֵיכֶם תִּדְבָּקוּ כַּאֲשֶׁר עֲשִׂיתֶם עַד הַיּוֹם הַזֶּה:

9   "*Hashem* has driven out great, powerful nations on your account, and not a man has withstood you to this day.

ט   וַיּוֹרֶשׁ יְהוָה מִפְּנֵיכֶם גּוֹיִם גְּדֹלִים וַעֲצוּמִים וְאַתֶּם לֹא־עָמַד אִישׁ בִּפְנֵיכֶם עַד הַיּוֹם הַזֶּה:

10   A single man of you would put a thousand to flight, for *Hashem* your God Himself has been fighting for you, as He promised you.

י   אִישׁ־אֶחָד מִכֶּם יִרְדָּף־אָלֶף כִּי יְהוָה אֱלֹהֵיכֶם הוּא הַנִּלְחָם לָכֶם כַּאֲשֶׁר דִּבֶּר לָכֶם:

11   For your own sakes, therefore, be most mindful to love *Hashem* your God.

יא   וְנִשְׁמַרְתֶּם מְאֹד לְנַפְשֹׁתֵיכֶם לְאַהֲבָה אֶת־יְהוָה אֱלֹהֵיכֶם:

12   For should you turn away and attach yourselves to the remnant of those nations – to those that are left among you – and intermarry with them, you joining them and they joining you,

יב   כִּי אִם־שׁוֹב תָּשׁוּבוּ וּדְבַקְתֶּם בְּיֶתֶר הַגּוֹיִם הָאֵלֶּה הַנִּשְׁאָרִים הָאֵלֶּה אִתְּכֶם וְהִתְחַתַּנְתֶּם בָּהֶם וּבָאתֶם בָּהֶם וְהֵם בָּכֶם:

13   know for certain that *Hashem* your God will not continue to drive these nations out before you; they shall become a snare and a trap for you, a scourge to your sides and thorns in your eyes, until you perish from this good land that *Hashem* your God has given you.

יג   יָדוֹעַ תֵּדְעוּ כִּי לֹא יוֹסִיף יְהוָה אֱלֹהֵיכֶם לְהוֹרִישׁ אֶת־הַגּוֹיִם הָאֵלֶּה מִלִּפְנֵיכֶם וְהָיוּ לָכֶם לְפַח וּלְמוֹקֵשׁ וּלְשֹׁטֵט בְּצִדֵּיכֶם וְלִצְנִנִים בְּעֵינֵיכֶם עַד־אֲבָדְכֶם מֵעַל הָאֲדָמָה הַטּוֹבָה הַזֹּאת אֲשֶׁר נָתַן לָכֶם יְהוָה אֱלֹהֵיכֶם:

Hesder students studying *Torah* in Shilo

23:6 But be most resolute Throughout *Sefer Yehoshua*, the instructions to be "strong" and "resolute" are delivered repeatedly, both to *Yehoshua* himself and the Children of Israel as a whole. Significantly, this command applies both to spiritual tasks, such as the exhortation in this verse to observe the entire *Torah* of *Moshe*, and to physical tasks such as fighting battles to conquer the Land of Israel (see, e.g.,

Joshua 1:6). A complete national life requires both spiritual and physical fortitude. In today's Israeli army, many soldiers exemplify this devotion to both *Torah* study and military service by enlisting in the *Hesder* program that combines high level *Torah* study with mandatory army service. The students and graduates of these academies are exemplary soldiers as well as scholars, thereby serving as role models for all.

14 "I am now going the way of all the earth. Acknowledge with all your heart and soul that not one of the good things that *Hashem* your God promised you has failed to happen; they have all come true for you, not a single one has failed.

יד וְהִנֵּה אָנֹכִי הוֹלֵךְ הַיּוֹם בְּדֶרֶךְ כָּל־הָאָרֶץ וִידַעְתֶּם בְּכָל־לְבַבְכֶם וּבְכָל־נַפְשְׁכֶם כִּי לֹא־נָפַל דָּבָר אֶחָד מִכֹּל הַדְּבָרִים הַטּוֹבִים אֲשֶׁר דִּבֶּר יְהֹוָה אֱלֹהֵיכֶם עֲלֵיכֶם הַכֹּל בָּאוּ לָכֶם לֹא־נָפַל מִמֶּנּוּ דָּבָר אֶחָד:

15 But just as every good thing that *Hashem* your God promised you has been fulfilled for you, so *Hashem* can bring upon you every evil thing until He has wiped you off this good land that *Hashem* your God has given you.

טו וְהָיָה כַּאֲשֶׁר־בָּא עֲלֵיכֶם כָּל־הַדָּבָר הַטּוֹב אֲשֶׁר דִּבֶּר יְהֹוָה אֱלֹהֵיכֶם אֲלֵיכֶם כֵּן יָבִיא יְהֹוָה עֲלֵיכֶם אֵת כָּל־הַדָּבָר הָרָע עַד־הַשְׁמִידוֹ אוֹתְכֶם מֵעַל הָאֲדָמָה הַטּוֹבָה הַזֹּאת אֲשֶׁר נָתַן לָכֶם יְהֹוָה אֱלֹהֵיכֶם:

16 If you break the covenant that *Hashem* your God enjoined upon you, and go and serve other gods and bow down to them, then *Hashem*'s anger will burn against you, and you shall quickly perish from the good land that He has given you."

טז בְּעָבְרְכֶם אֶת־בְּרִית יְהֹוָה אֱלֹהֵיכֶם אֲשֶׁר צִוָּה אֶתְכֶם וַהֲלַכְתֶּם וַעֲבַדְתֶּם אֱלֹהִים אֲחֵרִים וְהִשְׁתַּחֲוִיתֶם לָהֶם וְחָרָה אַף־יְהֹוָה בָּכֶם וַאֲבַדְתֶּם מְהֵרָה מֵעַל הָאָרֶץ הַטּוֹבָה אֲשֶׁר נָתַן לָכֶם:

24 1 *Yehoshua* assembled all the tribes of *Yisrael* at Schechem. He summoned *Yisrael*'s elders and commanders, magistrates and officers; and they presented themselves before *Hashem*.

כד א וַיֶּאֱסֹף יְהוֹשֻׁעַ אֶת־כָּל־שִׁבְטֵי יִשְׂרָאֵל שְׁכֶמָה וַיִּקְרָא לְזִקְנֵי יִשְׂרָאֵל וּלְרָאשָׁיו וּלְשֹׁפְטָיו וּלְשֹׁטְרָיו וַיִּתְיַצְּבוּ לִפְנֵי הָאֱלֹהִים:

2 Then *Yehoshua* said to all the people, "Thus said *Hashem*, the God of *Yisrael*: In olden times, your forefathers – *Terach*, father of *Avraham* and father of Nahor – lived beyond the Euphrates and worshiped other gods.

ב וַיֹּאמֶר יְהוֹשֻׁעַ אֶל־כָּל־הָעָם כֹּה־אָמַר יְהֹוָה אֱלֹהֵי יִשְׂרָאֵל בְּעֵבֶר הַנָּהָר יָשְׁבוּ אֲבוֹתֵיכֶם מֵעוֹלָם תֶּרַח אֲבִי אַבְרָהָם וַאֲבִי נָחוֹר וַיַּעַבְדוּ אֱלֹהִים אֲחֵרִים:

3 But I took your father *Avraham* from beyond the Euphrates and led him through the whole land of Canaan and multiplied his offspring. I gave him *Yitzchak*,

ג וָאֶקַּח אֶת־אֲבִיכֶם אֶת־אַבְרָהָם מֵעֵבֶר הַנָּהָר וָאוֹלֵךְ אוֹתוֹ בְּכָל־אֶרֶץ כְּנָעַן וָארֶב [וָאַרְבֶּה] אֶת־זַרְעוֹ וָאֶתֶּן־לוֹ אֶת־יִצְחָק:

4 and to *Yitzchak* I gave *Yaakov* and Esau. I gave Esau the hill country of Seir as his possession, while *Yaakov* and his children went down to Egypt.

ד וָאֶתֵּן לְיִצְחָק אֶת־יַעֲקֹב וְאֶת־עֵשָׂו וָאֶתֵּן לְעֵשָׂו אֶת־הַר שֵׂעִיר לָרֶשֶׁת אוֹתוֹ וְיַעֲקֹב וּבָנָיו יָרְדוּ מִצְרָיִם:

5 "Then I sent *Moshe* and *Aharon*, and I plagued Egypt with [the wonders] that I wrought in their midst, after which I freed you

ה וָאֶשְׁלַח אֶת־מֹשֶׁה וְאֶת־אַהֲרֹן וָאֶגֹּף אֶת־מִצְרַיִם כַּאֲשֶׁר עָשִׂיתִי בְּקִרְבּוֹ וְאַחַר הוֹצֵאתִי אֶתְכֶם:

6 I freed your fathers – from Egypt, and you came to the Sea. But the Egyptians pursued your fathers to the Sea of Reeds with chariots and horsemen.

ו וָאוֹצִיא אֶת־אֲבוֹתֵיכֶם מִמִּצְרַיִם וַתָּבֹאוּ הַיָּמָּה וַיִּרְדְּפוּ מִצְרַיִם אַחֲרֵי אֲבוֹתֵיכֶם בְּרֶכֶב וּבְפָרָשִׁים יַם־סוּף:

7 They cried out to *Hashem*, and He put darkness between you and the Egyptians; then He brought the Sea upon them, and it covered them. Your own eyes saw what I did to the Egyptians. "After you had lived a long time in the wilderness,

ז וַיִּצְעֲקוּ אֶל־יְהֹוָה וַיָּשֶׂם מַאֲפֵל בֵּינֵיכֶם וּבֵין הַמִּצְרִים וַיָּבֵא עָלָיו אֶת־הַיָּם וַיְכַסֵּהוּ וַתִּרְאֶינָה עֵינֵיכֶם אֵת אֲשֶׁר־עָשִׂיתִי בְּמִצְרָיִם וַתֵּשְׁבוּ בַמִּדְבָּר יָמִים רַבִּים:

Joshua

8 I brought you to the land of the Amorites who lived beyond the *Yarden*. They gave battle to you, but I delivered them into your hands; I annihilated them for you, and you took possession of their land.

ח וָאָבִאָה [וָאָבִיא] אֶתְכֶם אֶל־אֶרֶץ הָאֱמֹרִי הַיּוֹשֵׁב בְּעֵבֶר הַיַּרְדֵּן וַיִּלָּחֲמוּ אִתְּכֶם וָאֶתֵּן אוֹתָם בְּיֶדְכֶם וַתִּירְשׁוּ אֶת־אַרְצָם וָאַשְׁמִידֵם מִפְּנֵיכֶם:

9 Thereupon Balak son of Zippor, the king of Moab, made ready to attack *Yisrael*. He sent for Balaam son of Beor to curse you,

ט וַיָּקָם בָּלָק בֶּן־צִפּוֹר מֶלֶךְ מוֹאָב וַיִּלָּחֶם בְּיִשְׂרָאֵל וַיִּשְׁלַח וַיִּקְרָא לְבִלְעָם בֶּן־בְּעוֹר לְקַלֵּל אֶתְכֶם:

10 but I refused to listen to Balaam; he had to bless you, and thus I saved you from him.

י וְלֹא אָבִיתִי לִשְׁמֹעַ לְבִלְעָם וַיְבָרֶךְ בָּרוֹךְ אֶתְכֶם וָאַצִּל אֶתְכֶם מִיָּדוֹ:

11 "Then you crossed the *Yarden* and you came to *Yericho*. The citizens of *Yericho* and the Amorites, Perizzites, Canaanites, Hittites, Girgashites, Hivites, and Jebusites fought you, but I delivered them into your hands.

יא וַתַּעַבְרוּ אֶת־הַיַּרְדֵּן וַתָּבֹאוּ אֶל־יְרִיחוֹ וַיִּלָּחֲמוּ בָכֶם בַּעֲלֵי־יְרִיחוֹ הָאֱמֹרִי וְהַפְּרִזִּי וְהַכְּנַעֲנִי וְהַחִתִּי וְהַגִּרְגָּשִׁי הַחִוִּי וְהַיְבוּסִי וָאֶתֵּן אוֹתָם בְּיֶדְכֶם:

12 I sent a plague ahead of you, and it drove them out before you – [just like] the two Amorite kings – not by your sword or by your bow.

יב וָאֶשְׁלַח לִפְנֵיכֶם אֶת־הַצִּרְעָה וַתְּגָרֶשׁ אוֹתָם מִפְּנֵיכֶם שְׁנֵי מַלְכֵי הָאֱמֹרִי לֹא בְחַרְבְּךָ וְלֹא בְקַשְׁתֶּךָ:

13 I have given you a land for which you did not labor and towns which you did not build, and you have settled in them; you are enjoying vineyards and olive groves which you did not plant.

יג וָאֶתֵּן לָכֶם אֶרֶץ אֲשֶׁר לֹא־יָגַעְתָּ בָּהּ וְעָרִים אֲשֶׁר לֹא־בְנִיתֶם וַתֵּשְׁבוּ בָּהֶם כְּרָמִים וְזֵיתִים אֲשֶׁר לֹא־נְטַעְתֶּם אַתֶּם אֹכְלִים:

va-e-TAYN la-KHEM E-retz a-SHER lo ya-GA-ta BAH v'-a-REEM
a-SHER lo v'-nee-TEM va-tay-sh'-VU ba-HEM k'-ra-MEEM
v'-zay-TEEM a-SHER lo n'-ta-TEM a-TEM o-kh'-LEEM

14 "Now, therefore, revere *Hashem* and serve Him with undivided loyalty; put away the gods that your forefathers served beyond the Euphrates and in Egypt, and serve *Hashem*.

יד וְעַתָּה יְראוּ אֶת־יְהֹוָה וְעִבְדוּ אֹתוֹ בְּתָמִים וּבֶאֱמֶת וְהָסִירוּ אֶת־אֱלֹהִים אֲשֶׁר עָבְדוּ אֲבוֹתֵיכֶם בְּעֵבֶר הַנָּהָר וּבְמִצְרַיִם וְעִבְדוּ אֶת־יְהֹוָה:

24:13 I have given you a land *Yehoshua*'s final speech to the nation includes a review of their history, starting from before the birth of *Avraham*, continuing through the enslavement in Egypt and subsequent exodus, and concluding with their recent conquest and possession of the Promised Land. In addition to fostering loyalty to *Hashem*, this farewell address serves as a powerful reminder that what God wants is for the People of Israel to serve Him specifically in *Eretz Yisrael*. We, who live in an era that has seen the Jewish exiles gather from around the world to live together as a free nation in the State of Israel, are especially privileged to witness the words of *Yehoshua* realized before our very eyes.

Hurva Synagogue in the Old City of *Yerushalayim*

¹⁵ Or, if you are loath to serve *Hashem*, choose this day which ones you are going to serve – the gods that your forefathers served beyond the Euphrates, or those of the Amorites in whose land you are settled; but I and my household will serve *Hashem*."

טו וְאִם רַע בְּעֵינֵיכֶם לַעֲבֹד אֶת־יְהֹוָה בַּחֲרוּ לָכֶם הַיּוֹם אֶת־מִי תַעֲבֹדוּן אִם אֶת־אֱלֹהִים אֲשֶׁר־עָבְדוּ אֲבוֹתֵיכֶם אֲשֶׁר בְּעֵבֶר [מֵעֵבֶר] הַנָּהָר וְאִם אֶת־אֱלֹהֵי הָאֱמֹרִי אֲשֶׁר אַתֶּם יֹשְׁבִים בְּאַרְצָם וְאָנֹכִי וּבֵיתִי נַעֲבֹד אֶת־יְהֹוָה:

¹⁶ In reply, the people declared, "Far be it from us to forsake *Hashem* and serve other gods!

טז וַיַּעַן הָעָם וַיֹּאמֶר חָלִילָה לָּנוּ מֵעֲזֹב אֶת־יְהֹוָה לַעֲבֹד אֱלֹהִים אֲחֵרִים:

¹⁷ For it was *Hashem* our God who brought us and our fathers up from the land of Egypt, the house of bondage, and who wrought those wondrous signs before our very eyes, and guarded us all along the way that we traveled and among all the peoples through whose midst we passed.

יז כִּי יְהֹוָה אֱלֹהֵינוּ הוּא הַמַּעֲלֶה אֹתָנוּ וְאֶת־אֲבוֹתֵינוּ מֵאֶרֶץ מִצְרַיִם מִבֵּית עֲבָדִים וַאֲשֶׁר עָשָׂה לְעֵינֵינוּ אֶת־הָאֹתוֹת הַגְּדֹלוֹת הָאֵלֶּה וַיִּשְׁמְרֵנוּ בְּכָל־הַדֶּרֶךְ אֲשֶׁר הָלַכְנוּ בָהּ וּבְכֹל הָעַמִּים אֲשֶׁר עָבַרְנוּ בְּקִרְבָּם:

¹⁸ And then *Hashem* drove out before us all the peoples – the Amorites – that inhabited the country. We too will serve *Hashem*, for He is our God."

יח וַיְגָרֶשׁ יְהֹוָה אֶת־כָּל־הָעַמִּים וְאֶת־הָאֱמֹרִי יֹשֵׁב הָאָרֶץ מִפָּנֵינוּ גַּם־אֲנַחְנוּ נַעֲבֹד אֶת־יְהֹוָה כִּי־הוּא אֱלֹהֵינוּ:

¹⁹ *Yehoshua*, however, said to the people, "You will not be able to serve *Hashem*, for He is a holy *Hashem*. He is a jealous *Hashem*; He will not forgive your transgressions and your sins.

יט וַיֹּאמֶר יְהוֹשֻׁעַ אֶל־הָעָם לֹא תוּכְלוּ לַעֲבֹד אֶת־יְהֹוָה כִּי־אֱלֹהִים קְדֹשִׁים הוּא אֵל־קַנּוֹא הוּא לֹא־יִשָּׂא לְפִשְׁעֲכֶם וּלְחַטֹּאותֵיכֶם:

²⁰ If you forsake *Hashem* and serve alien gods, He will turn and deal harshly with you and make an end of you, after having been gracious to you."

כ כִּי תַעַזְבוּ אֶת־יְהֹוָה וַעֲבַדְתֶּם אֱלֹהֵי נֵכָר וְשָׁב וְהֵרַע לָכֶם וְכִלָּה אֶתְכֶם אַחֲרֵי אֲשֶׁר־הֵיטִיב לָכֶם:

²¹ But the people replied to *Yehoshua*, "No, we will serve *Hashem*!"

כא וַיֹּאמֶר הָעָם אֶל־יְהוֹשֻׁעַ לֹא כִּי אֶת־יְהֹוָה נַעֲבֹד:

²² Thereupon *Yehoshua* said to the people, "You are witnesses against yourselves that you have by your own act chosen to serve *Hashem*." "Yes, we are!" they responded.

כב וַיֹּאמֶר יְהוֹשֻׁעַ אֶל־הָעָם עֵדִים אַתֶּם בָּכֶם כִּי־אַתֶּם בְּחַרְתֶּם לָכֶם אֶת־יְהֹוָה לַעֲבֹד אוֹתוֹ וַיֹּאמְרוּ עֵדִים:

²³ "Then put away the alien gods that you have among you and direct your hearts to *Hashem*, the God of *Yisrael*."

כג וְעַתָּה הָסִירוּ אֶת־אֱלֹהֵי הַנֵּכָר אֲשֶׁר בְּקִרְבְּכֶם וְהַטּוּ אֶת־לְבַבְכֶם אֶל־יְהֹוָה אֱלֹהֵי יִשְׂרָאֵל:

²⁴ And the people declared to *Yehoshua*, "We will serve none but *Hashem* our God, and we will obey none but Him."

כד וַיֹּאמְרוּ הָעָם אֶל־יְהוֹשֻׁעַ אֶת־יְהֹוָה אֱלֹהֵינוּ נַעֲבֹד וּבְקוֹלוֹ נִשְׁמָע:

²⁵ On that day at *Shechem*, *Yehoshua* made a covenant for the people and he made a fixed rule for them.

כה וַיִּכְרֹת יְהוֹשֻׁעַ בְּרִית לָעָם בַּיּוֹם הַהוּא וַיָּשֶׂם לוֹ חֹק וּמִשְׁפָּט בִּשְׁכֶם:

²⁶ *Yehoshua* recorded all this in a book of divine instruction. He took a great stone and set it up at the foot of the oak in the sacred precinct of *Hashem*;

כו וַיִּכְתֹּב יְהוֹשֻׁעַ אֶת־הַדְּבָרִים הָאֵלֶּה בְּסֵפֶר תּוֹרַת אֱלֹהִים וַיִּקַּח אֶבֶן גְּדוֹלָה וַיְקִימֶהָ שָּׁם תַּחַת הָאַלָּה אֲשֶׁר בְּמִקְדַּשׁ יְהֹוָה:

27 and *Yehoshua* said to all the people, "See, this very stone shall be a witness against us, for it heard all the words that *Hashem* spoke to us; it shall be a witness against you, lest you break faith with your God."

28 *Yehoshua* then dismissed the people to their allotted portions.

29 After these events, *Yehoshua* son of *Nun*, the servant of *Hashem*, died at the age of one hundred and ten years.

30 They buried him on his own property, at Timnath-serah in the hill country of *Efraim*, north of Mount Gaash.

31 *Yisrael* served *Hashem* during the lifetime of *Yehoshua* and the lifetime of the elders who lived on after *Yehoshua*, and who had experienced all the deeds that *Hashem* had wrought for *Yisrael*.

32 The bones of *Yosef*, which the Israelites had brought up from Egypt, were buried at *Shechem*, in the piece of ground which *Yaakov* had bought for a hundred *kesita* from the children of Hamor, *Shechem*'s father, and which had become a heritage of the Josephites.

33 *Elazar* son of *Aharon* also died, and they buried him on the hill of his son *Pinchas*, which had been assigned to him in the hill country of *Efraim*.

כז וַיֹּאמֶר יְהוֹשֻׁעַ אֶל־כָּל־הָעָם הִנֵּה הָאֶבֶן הַזֹּאת תִּהְיֶה־בָּנוּ לְעֵדָה כִּי־הִיא שָׁמְעָה אֵת כָּל־אִמְרֵי יְהוָה אֲשֶׁר דִּבֶּר עִמָּנוּ וְהָיְתָה בָכֶם לְעֵדָה פֶּן־תְּכַחֲשׁוּן בֵּאלֹהֵיכֶם:

כח וַיְשַׁלַּח יְהוֹשֻׁעַ אֶת־הָעָם אִישׁ לְנַחֲלָתוֹ:

כט וַיְהִי אַחֲרֵי הַדְּבָרִים הָאֵלֶּה וַיָּמָת יְהוֹשֻׁעַ בִּן־נוּן עֶבֶד יְהוָה בֶּן־מֵאָה וָעֶשֶׂר שָׁנִים:

ל וַיִּקְבְּרוּ אֹתוֹ בִּגְבוּל נַחֲלָתוֹ בְּתִמְנַת־סֶרַח אֲשֶׁר בְּהַר־אֶפְרָיִם מִצְּפוֹן לְהַר־גָּעַשׁ:

לא וַיַּעֲבֹד יִשְׂרָאֵל אֶת־יְהוָה כֹּל יְמֵי יְהוֹשֻׁעַ וְכֹל יְמֵי הַזְּקֵנִים אֲשֶׁר הֶאֱרִיכוּ יָמִים אַחֲרֵי יְהוֹשֻׁעַ וַאֲשֶׁר יָדְעוּ אֵת כָּל־מַעֲשֵׂה יְהוָה אֲשֶׁר עָשָׂה לְיִשְׂרָאֵל:

לב וְאֶת־עַצְמוֹת יוֹסֵף אֲשֶׁר־הֶעֱלוּ בְנֵי־יִשְׂרָאֵל מִמִּצְרַיִם קָבְרוּ בִשְׁכֶם בְּחֶלְקַת הַשָּׂדֶה אֲשֶׁר קָנָה יַעֲקֹב מֵאֵת בְּנֵי־חֲמוֹר אֲבִי־שְׁכֶם בְּמֵאָה קְשִׂיטָה וַיִּהְיוּ לִבְנֵי־יוֹסֵף לְנַחֲלָה:

לג וְאֶלְעָזָר בֶּן־אַהֲרֹן מֵת וַיִּקְבְּרוּ אֹתוֹ בְּגִבְעַת פִּינְחָס בְּנוֹ אֲשֶׁר נִתַּן־לוֹ בְּהַר אֶפְרָיִם:

List of Transliterated Words in *The Israel Bible*

The following is a list of nouns which have been transliterated into Hebrew in the English translation and commentary of *The Israel Bible*:

Hebrew Name	English Name	Pronunciation	Hebrew
Achan	Achan	a-KHAN	עָכָן
Achav	Ahab	akh-AV	אַחְאָב
Achaz	Ahaz	a-KHAZ	אָחָז
Achazyahu	Ahaziah	a-khaz-YA-hu	אֲחַזְיָהוּ
Achiezer	Ahiezer	a-khee-E-zer	אֲחִיעֶזֶר
Achihud	Ahihud	a-khee-HUD	אֲחִיהוּד
Achikam	Ahikam	a-khee-KAM	אֲחִיקָם
Achilud	Ahilud	a-khee-LUD	אֲחִילוּד
Achimelech	Ahimelech	a-khee-ME-lekh	אֲחִימֶלֶךְ
Achira	Ahira	a-khee-RA	אֲחִירַע
Achisamach	Ahisamach	a-khee-sa-MAKH	אֲחִיסָמָךְ
Achitofel	Ahithophel	a-khee-TO-fel	אֲחִיתֹפֶל
Achituv	Ahitub	a-khee-TUV	אֲחִיטוּב
Achiya	Ahijah	a-khi-YAH	אֲחִיָּה
Adam	Adam	a-DAM	אָדָם
Adar	Adar	a-DAR	אֲדָר
Adoniyahu	Adonijah	a-do-ni-YA-hu	אֲדֹנִיָּהוּ
Adulam	Adullam	a-du-LAM	עֲדֻלָּם
Agur	Agur	a-GUR	אָגוּר
Aharon	Aaron	a-ha-RON	אַהֲרֹן
Amasa	Amasa	a-ma-SA	עֲמָשָׂא
Amatzya	Amaziah	a-matz-YAH	אֲמַצְיָה
Amen	Amen	a-MAYN	אָמֵן
Amiel	Ammiel	a-mee-AYL	עַמִּיאֵל
Aminadav	Amminadab	a-mee-na-DAV	עַמִּינָדָב
Amitai	Amittai	a-mi-TAI	אֲמִתַּי
Amnon	Amnon	am-NON	אַמְנוֹן

Hebrew Name	English Name	Pronunciation	Hebrew
Amon	Amon	a-MON	אָמוֹן
Amos	Amos	a-MOS	עָמוֹס
Amotz	Amoz	a-MOTZ	אָמוֹץ
Amram	Amram	am-RAM	עַמְרָם
Anatot	Anathoth	a-na-TOT	עֲנָתוֹת
Aron	Ark	a-RON	אָרוֹן
Aron HaBrit	Ark of the Covenant	a-RON ha-b'-REET	אֲרוֹן הַבְּרִית
Arpachshad	Arpachshad	ar-pakh-SHAD	אַרְפַּכְשָׁד
Asa	Asa	a-SA	אָסָא
Asael	Asahel	a-sah-AYL	עֲשָׂהאֵל
Asaf	Asaph	a-SAF	אָסָף
Ashdod	Ashdod	ash-DOD	אַשְׁדּוֹד
Asher	Asher	a-SHAYR	אָשֵׁר
Ashkelon	Ashkelon	ash-k'-LON	אַשְׁקְלוֹן
Atalya	Athaliah	a-tal-YAH	עֲתַלְיָה
Avdon	Abdon	av-DON	עַבְדּוֹן
Avichayil	Abihail	a-vee-KHA-yil	אֲבִיחַיִל
Avidan	Abidan	a-vee-DAN	אֲבִידָן
Avigail	Abigail	a-vee-GA-yil	אֲבִיגַיִל
Avihu	Abihu	a-vee-HU	אֲבִיהוּא
Avimelech	Abimelech	a-vee-ME-lekh	אֲבִימֶלֶךְ
Avinadav	Abinadab	a-vee-na-DAV	אֲבִינָדָב
Aviram	Abiram	a-vee-RAM	אֲבִירָם
Avishai	Abishai	a-vee-SHAI	אֲבִישַׁי
Aviya	Abijah	a-vi-YAH	אֲבִיָּה
Aviyam	Abijam	a-vi-YAM	אֲבִיָּם
Avner	Abner	av-NAYR	אַבְנֵר
Avraham	Abraham	av-ra-HAM	אַבְרָהָם
Avram	Abram	av-RAM	אַבְרָם
Avshalom	Absalom	av-sha-LOM	אַבְשָׁלוֹם
Azarya	Azariah	a-zar-YAH	עֲזַרְיָה
Azeika	Azekah	a-zay-KAH	עֲזֵקָה
Azza	Gaza	a-ZAH	עַזָּה

Hebrew Name	English Name	Pronunciation	Hebrew
B'nei Yisrael	The Children of Israel	b'-NAY yis-ra-AYL	בְּנֵי יִשְׂרָאֵל
Barak	Barak	ba-rakh-AYL	בָּרָק
Baruch	Baruch	ba-RUKH	בָּרוּךְ
Barzilai	Barzillai	bar-zi-LAI	בַּרְזִלַּי
Basha	Baasa	ba-SHA	בַּעְשָׁא
Batsheva	Bath-sheba	bat-SHE-va	בַּת־שֶׁבַע
Be'er Sheva	Beer-sheba	b'-AYR SHE-va	בְּאֵר שֶׁבַע
Be'eri	Beeri	b'-ay-REE	בְּאֵרִי
Beit Aven	Beth-aven	bayt A-ven	בֵּית אָוֶן
Beit El	Beth-el	bayt el	בֵּית אֵל
Beit Hamikdash	Temple	bayt ha-mik-DASH	בֵּית הַמִּקְדָּשׁ
Beit Lechem	Beth-lehem	bayt LE-khem	בֵּית לֶחֶם
Beit Shean	Beth-shean	bayt sh'-AN	בֵּית שְׁאָן
Beit Shemesh	Beth-shemesh	bayt SHE-mesh	בֵּית שָׁמֶשׁ
Berechya	Berechiah	be-rekh-YAH	בֶּרֶכְיָה
Betzalel	Bezalel	b'-tzal-AYL	בְּצַלְאֵל
Bilha	Bilhah	bil-HAH	בִּלְהָה
Binyamin	Benjamin	bin-ya-MIN	בִּנְיָמִין
Boaz	Boaz	BO-az	בֹּעַז
Buki	Bukki	bu-KEE	בֻּקִּי
Buzi	Buzi	bu-ZEE	בּוּזִי
Carmel	Carmel	kar-MEL	כַּרְמֶל
Chachalya	Hacaliah	kha-khal-YAH	חֲכַלְיָה
Chagai	Haggai	kha-GAI	חַגַּי
Chana	Hannah	kha-NAH	חַנָּה
Chanamel	Hanamel	kha-nam-AYL	חֲנַמְאֵל
Chanani	Hanani	kha-NA-nee	חֲנָנִי
Chananya	Hananiah	kha-nan-YAH	חֲנַנְיָה
Chaniel	Hanniel	kha-nee-AYL	חַנִּיאֵל
Chanoch	Enoch	kha-NOKH	חֲנוֹךְ
Chava	Eve	kha-VAH	חַוָּה
Chavakuk	Habakkuk	kha-va-KUK	חֲבַקּוּק

Hebrew Name	English Name	Pronunciation	Hebrew
Chermon	Hermon	kher-MON	חֶרְמוֹן
Chetzron	Hezron	khetz-RON	חֶצְרוֹן
Chever	Heber	KHE-ver	חֶבֶר
Chevron	Hebron	khev-RON	חֶבְרוֹן
Chilkiyahu	Hilkiah	khil-ki-YA-hu	חִלְקִיָּהוּ
Chizkiyahu	Hezekiah	khiz-ki-YA-hu	חִזְקִיָּהוּ
Chofni	Hophni	khof-NEE	חׇפְנִי
Chogla	Hoglah	khog-LAH	חׇגְלָה
Chulda	Hulda	khul-DAH	חֻלְדָּה
Chur	Hur	Khur	חוּר
Dan	Dan	Dan	דָּן
Daniel	Daniel	da-ni-YAYL	דָּנִיֵּאל
Datan	Dathan	da-TAN	דָּתָן
David	David	da-VID	דָּוִד
Devora	Deborah	d'-vo-RAH	דְּבוֹרָה
Dina	Dinah	DEE-nah	דִּינָה
Doeg Ha'adomi	Doeg the Edomite	do-AYG ha-a-do-MEE	דּוֹאֵג הָאֲדֹמִי
Efraim	Ephraim	ef-RA-yim	אֶפְרָיִם
Efrat	Ephrat	ef-RAT	אֶפְרָתָה
Efrat	Ephrathah	ef-RA-tah	אֶפְרָתָה
Ehud	Ehud	ay-HUD	אֵהוּד
Eila	Elah	AY-lah	אֵלָה
Eilon	Elon	ay-LON	אֵילוֹן
Ein Gedi	En-gedi	ayn GE-dee	עֵין גֶּדִי
Elazar	Eleazar	el-a-ZAR	אֶלְעָזָר
Elchanan	Elhanan	el-kha-NAN	אֶלְחָנָן
Eli	Eli	ay-LEE	עֵלִי
Eliav	Eliab	e-lee-AV	אֱלִיאָב
Elidad	Elidad	e-lee-DAD	אֱלִידָד
Eliezer	Eliezer	e-lee-E-zer	אֱלִיעֶזֶר
Elimelech	Elimelech	e-lee-ME-lekh	אֱלִימֶלֶךְ
Elisha	Elisha	e-lee-SHA	אֱלִישָׁע

Hebrew Name	English Name	Pronunciation	Hebrew
Elishama	Elishama	e-lee-sha-MA	אֱלִישָׁמָע
Elisheva	Elisheba	e-lee-SHE-va	אֱלִישֶׁבַע
Elitzafan	Eli-zaphan	e-lee-tza-FAN	אֱלִיצָפָן
Elitzur	Elizur	e-lee-TZUR	אֱלִיצוּר
Eliyahu	Elijah	ay-li-YA-hu	אֵלִיָּהוּ
Elkana	Elkanah	el-ka-NAH	אֶלְקָנָה
Elyasaf	Eliasaph	el-ya-SAF	אֶלְיָסָף
Elyashiv	Eliashib	el-ya-SHEEV	אֶלְיָשִׁיב
Enosh	Enosh	e-NOSH	אֱנוֹשׁ
Er	Er	ayr	עֵר
Eshtaol	Eshtaol	esh-ta-OL	אֶשְׁתָּאֹל
Esther	Esther	es-TAYR	אֶסְתֵּר
Eved Melech	Ebed-melech	E-ved ME-lekh	עֶבֶד־מֶלֶךְ
Even Ha-Ezer	Eben-Ezer	E-ven ha-E-zer	אֶבֶן הָעֶזֶר
Ever	Eber	AY-ver	עֵבֶר
Evyatar	Abiathar	ev-ya-TAR	אֶבְיָתָר
Ezra	Ezra	ez-RA	עֶזְרָא
Gad	Gad	gad	גָּד
Gadi	Gaddi	ga-DEE	גַּדִּי
Gadiel	Gaddiel	ga-dee-AYL	גַּדִּיאֵל
Gamliel	Gamaliel	gam-lee-AYL	גַּמְלִיאֵל
Gedalia	Gedaliah	g'-dal-YA (hu)	גְּדַלְיָהוּ
Gedera	Gederah	g'-day-RAH	גְּדֵרָה
Gershom	Gershom	gay-r'-SHOM	גֵּרְשׁוֹם
Gershon	Gershon	gay-r'-SHON	גֵּרְשׁוֹן
Geshem	Geshem	GE-shem	גֶּשֶׁם
Geuel	Geuel	g'-u-AYL	גְּאוּאֵל
Gidon	Gideon	gid-ON	גִּדְעוֹן
Gilad	Gilead	gil-AD	גִּלְעָד
Gilgal	Gilgal	gil-GAL	גִּלְגָּל
Giva	Gibeah	giv-AH	גִּבְעָה
Givon	Gibeon	giv-ON	גִּבְעוֹן

66

Hebrew Name	English Name	Pronunciation	Hebrew
Hadassa	Hadassah	ha-da-SAH	הֲדַסָּה
Har Eival	Mount Ebal	ay-VAL	הַר עֵיבָל
Har Gerizim	Mount Gerizim	g'-ri-ZEEM	הַר גְּרִזִים
Har HaBayit	Temple Mount	har ha-BA-yit	הַר הַבַּיִת
Har HaZeitim	the Mount of Olives	har ha-zay-TEEM	הַר הַזֵּיתִים
Hashem	Lord/God		
Hayman	Heman	hay-MAN	הֵימָן
Hoshea	Hosea	ho-SHAY-a	הוֹשֵׁעַ
Ido	Iddo	i-DO	עִדּוֹ
Imanu-El	Immanuel	i-MA-nu ayl	עִמָּנוּ אֵל
Ish-boshet	Ish-bosheth	eesh BO-shet	אִישׁ־בֹּשֶׁת
Itamar	Ithamar	ee-ta-MAR	אִיתָמָר
Itiel	Ithiel	ee-tee-AYL	אִיתִיאֵל
Ivtzan	Ibzan	iv-TZAN	אִבְצָן
Iyov	Job	i-YOV	אִיּוֹב
Kadmiel	Kadmiel	kad-mee-AYL	קַדְמִיאֵל
Kalev	Caleb	ka-LAYV	כָּלֵב
Keesh	Kish	keesh	קִישׁ
Kehat	Kohath	k'-HAT	קְהָת
Keinan	Kenan	kay-NAN	קֵינָן
Kemuel	Kemuel	k'-mu-AYL	קְמוּאֵל
Keruvim	Cherubim	k'-ru-VEEM	כְּרוּבִים
Kilyon	Chilion	kil-YON	כִּלְיוֹן
Kiryat Arba	Kiriath-arba	keer-YAT AR-bah	קִרְיַת אַרְבַּע
Kiryat Sefer	Kiriath-sepher	keer-YAT SAY-fer	קִרְיַת־סֵפֶר
Kiryat Ye'arim	Kiriath-jearim	keer-YAT y'-a-REEM	קִרְיַת יְעָרִים
Kislev	Chislev	kis-LAYV	כִּסְלֵו
Kohanim	Priests	ko-ha-NEEM	כֹּהֲנִים
Kohelet	Koheleth	ko-HE-let	קֹהֶלֶת
Kohen	Priest	ko-HAYN	כֹּהֵן
Kohen Gadol	High Priest	ko-HAYN ga-DOL	כֹּהֵן גָּדוֹל
Korach	Korah	KO-rakh	קֹרַח

Hebrew Name	English Name	Pronunciation	Hebrew
Kushi	Cushi	ku-SHEE	כּוּשִׁי
Lachish	Lachish	la-KHEESH	לָכִישׁ
Leah	Leah	lay-AH	לֵאָה
Lemech	Lamech	LE-mekh	לֶמֶךְ
Lemuel	Lemuel	l'-mu-AYL	לְמוּאֵל
Levi	Levi	lay-VEE	לֵוִי
Leviim	Levites	l'-vee-IM	לְוִים
Machla	Mahlah	makh-LAH	מַחְלָה
Machlon	Mahlon	makh-LON	מַחְלוֹן
Machseya	Mahseiah	makh-say-YAH	מַחְסֵיָה
Malachi	Malachi	mal-a-KHEE	מַלְאָכִי
Manoach	Manoah	ma-NO-akh	מָנוֹחַ
Mashiach	Messiah	ma-SHEE-akh	מָשִׁיחַ
Mefiboshet	Mephibosheth	m'-fee-VO-shet	מְפִיבֹשֶׁת
Mehalalel	Mahalalel	ma-ha-lal-AYL	מְהַלַלְאֵל
Menachem	Menahem	m'-na-KHAYM	מְנַחֵם
Menashe	Menasseh	m'-na-SHEH	מְנַשֶּׁה
Menorah	Candlestick	m'-no-RAH	מְנֹרה
Merari	Merari	m'-ra-REE	מְרָרִי
Metushelach	Methusaleh	m'-tu-SHE-lakh	מְתוּשֶׁלַח
Micha	Micah	mee-KHAH	מִיכָה
Michael	Michael	mee-kha-AYL	מִיכָאֵל
Michaihu	Micaiah	mee-KHAI-hu	מִיכָיְהוּ
Michal	Michal	mee-KHAL	מִיכַל
Milka	Milcah	mil-KAH	מִלְכָּה
Miriam	Miriam	mir-YAM	מִרְיָם
Mishael	Mishael	mee-sha-AYL	מִישָׁאֵל
Mishkan	Tabernacle	mish-KAN	מִשְׁכַּן
Mitzpa	Mizpah	mitz-PAH	מִצְפָּה
Mizbayach	Altar	miz-BAY-akh	מִזְבֵּחַ
Mordechai	Mordecai	mor-d'-KHAI	מָרְדֳּכַי
Moriah	Moriah	mo-ri-YAH	מוֹרִיָּה

Hebrew Name	English Name	Pronunciation	Hebrew
Moshe	Moses	mo-SHEH	מֹשֶׁה
Nachbi	Nahbi	nakh-BEE	נַחְבִּי
Nachor	Nahor	na-KHOR	נָחוֹר
Nachshon	Nahshon	nakh-SHON	נַחְשׁוֹן
Nachum	Nahum	na-KHUM	נַחוּם
Nadav	Nadab	na-DAV	נָדָב
Naftali	Naphtali	naf-ta-LEE	נַפְתָּלִי
Naomi	Naomi	na-o-MEE	נָעֳמִי
Natan	Nathan	na-TAN	נָתָן
Naval	Nabal	na-VAL	נָבָל
Navi	Prophet	na-VEE	נָבִיא
Navot	Naboth	na-VAL	נָבָל
Nechemya	Nehemiah	n'-khem-YAH	נְחֶמְיָה
Negev	Negeb	NE-gev	נֶגֶב
Nerya	Neriah	nay-ri-YAH	נֵרִיָּה
Netanel	Nethanel	n'-tan-AYL	נְתַנְאֵל
Neviah	Prophetess	n'-vee-AH	נְבִיאָה
Neviim	Prophets	n'-vee-EEM	נְבִיאִים
Nisan	Nisan	nee-SAN	נִיסָן
Noa	Noah	no-AH	נֹעָה
Noach	Noah	NO-akh	נֹחַ
Nov	Nob	nov	נֹב
Nun	Nun	nun	נוּן
Oded	Oded	o-DAYD	עוֹדֵד
Ohola	Oholah	a-ho-LAH	אָהֳלָה
Oholiav	Oholiab	o-ha-lee-AV	אָהֳלִיאָב
Oholiva	Oholibah	a-ho-lee-VAH	אָהֳלִיבָה
Omri	Omri	om-REE	עָמְרִי
Onan	Onan	o-NAN	אוֹנָן
Otniel	Othniel	ot-nee-AYL	עָתְנִיאֵל
Ovadya	Obadiah	o-vad-YAH	עֹבַדְיָה
Oved	Obed	o-VAYD	עוֹבֵד

Hebrew Name	English Name	Pronunciation	Hebrew
Oved Edom	Obed Edom	o-VAYD e-DOM	עוֹבֵד אֱדוֹם
Pagiel	Pagiel	pag-ee-AYL	פַּגְעִיאֵל
Palti	Palti	pal-TEE	פַּלְטִי
Paltiel	Paltiel	pal-tee-AYL	פַּלְטִיאֵל
Pekach	Pekah	PE-kakh	פֶּקַח
Pedael	Pedahel	p'-da-AYL	פְּדַהְאֵל
Pekachya	Pekahiah	p'-kakh-YAH	פְּקַחְיָה
Peleg	Peleg	PE-leg	פֶּלֶג
Penina	Peninnah	p'-ni-NAH	פְּנִנָּה
Peretz	Perez	PE-retz	פֶּרֶץ
Petuel	Pethuel	p'-tu-AYL	פְּתוּאֵל
Pinchas	Phinehas	peen-KHAS	פִּינְחָס
Rachel	Rachel	ra-KHAYL	רָחֵל
Ram	Ram	ram	רָם
Rama	Ramah	ra-MAH	רָמָה
Re'u	Reu	r'-U	רְעוּ
Rechovam	Rehoboam	r'-khav-AM	רְחַבְעָם
Reuven	Reuben	r'-u-VAYN	רְאוּבֵן
Rivka	Rebecca	riv-KAH	רִבְקָה
Rut	Ruth	rut	רוּת
Salma	Salmon/Salmah	sal-MAH	שַׂלְמָה
Salmon	Salmon	sal-MON	שַׂלְמוֹן
Sara	Sarah	sa-RAH	שָׂרָה
Sarai	Sarai	sa-RAI	שָׂרַי
Selah	Selah	SE-lah	סֶלָה
Seraya	Seraiah	s'-ra-YAH	שְׂרָיָה
Serug	Serug	s'-RUG	שְׂרוּג
Setur	Sethur	s'-TUR	סְתוּר
Shaarayim	Shaaraim	sha-a-RA-yim	שַׁעֲרַיִם
Shabbat	Sabbath	sha-BAT	שַׁבָּת
Shabbatot	Sabbaths	sha-ba-TOT	שַׁבָּתוֹת
Shafan	Shaphan	sha-FAN	שָׁפָן

Hebrew Name	English Name	Pronunciation	Hebrew
Shafat	Shaphat	sha-FAT	שָׁפָט
Shalem	Salem	sha-LAYM	שָׁלֵם
Shalum	Shallum	sha-LUM	שַׁלּוּם
Shamgar	Shamgar	sham-GAR	שַׁמְגַּר
Shamua	Shammua	sha-MU-a	שַׁמּוּעַ
Shaul	Saul	sha-UL	שָׁאוּל
Shealtiel	Shealtiel	sh'-al-tee-AYL	שְׁאַלְתִּיאֵל
Shear Yashuv	Shear-Jashub	sh'-AR ya-SHUV	שְׁאָר יָשׁוּב
Shechanya	Shecaniah	sh'-khan-YAH	שְׁכַנְיָה
Shechem	Shechem	sh'-KHEM	שְׁכֶם
Sheila	Shelah	shay-LAH	שֵׁלָה
Shelach	Shelah	SHE-lakh	שָׁלַח
Shelumiel	Shelumiel	sh'-lu-mee-AYL	שְׁלֻמִיאֵל
Shem	Shem	Shaym	שֵׁם
Shemaya	Shemaiah	sh'-ma-YAH	שְׁמַעְיָה
Sheshbatzar	Sheshbazzar	shaysh-ba-TZAR	שֵׁשְׁבַּצַּר
Shet	Seth	Shayt	שֵׁת
Shevat	Shebat	sh'-VAT	שְׁבָט
Shilo	Shiloh	shi-LOH	שִׁלֹה
Shim'i	Shimei	shim-EE	שִׁמְעִי
Shimon	Simeon	shim-ON	שִׁמְעוֹן
Shimshon	Samson	shim-SHON	שִׁמְשׁוֹן
Shlomo	Solomon	sh'-lo-MOH	שְׁלֹמֹה
Shmuel	Samuel	sh'-mu-AYL	שְׁמוּאֵל
Shofar	Horn	sho-FAR	שׁוֹפָר
Shofarot	Horns	sho-fa-ROT	שׁוֹפָרוֹת
Shomron	Samaria	sho-m'-RON	שֹׁמְרוֹן
Sivan	Sivan	see-VAN	סִיוָן
Tamar	Tamar	ta-MAR	תָּמָר
Tanakh	Hebrew Bible	ta-NAKH	תָּנַ"ךְ
Tapuach	Tappuah	ta-PU-akh	תַּפּוּחַ
Tavor	Tabor	ta-VOR	תָּבוֹר

Hebrew Name	English Name	Pronunciation	Hebrew
Tekoa	Tekoa	t'-KO-a	תְּקוֹעָה
Terach	Terah	TE-rakh	תֶּרַח
Teveria	Tiberias	t'-ver-YAH	טְבֶרְיָה
Tevet	Tebeth	tay-VAYT	טֵבֵת
Tirtza	Tirzah	tir-TZAH	תִּרְצָה
Tola	Tola	to-LA	תּוֹלָע
Tzadok	Zadok	tza-DOK	צָדוֹק
Tzefanya	Zephaniah	tz'-fan-YAH	צְפַנְיָה
Tzelofchad	Zelophehad	tz'-la-f'-KHAD	צְלָפְחָד
Tzeruya	Zeruiah	tz'-ru-YAH	צְרוּיָה
Tzfat	Safed	tz'-FAT	צְפַת
Tzidkiyahu	Zedekiah	tzid-ki-YA-hu	צִדְקִיָּהוּ
Tziklag	Ziklag	tzi-k'-LAG	צִקְלַג
Tzion	Zion	tzi-YON	צִיּוֹן
Tzipora	Zipporah	tzi-po-RAH	צִפֹּרָה
Tzora	Zorah	tzor-AH	צָרְעָה
Tzuriel	Zuriel	tzu-ree-AYL	צוּרִיאֵל
Ukal	Ucal	u-KAL	אֻכָל
Uri	Uri	u-REE	אוּרִי
Uriya	Uriah	u-ri-YAH	אוּרִיָּה
Utz	Uz	Utz	עוּץ
Uzziyahu	Uzziah	u-zi-YA-hu	עֻזִּיָּהוּ
Yaakov	Jacob	ya-a-KOV	יַעֲקֹב
Yachaziel	Jahaziel	ya-kha-zee-AYL	יַחֲזִיאֵל
Yael	Jael	ya-AYL	יָעֵל
Yaffo	Joppa/Jaffa	ya-FO	יָפוֹ
Yair	Jair	ya-EER	יָאִיר
Yakeh	Jakeh	ya-KEH	יָקֶה
Yarden	Jordan	yar-DAYN	יַרְדֵּן
Yarmut	Jarmuth	yar-MUT	יַרְמוּת
Yechezkel	Ezekiel	y'-khez-KAYL	יְחֶזְקֵאל
Yechiel	Jehiel	y'-khee-AYL	יְחִיאֵל

Hebrew Name	English Name	Pronunciation	Hebrew
Yechonya	Jeconiah	y'-khon-YAH	יְכָנְיָה
Yedutun	Jeduthun	y'-du-TUN	יְדוּתוּן
Yehoachaz	Jehoahaz	y'-ho-a-KHAZ	יְהוֹאָחָז
Yehoash	Jehoash	y'-ho-ASH	יְהוֹאָשׁ
Yehochanan	Jehohanan	y'-ho-kha-NAN	יְהוֹחָנָן
Yehonatan	Jonathan	y'-ho-na-TAN	יְהוֹנָתָן
Yehoram	Jehoram	y'-ho-RAM	יְהוֹרָם
Yehoshafat	Jehoshaphat	y'-ho-sha-FAT	יְהוֹשָׁפָט
Yehoshavat	Jehoshabeath	y'-ho-shav-AT	יְהוֹשַׁבְעַת
Yehosheva	Jehosheba	y-ho-SHE-va	יְהוֹשֶׁבַע
Yehoshua	Joshua	y'-ho-SHU-a	יְהוֹשֻׁעַ
Yehotzadak	Jehozadak	y'-ho-tza-DAK	יְהוֹצָדָק
Yehoyachin	Jehoiachin	y'-ho-ya-KHEEN	יְהוֹיָכִין
Yehoyada	Jehoiada	y'-ho-ya-DA	יְהוֹיָדָע
Yehoyakim	Jehoiakim	y'-ho-ya-KEEM	יְהוֹיָקִים
Yehu	Jehu	yay-HU	יֵהוּא
Yehuda	Judah	y'-hu-DAH	יְהוּדָה
Yehudi	Jew	y'-hu-DEE	יְהוּדִי
Yehudim	Jews	y'-hu-DEEM	יְהוּדִים
Yered	Jared	YE-red	יֶרֶד
Yericho	Jericho	y'-ree-KHO	יְרִיחוֹ
Yerovam	Jeroboam	ya-rov-AM	יָרָבְעָם
Yerubaal	Jerubbaal	y'-ru-BA-al	יְרֻבַּעַל
Yerushalayim	Jerusalem	y'-ru-sha-LA-yim	יְרוּשָׁלַיִם
Yeshayahu	Isaiah	y'-sha-YA-hu	יְשַׁעְיָהוּ
Yeshua	Jeshua	yay-SHU-a	יֵשׁוּעַ
Yiftach	Jephthah	yif-TAKH	יִפְתָּח
Yigal	Igal	yig-AL	יגְאָל
Yirmiyahu	Jeremiah	yir-m'-YA-hu	יִרְמְיָהוּ
Yishai	Jesse	yi-SHAI	יִשַׁי
Yisrael	Israel	yis-ra-AYL	יִשְׂרָאֵל
Yissachar	Issachar	yi-sa-KHAR	יִשָּׂשכָר

Hebrew Name	English Name	Pronunciation	Hebrew
Yitzchak	Issac	yitz-KHAK	יִצְחָק
Yizrael	Jezreel	yiz-r'-EL	יִזְרְעֶאל
Yoash	Joash	yo-ASH	יוֹאָשׁ
Yoav	Joab	yo-AV	יוֹאָב
Yochanan	Johanan	yo-kha-NAN	יוֹחָנָן
Yocheved	Jochebed	yo-KHE-ved	יוֹכֶבֶד
Yoel	Joel	yo-AYL	יוֹאֵל
Yona	Jonah	yo-NAH	יוֹנָה
Yonadav	Jonadab	yo-na-DAV	יוֹנָדָב
Yonatan	Jonathan	yo-na-TAN	יוֹנָתָן
Yoram	Joram	yo-RAM	יוֹרָם
Yosef	Joseph	yo-SAYF	יוֹסֵף
Yoshiyahu	Josiah	yo-shi-YA-hu	יֹאשִׁיָהוּ
Yotam	Jotham	yo-TAM	יוֹתָם
Yotzadak	Jozadak	yo-tza-DAK	יוֹצָדָק
Yozavad	Jozabad	yo-za-VAD	יוֹזָבָד
Zanoach	Zanoah	za-NO-akh	זָנוֹחַ
Zecharya	Zechariah	z'-khar-YAH	זְכַרְיָה
Zerach	Zerah	ZE-rakh	זֶרַח
Zerubavel	Zerubbabel	z'-ru-ba-VEL	זְרֻבָּבֶל
Zevulun	Zebulun	z'-vu-LUN	זְבוּלֻן
Zilpa	Zilpah	zil-PAH	זִלְפָּה
Zimri	Zimri	zim-REE	זִמְרִי

Jewish Holidays

Hebrew Name	English Name	Pronunciation	Hebrew
Chanukah	Hanukkah	kha-nu-KAH	חֲנוּכָּה
Pesach	Passover	PE-sakh	פֶּסַח
Purim	Purim	pu-REEM	פוּרִים
Rosh Hashana	Jewish New Year	rosh ha-sha-NAH	רֹאשׁ הַשָׁנָה
Shavuot	Feast of Weeks	sha-vu-OT	שָׁבוּעוֹת
Shemini Atzeret	Eight Day of Assembly	sh'-mee-NEE a-TZE-ret	שְׁמִינִי עֲצֶרֶת
Sukkot	Feast of Tabernacles	su-KOT	סֻכּוֹת

Hebrew Name	English Name	Pronunciation	Hebrew
Yom Kippur	Day of Atonement	yom kee-PUR	יוֹם כִּיפּוּר

Biblical Measurements

Hebrew Name	English Name	Pronunciation	Hebrew
Amah	Cubit	a-MAH	אַמָּה
Amot	Cubits	a-MOT	אַמוֹת
Bat	Bath	bat	בַּת
Batim	Baths	ba-TEEM	בָּתִּים
Beka	half-shekel	BE-ka	בֶּקַע
Chomarim	Homers	kho-ma-REEM	חֳמָרִים
Chomer	Homer	KHO-mer	חֹמֶר
Efah	Ephah	ay-FAH	אֵיפָה
Geira	Gerah	gay-RAH	גֵּרָה
Gomed	Gomed	GO- med	גֹּמֶד
Hin	Hin	heen	הִין
Kav	kab	kav	קַב
Kesita	kesitah	k'-see-TAH	קְשִׂיטָה
Kikar	talent	ki-KAR	כִּכָּר
Kikarim	talents	ki-ka-RIM	כִּכָּרִים
Kor	kor	kor	כֹּר
Letek	lethech	LE-tek	לֶתֶךְ
Log	Log	log	לֹג
Maneh	Mina	ma-NEH	מָנֶה
Manim	Minas	ma-NEEM	מָנִים
Omer	Omer	O-mer	עֹמֶר
Pim	Pim	peem	פִּים
Se'ah	Seah	say-AH	סְאָה
Se'eem	Seahs	s'-EEM	סְאִים
Shekalim	Shekels	sh'-ka-LEEM	שְׁקָלִים
Shekel	Shekel	SHE-kel	שֶׁקֶל
Tefach	Handbreadth	TE-fakh	טֶפַח
Zeret	Span	ZE-ret	זֶרֶת

Photo Credits

Map of Modern-Day Israel and its Neighbors

The following is a map of modern-day Israel and the surrounding countries

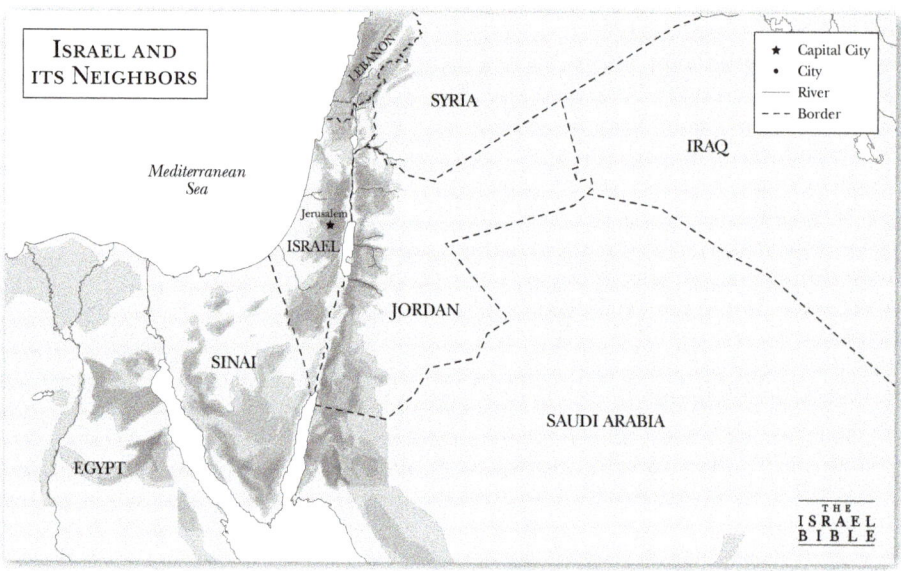

NOTES

NOTES

NOTES

NOTES

NOTES

NOTES

For more inspiring commentary,
interactive maps, educational videos,
vivid photographs and more,
please visit our website

www.TheIsraelBible.com

THE
ISRAEL
BIBLE